Preface

This book is one of three books that we are publishing in the area of Interactive Learning:

Interactive Video, by Eric Parsloe (EPIC Ltd) and Myth of the Learning Machine, by John Heaford (Deltak Ltd)

In the context of these books, we are constraining our discussion to interaction with a computer and, in particular, a microcomputer. This book is intended to give a complete introduction to the field, whilst the other two books, also due for publication this year, cover Video Disk technology and the broader issues of Computer Based Learning (or CBL as it is called) including the psychological issues.

In this book, for the first time, we bring together a discussion of the fundamental aspects of CBL and then go on to show how a low-cost microcomputer can be used to prepare effective CBL lessons. As such, it draws on some 10 years of my experience, beginning with mainframe computers and ending, now, with a belief in micros as the most convincing way of promoting CBL to the great mass of trainers and teachers. A year or so ago, this view was regarded as heresy, and I well remember annoying manufacturers of megacomputers with correspondingly highly-priced CBL packages, when I preached that the micro was the way to go for most CBL applications. Nowadays, those same indutry giants are introducing micro-implementations of their systems!

But, I would be the first to agree that CBL on a micro can lead to problems. This was only too apparent when I taught the subject on numerous courses whilst working for a large software consultancy organisation. So, this book draws on what I hope I have learned in the past 10 years and it is about the practical methods and problems that arise when we start to use a microcomputer to teach people how to learn just about any sort of knowledge. I hope that it will be just as useful to:

Parents:	with home computers and the need to prepare useful and effective lessons for their children to use at home.
Teachers:	requiring to enliven parts of the syllabus, or to provide routine remedial lessons.
Trainers:	needing to save company money on travel and accomodation.
Businessmen:	who also act as trainers, but in a more informal way.
Consultants:	they need to understand this new training technology so that they can advise their clients.
Entrepreneurs:	there will be many openings for people who can write computer based learning programs, either speculatively or on a bespoke basis.

Of course, writing a book for such a diverse range of people is not an easy task. It is all too easy to fall into the trap of being very general and talking in vague terms about the academic niceties of CBL. There is also the problem of a great diversity of computers and languages that are suitable for CBL authors. Therefore, I have taken the radical step of writing the book from an entirely practical standpoint, except for two or three chapters which are intended for the the more advanced reader. Also, I decided that if the book were to be at all meaningful, it must be built around one practical programming language. There was a large choice confronting me, each promising more than the other and ranging in price from £100 to £20,000. I took the view that the book should make its appeal to the largest possible readership, so again I took a practical step and chose, as my demonstration system, the popular Apple II microcomputer, complete with the SuperPILOT author language. Although this is an inexpensive combination, I hope to demonstrate that it is surprisingly flexible and powerful and, indeed can often out-perform many systems costing ten or a hundred times more. BUT, I am not suggesting that the Apple is the best microcomputer, and I am not suggesting that SuperPILOT is the best author language: like anything else in computing it depends on the application.

However, even though this particular combination has been chosen, there is so much in common between SuperPILOT and other author languages, that you will have very little trouble in converting the programs from this book into the language of your choice - whether that be some other version of PILOT, the BBC Microtext language, PASS, TUTOR or whatever else you intend to use. In fact, the chapters on PILOT tell you which are the Apple-specific features, which are to be found in all versions of PILOT, and some of the features found in other versions.

To form a bridge between this simple, low cost approach and the so-called mainline computer based training systems such as PLATO, there is a special chapter that shows you how to write your own program generator, such that you need never write any actual program language statements. Intriguingly, this generator is written in PILOT and produces PILOT statements, though the user need never be aware of this!

The final chapter is intended to be the most provocative of all. It presents a model of cost effectiveness that should help you in deciding which is the most cost-effective combination of hardware and software. The idea is to use a simple, objective mathematical model that most people agree is acceptable in itself. You then plug in the data and out pops a value. You can discuss the input data endlessly, but the model itself is consistent and realistic. I won't tell you the outcome yet, otherwise perhaps you won't buy the book!

Whatever happens, I hope that you have as much fun from computer based learning as I have had over the past few years. And, I'll always be pleased to hear from you if you have a different point of view from mine.

Graham Beech, Wilmslow, 1983.

Acknowledgments

I am greatly indebted to Apple Computer Ltd for the extended loan of a complete Apple II system, complete with SuperPILOT and Applewriter II. The foregoing names are all registered trademarks.

Richard Stanley of Control Data Limited provided considerable help and many useful ideas during the preparation of this book. In particular, thanks Richard for supplying me with various photographs of the PLATO system and especially for the financial model used towards the end of the book.

In no particular order, many thanks also to:

Len Gould of the Manpower Sevices Commission and Richard Freeman of the National Extension College, for reading through the manuscript and suggesting some important changes.

Ron Bartholomew of British Airways for details of their pilot training package and for checking my ignorance of matters aeronautical.

M. David Merrill of the University of Southern California, for reading through my summary of Component Display Theory.

David Welham of Wicat Ltd for information on Wise and its use at American Express.

John C. Lord of Mobil Oil Corporation, for details of their process simulator based on the Regency Systems RC-2.

Ian Every, the Academic Computing Service of the Open University for details of their TERAK system.

Ronnie Goldstein of SMILE for details and pictures of PREDICT and BOAT.

Margaret Hathaway and Karen Pitcher of the Advisory Unit for Computer Based Education, for helpful advice on MicroQUERY.

Tim Morris of BP Educational Service, for details of Slick!

Paul Chapman of ICI Organics Division, for permission to describe their Ice Making project.

And.. lots more people I've met over the past 10 years who've made me stop and think!

How to Use This Book

This book is intended to be a comprehensive guide to computer based learning, as practised in the mid-1980's on contemproray microcomputers.

It is divided into four parts which, together, cover all of the necessary theoretical and practical aspects of the subject. From my own experience, the book is an excellent support to a training course and organised as follows:

1: Introduction and background.

2: Planning methodology; terminology associated with the subject.

3: PILOT as an example authoring language, and SuperPILOT as an authoring system.

4: Other authoring systems.

5: Summary, discussion and review of practical work.

From Stage 2 onwards, it is suggested that participants start work on a course project. This should be very small (perhaps representing 5 to 10 minutes on the computer) and of interest to participants. Ideally, groups of two people working together are best.

The project work can be mixed in with lecture presentations and practical exercises to suit the course. Background readings of this book can be selected and recommended as necessary.

Contents

PART ONE: BACKGROUND TO CBL

PART TWO: PLANNING - THE KEY TO SUCCESSFUL LESSON DESIGN

PART THREE: PILOT - As An Example Authoring Language and Apple SuperPILOT As An Authoring System

PART FOUR: BEYOND PILOT

Part One:

Background to Computer Based Learning

These first two chapters give a quick survey of the field and summarise how various people have succeeded in using the medium.

You'll see that a wide aspectrum of applications is covered- from simple school-level applications on a Sinclair Spectrum, through to airline pilot training on the PLATO system.

Although these chapters may not deal with exactly the problem you had in mind, you should be able to relate your own applications to some of the work about to be described.

Chapter 1

A Short History of the Future

The fact that Computer Based Learning (CBL) is a young and fast-growing method of instruction could hardly be more timely. We live in a world where scarcely anyone contemplates a career for life. The majority of us will have several changes in direction- I have had three in fifteen years- when we have to learn a totally new set of skills and knowledge. Even those who stay in a career must constantly update themselves: learning, unlearning and relearning. It is estimated, for example, that half of a graduate engineer's knowledge will be out of date in 5 to 7 years. If this is the case, the medium of CBL must be put to good use: it promises faster, cheaper and more effective learning than most other methods.

So, what is this method all about?

Quite simply, it is all about using a computer to learn about something which may previously have been taught by more traditional methods- these include books, tape-slide and, of course, human teachers. But, before we find out exactly what CBL is all about, it is worth seeing how the world began:

1.1 Pre-History

CBL first began at a most unfortunate time in the history of computing. It started way back in the 1960's when computers were all of the type that filled very large rooms and the only respectable languages were COBOL and FORTRAN. Data input was usually by punched cards, or by print-on-paper teletypes that chattered noisily and gave response times between several seconds and a minute or so. It says something for the perseverance of the 60's pioneers that they attempted to produce learning programs with such equipment. It also says a lot for two manufacturers who have stayed with CBL from those early days to the present micro era: Control Data Corporation (CDC) and International Business Machines (IBM).

A Tale of Two Giants

We'll be looking in detail at the products on offer from the various vendors, but those from CDC and IBM do deserve special mention. Taking IBM first, they developed a language called COURSEWRITER which was designed specifically for CBL, unlike the commercial and scientific languages around at the time, good old COBOL and FORTRAN. The Coursewriter language was (and still is) able to match student answers against anticipated key words, provide 'help' or 'hint' materials and to keep records of the student as progress is made through the course. Although Coursewriter can do these fancy things, it is still a computer language, which must be learnt before a lesson can be written. Later on, we'll see some examples of actual programs written in languages of this type, but this is the sort of typed dialogue that a student might have with a lesson written in Coursewriter, and running on an IBM computer:

computer	Are you ready to take the test?
student	PARDON?
computer	Please answer Yes or No.
student	YES
computer	OK, grab your calculator and press any key.

The Coursewriter program is looking for the words YES or NO. Depending on how it had been designed, the program might accept a reply like 'YES, I AM READY' or it may require just the single words YES or NO. Such matching lies at the heart of 'Authoring Languages' of which Coursewriter is an example.

This example was concerned solely with text. The programming language was used to present text, analyse text answers for likely words, and to skip to new parts of the lesson. On the way, it would be keeping a count of how many right and wrong answers were given, updating test scores and so on. IBM have stuck with this text-oriented philosophy, but Coursewriter has developed considerably and has been assimilated into an easier-to-use product called the "IBM Instructional Systems". These are actually comprised of two companion products, IIPS (the presentation system) and IIAS (the authoring system). This latter IBM product allows people who are not expert in programming to prepare lessons by filling in pre-printed forms. For example, there is a form to be used in the preparation of

3

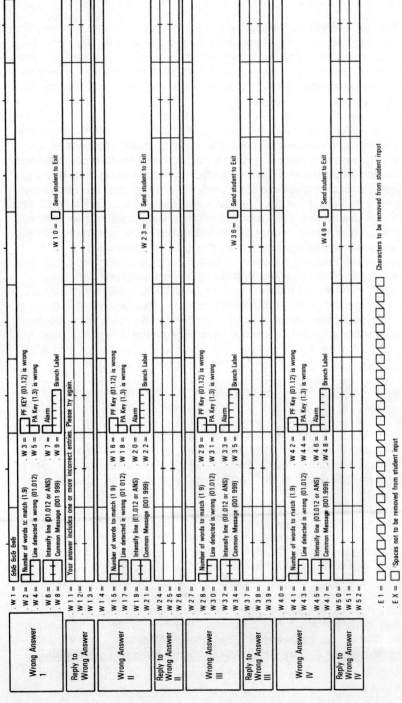

Figure 1.1 IIS Question Worksheet

4

student tests, and all the teacher needs to do is to complete the section containing the text of the question, and to fill in the answer section in the form of keywords or a letter or number indicating the correct answer on a list. There is also space on the form to give replies to correct or unanticipated answers, hints and so on. A copy of this form is shown in Figure 1.1.

The way that IBM developed their CBL system is representative of several other suppliers. There has been a move away from program coding towards easy lesson entry for non experts, in the belief that productivity will be increased. Another important supplier we will look at, who has also taken this approach, is Control Data Corporation with its PLATO system.

Without any doubt, PLATO has been the most important and most influential system. It was originally funded by the US government, and all of the early work was completed at the University of Illinois, in their Computer Based Education Research Laboratory. Development was then supported by Control Data Corporation, who now continue with the day-to-day development and marketing of PLATO. CDC have invested $600 million over a period of 20 years in this product, encouraged by the almost missionary zeal of their chairman, William Norris. Both the software and hardware are remarkable and innovative, and it is worth examining each of them briefly. Figure 1.2 illustrates the main components of a PLATO learning station (a fancy phrase for the collection of hardware!).

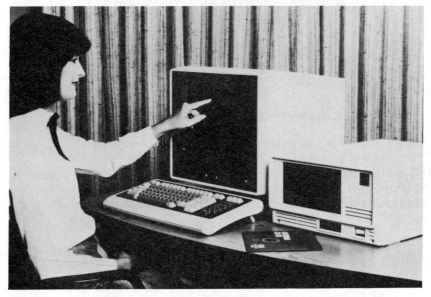

Figure 1.2 A PLATO Learning Station   (CDC Viking terminal with disk drive)

Until very recently, PLATO has depended very heavily on the use of a networked mainframe computer, the CDC Cyber 70 series. Communication is mainly achieved by telphone lines to special-purpose terminals, which originally used plasma (discharge) screens. These are made of flat plastic sheets which distort when touched; without going into exactly how it works, the electrical properties of the plasma screen are changed so that the position at which it was touched can be detected. Because of this property, the screen itself is touch-sensitive and permits students to 'touch' correct answers and so on. CDC no longer use the plasma screen, but the more conventional screens have a 'soft' front plastic layer which is also touch sensitive screen. In Figure 1.2, we can see how PLATO permits you to touch the screen as an alternative to the keyboard.

Figure 1.3 PLATO in use, illustrating the text and graphics features,

Figure 1.3 shows that the screen also has very good graphics capability, albeit monochrome. The keyboard is standard QWERTY layout with many extra keys such as HELP, NEXT, BACK and DATA which are used by the author.

At the heart of the PLATO software is TUTOR, the authoring language. As with IIS, this was originally the only way to create PLATO lessons. Like Coursewriter, it can present text and analyse typed answers but, also it can:

6

Create graphics.
Animate objects.
Specify various styles and sizes of text.
Detect which area of the screen was touched.
Use large groups of synonyms in answer matching.

Figure 1.4 Example of Multiple Choice Question, as Edited

... and a lot more besides. But it still just a language, and a large complex one too (there are hundreds of commands). So, to improve productivity, CDC have introduced a number of go-faster tools. For example, a graphics editor was introduced which enables a programmer to design outline pictures interactively on the screen and, when the result looks correct, a single command translates the picture into TUTOR language statements.

Also, a 'show-display' mode was introduced which enables an author to quickly test out a program to see how it looks on the screen and make changes to the code interactively by, for example, asking to move an object to a new location. On-line aids were introduced, so that authors could consult help-screens to find out how to do particular things without wading through a large manual. And, on-line consultants were made available: experts in all aspects of PLATO who could be called up through the system, "talked with" through the terminal, and who could monitor the author's screen to talk them through their difficulties. But, the biggest advance came with PLM (PLATO Learning Management) which dispensed with the necessity of learning any author language.

As the name suggests, this manages learning as opposed to giving it. PLM enables an author to design a course as a collection of modules which ,in turn, are made up of small segments called 'Instructional Units', or IU's.

Each IU has associated with it a collection of Learning Resources (LR), but an LR need not necessarily be delivered through the medium of a computer. It might be a videotape, part of a book or whatever; it might even be a lesson written in TUTOR. But, the time-consuming part of testing is all within PLM. An author specifies what kind of test is required and answers prompts on the screen, as in Figure 1.4.

PLM can be used to administer tests, collect marks, and route students to new lessons- all those things that are tedious for human instructors.

Recently, CDC have introduced a stand-alone authoring system on their own Viking terminals with some, but by no means all, of the features of the on-line system (see Fig.1.2). A stand-alone version of PLM is expected shortly- all indicating a move away from the traditional mega-computers that were the hallmark of CBL. Even more recently, CDC have announced development plans to transfer PLATO authoring systems and many existing lessons to popular microcomputers, such as the IBM PC, BBC, Apple II, Commodore, Zenith and Sirius machines. An example of a PLATO lesson being used on the Apple is shown in Figure 1.5.

The authoring systems will not, of course, be full-blown PLATO- that would be impossible to fit onto a standard micro. But, even a part of PLATO combined with low cost hardware, which many potential customers already own, will be a very attractive sales proposition and further justify CDC's massive investment in CBL.

Figure 1.5 School children using PLATO mathematics software on the Apple II plus.

Educational CBL - A Case of Retarded Development

The two systems that we have described have mainly found application in commercial training, with the notable exception of PLATO at several universities world-wide. With the aid of systems like IIS and PLATO, people have been trained in such diverse skills as salesmanship, touch-typing, financial accounting and flying jet aircraft. In every case, it is claimed that the training has been delivered at a lower cost than before and the effectiveness of the training has improved dramatically.

In contrast, the take-up of CBL within education has been slow and patchy. There are two main reasons for this. One is that CBL was developed originally as a method of programmed learning, closely related to'the work done by behavioural psychologists such as Pressey, Skinner and Crowder. Skinner did some convincing work in training pigeons to perform tasks in exchange for food and drink. He thought that this would work on students who, he thought, have a similar reward mechanism.

Skinner's method was essentially a linear series of small learning steps, whereas Crowder advocated a branching approach involving a multi-choice question format. Each methodology was incorporated into self-instructional "programmed learning" text books, where the reader is directed to different sections depending on the answer given to a question. Also, "teaching machines" were introduced: elctro-mechanical devices that had a simple keyboard and some type of projector to display a slide or piece of filmstrip, analogous to sections of a book.

It was realised that the computer offered a more flexible presentation device, albeit more expensive at the time. An over-enthusiastic reception of this idea, combined with the American love of technology, led many 1960's educators to produce CBL in the form of umptcen-thousands of pages of text with questions of the form 'Which is correct: 1,2, or 3'. This type of CBL was called Computer Assisted Instruction (CAI) and we shall use this term to refer solely to this page-turning mode of CBL. Thankfully, this method was a failure, and any teachers who thought that the computer might do them out of a job could breathe again. The computer terminals were disconnected and consigned to the broom cupboards of the USA.

The second reason for a slow uptake of CBL has been inappropriate technology. In the United Kingdom, a modestly-funded Government programme (National Development Programme in Computer Assisted Learning) was allocated £2.5 million from 1972 to 1977. The money was spread amongst several UK universities and polytechnics with the twin aims of developing CBL materials, within over 30 projects embracing over 100 educational institutions, and assimilating them into syllabuses. The whole thing swept along under the charismatic infuence of Richard Hooper, now head of Prestel. Many excellent CBL packages were developed, displaying a range of teaching styles that made use of 'respectable' methods such as simulation and discovery learning. Tens of thousands of students used the packages and hundreds of eager and ambitious academics became involved. After such a promising start, you might imagine that the Universities, Colleges and Training Centres in the UK would now be bulging with CBL packages. They aren't, and one reason is certainly that many of the packages were just plain boring. For the remainder, they suffered from being implemented on the wrong hardware: most of the work was done on mainframe and mini-computers because the micro technology was simply not available. In fact, NDPCAL ended in 1977 at just about the time that cheaper micros began to appear. If only, with hindsight, NDPCAL had been delayed by 5 years, we might have seen a much greater use of CBL in higher education.

As it was, a very small amount of post-NDPCAL funding was available, but most of the innovators went in different directions- presumably to squeeze money from the Government for more fashionable projects. Also, Richard Hooper- a sort of Michael Heseltine of CBL- had gone to pastures new, and no new messiah had appeared. So, CBL in higher education went into a decline in the UK (or, leastways, the momentum was very considerably decreased).

Some new activity has appeared at primary and secondary school level, encouraged in the UK by the Microelectronics in Education Programme. MEP began life in 1980, and runs until 1986. It is funded by the UK government, and covers 14 geographical regions, each one having its own resource centre equipped with a range of hardware. MEP supports a small number of national projects (Computers in the Curriculum; Five Ways Software; and Investigation on Teaching with Computers as an Aid) as well as numerous regional projects.

MEP is concerned with CBL in schools. The emphasis here is on investigatory learning, so LOGO and database enquiry programs are very much in vogue. Several packages have also been produced with the aid of commercial publishers, using more conventional programming (mainly BASIC), with financial subsidies from MEP. The main thrust of this type of CBL is to encourage 'high-level' problem solving skills. For example, a program of this type may involve a simulation of finding one's way from one town to another, through a list of specified villiages. The student would be provided with a map, a compass and the computer program.

Map bearings would be taken from an actual map with a real compass, the apparent bearing would be adjusted for a 'true-North' bearing and a direction entered into the computer. This might cause a little man to walk from the present point to a new destination, and the student would be told how near to the destination the directions had taken the simulated man. Unlike conventional training programs, this would demand and encourage the subordinate skills of map reading, reading off scales, adding magnetic corrections and so on. There is certainly a place for experimental learing of this sort which is, to some extent, rather like taking a car apart to find out how it works. Time will tell if large scale use will be made of CBL in schools: many teachers distrust technological teaching, or fear for their jobs, and most UK schools have only one microcomputer per school. Successful CBL requires a 1:1 ratio of student to computer; whilst this is possible in higher education (most Universities have clusters of terminals) it is not generally feasible in most state schools.

Interestingly, the environment that is now most attractive for CBL is the home. A large percentage of parents now own a computer, its purchase being justified either as a games machine or to give their children a computer advantage over those poor souls who share one between 30.

Any entrepreneur can see that these same parents will be equally willing to pay for good CBL programs that give their children the edge on others in mathematics, history, science, languages and what have you. It is just the natural development of the Space Invaders era.

1.2 What is CBL?

We've already hinted at this: the concept of using a computer as some sort of teaching medium. In this section, a better definition will be attempted and some of the many abbreviations will be spelled out.

CBL divides into two main areas: computer assisted learning (CAL) and computer managed learning (CML). If you are mainly interested in training, CBL is replaced by CBT, CAL by CAT and CML by CMT, the 'T' denoting training. There is no real difference between CBL and CBT except for the different perceptions that educators and trainers have.

These will include the relative importance of objectives, target populations, age ranges, motivational factors, testing and score keeping, to name but a few. But, most trainers regard training objectives as important, and CBT courses are intended to achieve such measurable objectives, whereas CBL lessons are often more informal, sometimes with no specified objectives.

For consistency, we will use the CAL and CML abbreviations. You will find many others; practioners in the USA still talk of CAI, which has a long-standing connotation of page-turning, so we won't mention it further in this book.

In a CAL lesson, the learner is engaged in an interactive dialogue with the computer. The dialogue can be through the screen and keyboard (usually) or by touching the screen, using joysticks, speech input or any of the other possible devices. Usually, the dialogue is under the control of the teaching program which will have been written in some suitable language such as TUTOR if you are using PLATO or, perhaps, if you are using a microcomputer, PILOT. The author of the CAL lesson must anticipate what possible responses can be made by the student, and what action should be taken after each response. For this reason, the production of a CAL lesson can be a lengthy process, sometimes requiring 100 hours for every single hour of student interaction.

CML, on the other hand, does not necessarily require any contact between student and computer. A CML system is a means of recording student marks, and directing students to the next part of the course (this process is called 'routeing'). In addition, a CML system may also do these things:

> Mark student tests automatically (e.g. by using an Optical Character Reader).
>
> Control student access to lessons (a process called 'rostering')
>
> Record when students use the computer.
>
> Record all student responses, for test validation.
>
> Maintain a bank of test questions for teachers to draw from.

You may remember having to do this tediously by hand! A further section enables you to set up models of any lens or mirror- something you could not previously do if you did not happen to have the real thing available.

Organisations like the armed services and universities make extensive use of CML, using it not only to administer tests, but to keep records on the progress of students throughout their courses. Military uses of CBL are rather different from civilian ones. It has been said that military CBL is as different from 'real' CBL as military music is from 'real' music!

In most cases, it is difficult to make an exact division between CAL and CML. Almost every CAL lesson of any size will have test points to direct students to different parts of the program, and most large CAL programs will collect some simplified test data. Even Apple SuperPILOT, a microcomputer CBL system, has an inbuilt CML sub-system.

So, CAL and CML are the main subdivisions. As a presentation medium, it is probably worth singling out Interactive Video (IV) as a third division since it seems to possess some attributes that are not displayed by conventional CAL. Its 'freeze-frame', slow-motion and other time compression / expansion features make it a unique tool for teaching psycho-motor skills and problem solving.

1.3 Why use CBL?

The most important reason for using CBL- certainly for using CAL- is that it is uniquely interactive. No other medium (except a human teacher) demands that a student makes frequent responses to ensure understanding. Similarly for the designer of CAL programs: you may think that you understand a topic well enough to teach it, but only when you have to express it as a CAL program do you realise the subtleties that you don't yet understand well enough: you can't bluff in a CAL program.

The interaction also leads to better retention. Psychologists have known for years that people retain knowledge better if they are made to DO something, and CAL interaction is certainly doing. It is interesting to contrast learning from a manual with learning from a computer. Manuals, once written, tend to stay that way except for pages of additions and corrections that scarcely make for easy reading. A manual can be replaced with a CAL lesson with many advantages, not the least being that it is easily updated. We will see an increasing trend for computer software and computers themselves to be self-documenting by way of built-in CAL lessons on their operation. For example, the Digital Equipment Corporation's range of personal computers each have CAL programs to give a quick overview of various languages and packages that are supplied. The packages are written in BASIC and involve the user taking part in an interactive simulation of the particular software. For example, the CAL lesson on BASIC lets the user type in simple BASIC statements and checks the statement for correct typing.

CAL lessons are also much shorter than traditional ones. Many studies, both in the UK and the USA, have shown a debatable time saving of around 30 percent, combined with the better retention we have already mentioned. We say 'debatable' because this 30% figure is often put about as propaganda by manufacturers. In fact, a large proportion of this saving is achieved by the redesign of a classroom course for self-instruction. But, whatever its origin, it means that students can attain the same standards as previously, in about two-thirds of the time. In commercial training, this means that trainees are back on the job more quickly as proficient workers. In schools and universities, students have more time for leisure or for studying other subjects. If a University course were completely CBL, students would need two, not three years of study to obtain a degree.

So far as most adults are concerned, they tend to prefer self-motivated and self-directed instruction. They want to acquire knowledge and skills now, not when the next course starts. CBL provides this immediacy, and is said to be RESPONSIVE to training needs. Hence the usefulness of the DEC lessons (described above) for its microcomputers- users can find out what they need to know immediately.

The best CAL programs possess all of the above, yet give the impression of INDIVIDUALISATION. The CAL lesson can find out, from pre-tests, not only the user's present state of knowledge, but also the preferred style of learning. Thus, the CAL lesson will train the user only in those skills presently lacking and it will do so in the manner preferred by the user. At the very least, any CAL program will only train for new skills, unlike many traditional courses that always go over old ground and progress too quickly or too slowly for the 'average' student. Good CAL lessons are tirelessly patient, able to give help, to review material quickly, and to present learning material at the correct speed for a given circumstance.

This adaptive speed of presentation is called 'self-pacing'.

A further reason for using CBL is that it is a secure medium. This has two meanings. On the one hand, it is secure in the sense that you can control who uses the lessons and you can ensure that unauthorised people do not see student data, even with a microcomputer system. Second, you can give people the opportunity to ask 'silly' questions or to give 'foolish' answers, in a way they could never do in a classroom. Invariably, the questions and answers did not seem foolish to the student. But, with the possibility of ridicule in front of a class, how many times have you kept silent? With CBL there is no embarrassment, the computer is impartial as to who are the learners, and they are free to experiment (in the better programs) whilst learning.

1.4 Some Cost Benefits

In the previous section, we left out one very good reason for using CBL - its low cost. Currently, the development cost of CBL is indeed high, but this is amortised over the lifetime of the product, given a sufficiently large audience. In chapter 3, we will take a more detailed look at costs, but here are some interim factors to bear in mind:

CBL can be presented in the office, on the shop-floor, at home- there is no need to stay in an expensive hotel nor pay high travel costs.

CBL courses can be around 30 percent shorter than traditional courses, so trainees spend less time away from their jobs.

Traditional training courses cost around £20 per hour per student, when everything is costed in. CBL can be delivered through popular micro-computers for between £2 to £5 per hour, after allowing for development costs.

1.5 A word about the future

CBL will certainly continue to be used in its traditional areas of industry and commerce. But, if I were to pick out one sector in which CBL will surely blossom, it must be the home. Think of how many people you know with home computers, and how many with video recorders. Very soon, the intermediate technology of the video tape will be replaced by video disk, which gives almost immediate access to thousands of pictures, under computer control. The arguments over whether it is economic to use video disk for CBL (the high cost of producing the master disk and so on) will disappear when entrepreneurs realise the vast potential for home education: not just of the children for whom, very often, the purchase of a computer was justified, but also those engineers we mentioned at the start of this chapter. With CBL courses delivered by videodisk and microcomputer, education will return to the home.

Schools will continue, but more as centres for acquiring skills in social behaviour, sports and the arts. The other aspects of learning will be achieved in a 1:1 domestic environment. If this is only half true, there will be an enormous market for educational software.

Just to show how quickly the field is moving, since first drafting this chapter, I have had to revise my optimism of the home market to even greater heights. A recent survey * predicts that the size of the market for educational software in homes and schools in the USA alone will reach 1.59 billion dollars by 1990. Parents in USA are already willing to pay up to $500 on a good program if they thought it would help their children. Schools, on the other hand, are still held back by the recession.

* (Educational Software: the next boost to the microcomputer market, published by IPI, Nordre Ringvej 201, 2600 - Glosttrup, Copenhagen, Denmark. $970).

Chapter 2

Success Stories

Many people have some strange ideas about CBL. Some think that it is just like programmed learning, whilst others think of it as purely the province of airlines and other large corporations. In fact, each of these views is incorrect. The CBL technique can equally well be applied to students in schools, colleges or in commercial training situations. Suitable computers range in price from the £100 personal micro, all the way up to time-shared mainframes. In other words, according to your training or learning problem, there is probably a way that CBL can help. And, many people will already have had similar problems to you, so this chapter is intended to demonstrate the sorts of successes that CBL has already achieved. We will look at examples from both the educational and training areas, using representative equipment:

2.1 CBL in Schools

As we mentioned in the previous chapter, educationalists tend to prefer CBL programs that develop high level skills rather than simply those that concentrate on acquiring a single skill, such as the ability to recite tables. Of course, given the correct educational scenario, the latter should not be denigrated because the high level programs invariably require the student to have good facility in basic skills such as multiplication. The following programs illustrate these differences in approach:

FOREST RANGER- a simple fantasy program (Blackboard Software-Sinclair Spectrum).

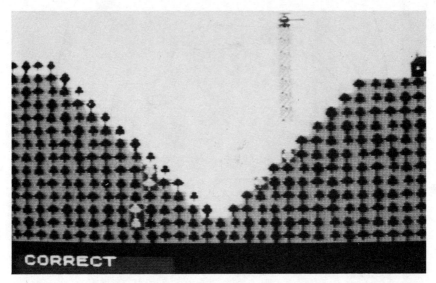

Figure 2.1 The "Speillicopter" Extinguishing a Fire in Exchange for a Correctly - Spelt Word.

This is an example of a program which is directed at one particular skill: spelling. The program runs on a Sinclair Spectrum and uses a vocabulary of 160 words. Initially, the young student sees a forest, the ranger's cabin and a 'spellicopter'. A word flashes briefly on the screen and it must be typed correctly, otherwise a fire breaks out in the forest. The only way to put out the fire is to spell subsequent words correctly, causing the spellicopter to be re-fuelled which enables it to fly to the fire.

This fairly simple program is representative of a large group of CBL programs in which the learning activity is embellished with a fantasy. In this case, the fantasy is the spellicopter but, of course, it could just as easily be a number-copter, a history-copter or whatever. A similar game, either on paper or on the computer, is 'hang-man' in which the fantasy is the construction of a gallows and the hanged man in a piecewise manner for each incorrect answer (usually an incorrectly guessed letter in a randomly-chosen word). Again, the fantasy could be applied to other situations and such fantasies are called 'extrinsic'.

As you might guess, there are also intrinsic fantasies, which can not be transferred out of the program. An example is the car-maze racing game in which a simulated car is 'driven' through an obstacle course on the screen:

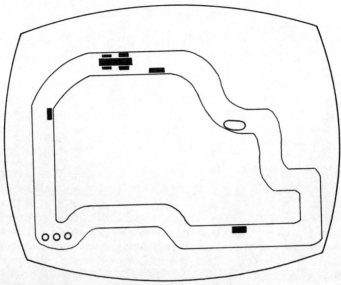

Figure 2.2 Car Maze

IMAGES (SciCAL Software, for the BBC Computer)

SciCAL is typical of several new software companies, in that their products are being marketed in the High Street to parents and students, whilst allowing for the fact that schools may also buy. Their programs are appealingly packaged, and cover many of the traditional O and A level topics. For example, IMAGES is concerned with ray diagram for mirrors and lenses. It is very straightforward- no fancy educational theory here- just good basic teaching. For example, one option allows you to construct ray diagrams like this:

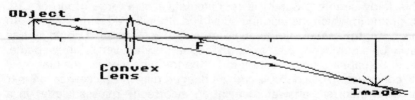

A real image is formed.Rays of light con
verge towards a real image.
Image is magnified
Image is inverted

SciCAL are at PO Box 6, Birkenhead L43 6XH.

20

LOGO- a language for exploring powerful ideas (Available for most popular microcomputers)

This is, of course, a language rather than a program. It is worth mentioning here because it typifies the 'high-level' problem solving approach that is favoured for computer activities with young children. In all respects LOGO, although seemingly just a computer language, provides a complete environment that typifies all CBL activities. Its main purposes are to get young children to program a computer and to encourage structured thinking.

The programming is achieved through a simple but powerful language that children can relate to in a physical way. This is because one of the main features of LOGO is TURTLE GRAPHICS: the commands of LOGO cause a 'turtle' to move about on the screen and, if required, the movements can be mirrored by a mechanical device called a 'floor turtle'. The floor turtle ressembles half a goldfish bowl, with elctric motors inside it to power its wheels, and it is attached to the controlling computer by an 'umbilical cord' set of control wires. Beneath the turtle there is a pen which can be raised or lowered, and it is this which is used to draw patterns on very large sheets of paper. Rather than use paper, patterns can be drawn solely on the screen, in which case the turtle is represented by a small triangle. The apex of this triangle points in the current forward direction of the turtle, and the following explanation should be sufficient to understand how the following sequence succeeds in drawing a triangle on the screen (Fig. 2.3):

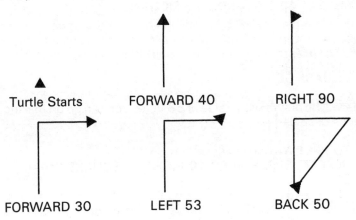

| Turtle Starts | FORWARD 40 | RIGHT 90 |
| FORWARD 30 | LEFT 53 | BACK 50 |

Figure 2.3 Drawing a Triangle with Logo

The commands FORWARD and BACK tell the turtle to travel forwards (or backwards) along the current direction by the specified number of units.

LEFT and RIGHT tell the turtle to change its direction by a particular number of degrees. In the above example, the attempted right angled triangle would not be quite perfect, so the student could make slight changes until perfection was achieved. One obvious attraction is that children can mimic the action of the turtle by walking around the floor themselves, thus verifying what happened or discovering new moves.

A LOGO user can invent new commands and store these in the computer for future use. For example, after perfecting a sequence of moves for a square, the definition SQUARE can be saved by writing, for example:

```
TO SQUARE
REPEAT 4(FORWARD 40 RIGHT 90)
END
```

And then, simply by typing

```
SQUARE
```

a square with side 40 units would appear. To make squares of any size, re-define SQUARE:

```
TO SQUARE:SIZE
REPEAT 4(FORWARD:SIZE RIGHT 90)
END
```

Then, if we type

```
SQUARE 55
```

a square will be drawn with a side of 55 units. You can go on making new definitions such as

```
TO PRETTY
REPEAT 10(FORWARD 10 RIGHT 36 SQUARE 90)
END
```

Most of the fun in LOGO for children is to build up definitions in this way and to use them in more complex patterns.

There's a lot more to LOGO than turtles, but this part of the language is presently having a great impact on children throughout the world. Turtle

Graphics also appear in certain versions of the PILOT language, about which we'll have much more to say later.

Basic Skills in Math for Florida High Schools (Florida State University using PLATO)

In this, and the following example, we take a look at how skills in mathematics can be improved with CBL. The two projects are quite different- one is a State-wide scheme based on the the PLATO system with a total budget of $792,000, the other is run on a shoe-string. Do not, however, conclude that either approach is better- it depends on the circumstances.

So, let's look firstly at the Florida experiment.

Starting in 1978, Florida State University (FSU) began a collaborative venture with Control Data (who supply the PLATO system) and three Florida High Schools in order to assess the mathematics part of the PLATO Basic Skills Learning System. This covers many fairly low level, yet important areas in reading, mathematics and language skills. The test sites were chosen in an urban, suburban and rural area and each was equipped with 8 PLATO terminals connected by telephone to the main Control Data computer at FSU. Each school assessed the PLATO lessons for suitability and assigned groups of students to study the lessons.

Typically, these students (usually the lowest achievers) would use PLATO for 20-30 minutes per day. The lessons covered the following areas:

> Basic Number Ideas
> Addition
> Subtraction
> Multiplication
> Division
> Fractions
> Decimals
> Ratios, proportions and percentages
> Geometry and measurement

Once a particular topic has been chosen, a student has the option to take a diagnostic test or to go through a tutorial lesson and then take a mastery test. In this way, time is not wasted on those areas with which students are familiar. Also, standardised tests were administered before and after the PLATO lessons and these showed that, on average, students progressed by 1.5 'grade equivalents' after spending an average of 20 hours on PLATO. This in itself is better than would have been possible with conventional teaching but the teachers report these other advantages:

> Longer retention of facts.
> Reduced discipline problems.
> All record keeping is done by PLATO.
> Students develop confidence in themselves through experiencing success.
> Attention spans are increased.

Students want to work in their own time, in addition to their allocated hours.

This last advantage is one of the oddest ones for teachers: students would sometimes resent having to give up their terminal for someone else and were disappointed if the equipment malfunctioned. One of the most effective disciplinary procedures was to threaten students with removal of their PLATO privileges! An explanation of this phenomenon is that the PLATO lessons constantly demonstrate concepts, draw excellent graphics and demand very frequent answers to questions in a way that no class teacher could possibly do. By presenting material in small increments, PLATO enables the student to build a history of successes, proving that he can learn: self esteem is improved.

As to cost, it was predicted that the lessons could be delivered for as little as $1.64 per hour, per student. It would be difficult to find many other media (except books, possibly) that could compete on cost alone.

SMILE- mathematics and CBL (RML 380-Z microcomputers)

This is an acronym for Secondary Mathematics in Inner London Education Authority (*). It is operated by a small group of teachers who offer to copy the collection of programs for other UK teachers who send two blank disks! The 30 or so programs run on the Research Machines 380-Z (a popular CP/M computer in British Secondary schools). The collection is varied and imaginative and includes:

PREDICT: This is a problem solving package which not only encourages

Details can be obtained from SMILE Centre, Middle Row School, Kensal Rd, London W10 5DB

children to THINK about numbers, but also encourages them to devise strategies of problem solving. The student types in a list of numbers, and the program uses one of twelve randomly-chosen rules to produce an outcome. For example, it might add all the numbers together, or subtract the two smallest numbers from each other: the student does not know what rule is being applied, only that

Figure 2.4 Using PREDICT

it is being used consistently. The point of the program is that the user must discover the rule by predicting the outcome correctly on three occasions. Initially, children tend to type in as many large numbers as the program permits, thinking that this will help them to discover the rule being used. Later, they develop the strategy of using a small number of carefully chosen numbers. For example, choosing just 2 numbers will quickly reveal if the computer is using a 'difference' rule.

BOAT: this program is based on the 'cannibals and missionaries' problem, but to bring it into an acceptable school context, SMILE use women and children. The idea is to successfully transport, say, 2 women and 2 children across a river in a boat that will hold no more than 2 women. The women and children wait on one bank of the river, and the student selects who will go in the boat which is then loaded and 'sails' to the opposite bank. You might start by putting two children in the boat, taking both of them across the river, then sailing back with one child and..... but it would spoil the fun to tell you how to do it!

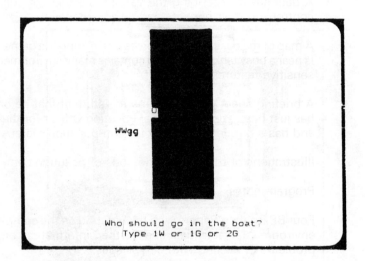

Figure 2.5 The start of the BOAT puzzle

In both of these programs, SMILE are doing more than teaching rote learning. Quite high mental processes of logic and deduction must be used, even though basic skills are still needed. The advantage of using programs of this sort in a classroom situation is that a small group of children can use the micro while the rest are engaged in more traditional learning activities.

SLICK! - a pollution game (BP Petroleum)

SLICK! is an interactive computer simulation from BP Educational Service. *

It has been designed for the 10-16 age range and focuses on the impact

---

(It has been designed to run on the BBC (cassette or disk), Apple II and RML 380-Z microcomputers. Details and prices from BP Educational Service, PO Box 5, Wetherby, West Yorkshire LS23 7EH)

of technology on society through a case study of oil pollution around the UK coast.

In addition to the program itself, the user is supplied with:

> Users Guide
>
> A data sheet describing the various methods of pollution control and their benefits and disadvantages.
>
> A map of the coastline to be protected during the game. This is near a busy tanker route and contains many environmentally sensitive features.
>
> A briefing sheet which informs the student that he or she has just been appointed Local Pollution Officer for the area and has a budget of £5000 for anti-pollution materials.
>
> Illustrations of the various methods of pollution control.
>
> Program notes.
>
> Four BP Briefing Papers with background on the company's environmental activities and further information on the problems of dealing with oil spillages.

At the start of the program, a replica of the map appears on the screen, in full colour. This is followed by a order form on which materials up to the value of £5000 are ordered. If desired, the program will automatically allocate this figure to help younger students.

An emergency is then announced. A tanker is leaking oil at a specified grid reference on the map. The screen shows information on wind speed and direction and the student must predict where the slick will move in a certain time period and type in the appropriate grid reference. The game is controlled by a time base and students have less and less time to make predictions and take action as the game progresses.

After each successful prediction of the slick's movement (there are 28 to make in each game) students can try to deal with the threat. This can include loading a tug with dispersant or absorbant materials, dispatching the tug to the slick and unloading the materials, placing booms at sensitive points, and deploying skimmers to mop up any oil the booms collect.

Feedback is given, such as the ramaining weight of their slick.

27

At the end of the game, the student is given a score reflecting the quality of their decisions and the accuracy of their predictions. The slick can take 50 different routes, so the game can be played many times by the same student or group of students.

Figure 2.6 Students using SLICK!

This program has several benefits: it teaches about pollution control whilst still requiring a range of numerical and other skills, such as map interpretation.

NATURAL LANGUAGE AND THE COMPUTER (Hull University, BBC Computer, marketed in the Acornsoft range)

These programs have been developed by members of the Educational Technology Research Group at the University of Hull. They are of interest in providing learning environments in which the user can explore the use and effects of language. In essence, the user takes part in a 'conversation' with the computer about objects that are displayed on the screen, and the programs are able to 'understand' most of the sentences- even quite complex grammatical ones- that can be formed from the allowed vocabularies.

The first package ('Language and Thought') developed by this group contains three programs called BOXES, COLOURS and SIZES; in addition to their interesting linguistic features, they also teach the concepts of relative position, colour and relative size. Taking one of the programs, BOXES, as an example, three coloured boxes appear on the screen with a triangle and a cross placed randomly inside two of the boxes. The user can choose either a 'pupil initiative' or 'computer initiative', as shown below:

PUPIL INITIATIVE

USER	Put the triangle in the red box
COMPUTER	(The computer does this)
USER	Where is the triangle?
COMPUTER	The triangle is in the red box.
USER	In what is the cross?
COMPUTER	The cross is in the blue box.

COMPUTER INITIATIVE

COMPUTER	Is the cross in the green box?
USER	No, the triangle is in the green box.
COMPUTER	No, the triangle is in the red box. I asked about the cross.
USER	Nothing in the green box.
COMPUTER	Well done!

A second package 'Hidden Sizes' has been developed by the Hull group. In this case the user is given a set of four objects (rectangles, crosses and diamonds) that are to be adjusted in height and width until they match a hidden set of shapes. As with the previous programs, the user interrogates the computer in a natural manner:

USER	What is taller than my blue cross?
COMPUTER	My yellow cross. Your yellow rectangle.
USER	What is shorter than my diamond?
COMPUTER	There is no diamond.
USER	Make my blue rectangle taller.
COMPUTER	(computer does this)

The user carries on until the set of four visible shapes is identical to the hidden ones. The computer reveals the hidden set when they match, or will tell the user (on request) how many shapes differ.

MicroQUERY- an information retrieval package (Advisory Unit for Computer Based Education, Hertfordshire, for the disk-based Research Machines 380-Z computer. Also, a related program, QUEST, is available for cassette based 380-Z, 480-Z or BBC model B computers, whilst QUEST-D and QUESTD are available for their disk-based counterparts).

By now, you will have seen that CBL is indeed very varied and does not consist simply of the student answering boring questions of the "which is correct... 1,2 or 3" type.

MicroQUERY turns the situation round. With this program, the student asks questions of the data stored in the computer, which contains suitably large files of information. There is a huge variety of data and examples include:

Local information on the settlements in Hertfordshire.

Data about Burgundy, as the basis of a school 'link'.

Local census data.

The datafiles can be set up and edited, or the teacher may simply choose a standard datafile from the dozens available. The program enables information to be extracted quickly and easily. Any data in the database can also be sorted, and there is a facility for histograms to be produced.

Ahah! you might say... this is computing, not CBL. But, in the unlikely event that you did say so, you'd be wrong. For example, children interrogate one of the datafiles of census data to find out how people lived over a hundred years ago; i.e. they learn about history but they do so by forming their own ideas, not by listening to a history lesson. They ask questions of the Burgundy datafile about what the climate is like, and what crops are grown, and so on.

MicroQUERY is not one, but a suite of programs. The most interesting one, from our point of view, is QUERY which retrieves data from the datafile, but firstly here are the subsdiary programs:

QEDIT:	this is used to set up datafiles and to edit or update them. Each datafile consists of a number of records, which in turn consist of fields. The user, setting up a new datafile, specifies the number of records, up to 20 fields per record and the name and size of each field. For example, a datafile of towns would have one record per town, and each record might contain NAME, POPULATION and GRID-REFERENCE as fields. Various datafiles have been built up for MicroQUERY by enthusiastic teachers, this being useful as it is the most laborious part of the process. More exciting is the idea of children developing their own files.
QSORT:	enables the result of a search to be sorted into alphabetical or numerical order.
QCLASS:	enables ranges to be specified for the classi-fication of numeric data in order to produce a table or a histogram.
QLABEL:	prints out labels (e.g. address labels for a mailing list) from the retrieved data.

Finally, we come to QUERY itself, "the interrogation software". Files can be searched for appropriate conditions. Apart from numeric processing features, there are about 20 different commands available to the QUERY user, for example:

INFILE- select the datafile you want to search.

HELP- provide assistance with any or all available commands.

GO- start the search.

Here is a sample search:

:INFILE DAT41	(Selects the 1841 census data for Datchworth, a small agricultural village.)
:STRUCTURE	(To see details of the fields in the datafile.)

:TITLE Working Children   (Give the table of results a title.)

:QUERY AGE LT 15 AGE   15 and greater than 10. Reject - NIDENT
GT 10 AND OCCUP NIDENT   means not identical - those with no
'''' AND OCCUP NIDENT   occupation at all or those that are
"SCHOLAR"   scholars.)

PRINT FORENAME SURNAME AGE OCCUP

:GO

The results would look like this:

Working Children

FORENAME	SURNAME	AGE	OCCUP
JAMES	GREGORY	12	HELPER IN GARDEN
ROSE	SMITH	14	SEAMSTRESS
SUSAN	GREGORY	13	TEACHER
THOMAS	WILLIAMS	12	FARM BOY

.... and so on. With a datafile of this sort, children can find out how many of their age were at work, what sort of jobs they did, and the size of the families. The emphasis is all on finding out, rather than being told.

2.2 CBL in Colleges and Universities

The sort of CBL practised in schools is very new and, mostly, innovatory. For this reason, it is difficult to define precisely what constitutes a good CBL program for schools. It is equally difficult to prescribe, given some educational need, exactly how to design such a program. Which leaves us with a bit of a problem until the dust has settled for a year or two. But, CBL in tertiary education (colleges, polytechnics and universities) has had longer to mature and the nature of the educational process in these institutions is somewhat different. Very often, students in these higher level courses are using computers as an everyday tool- to process results or to fit experimental data.

Unlike the education of young children, it is often necessary to train older students in the acquisition of more specific skills, such as how to perform a distillation experiment, to write programs in BASIC, to operate some piece of electronic equipment, or to interpret the readings from an instrument. In many ways, this is more similar to commercial training, more of which in section 2.3. In the following few paragraphs, we present just 3 examples chosen from the science area, to give a flavour of the type of programs in use:

Distillation (Stanley Smith, Illinois University, PLATO system)

Why should we teach distillation with a computer? Surely it is a manipulative skill that is being learned here?

That's true, but there is a lot of planning and logical thought that goes into such an experiment and what Professor Smith has done is to separate the planning elements and put them onto PLATO. Only when a student has demonstrated competence in carrying out a simulated distillation experiment are they allowed to go into the laboratory and do the real thing. The result is that those students who are inexpert must practise their planning skills longer, whilst the more expert are not being held back.

The program begins by displaying a collection of distillation glassware on the screen:

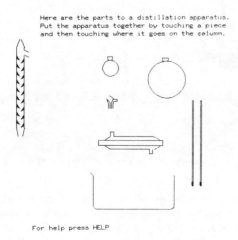

Here are the parts to a distillation apparatus.
Put the apparatus together by touching a piece
and then touching where it goes on the column.

For help press HELP

Figure 2.7 A screen print-out of the PLATO distillation program, at the start.

33

The student selects an item by touching it (the PLATO screen is touch sensitive) and then touching some other part of the screen where it is to be placed. Just as in real life, the equipment must be assembled in the correct order, so PLATO gives helpful messages such as 'No, the thermometer goes there' if someone tries to assemble it incorrectly.

In addition to touch-commands, sometimes the student must reply through the keyboard to questions such as 'What will you do next?'. A free text reply is expected and, depending on where the student has reached, it might be 'Heat the Oil Bath'. If this were correct, the rate of heating is selected by touching the screen. The distillation flask contains a mixture of pentane and hexane and, to achieve a 'success' grade, the two components must be separated in sufficient volume and to an acceptable purity. As the flask is heated, distillate passes through the distillation column to the receiving flask in a realistic manner.

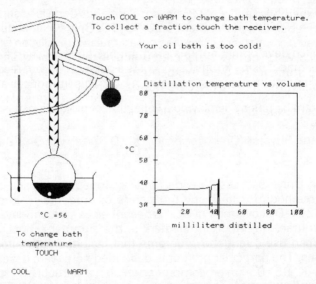

Figure 2.8 Distillation in progress. The graph displays distillate temperature

The receiving flask can be 'emptied' by touching it, otherwise PLATO warns you that the flask is overflowing! When the experiment is complete, the yield and purity are assessed and our expert chemist is now allowed into the lab! Oh, by the way, if the flask is heated too vigorously, the equipment 'explodes' on the screen, and you start again.

Organic Analysis (Central Program Exchange,* BASIC and FORTRAN versions)

This program is old-established, as can be seen from the fact that it started life as a mainframe FORTRAN program. There are several other similar programs, and like the distillation program described above, it attempts to separate the logical from the manipulative aspects of chemistry.

Essentially, the program contains a small database of 30 or so organic chemical compounds complete with their physical and chemical properties, and the results that would be obtained if certain chemical tests were carried out. Now, identifying a chemical compound is more than a guessing game; the process is shortened by a strategic choice of tests. So, the first thing to do is ask the program for the boiling point or melting point of the compound. Then, you might try buring a small sample - the program will tell you if the compound would burn with a smoky flame, thereby telling you if it contains benzene rings - an important fact. You might then shake it up in water and see if it is acid or alkaline - again usefully categorising it into broad chemical groups. Then, you go on to make more specific tests until the compound is finally identified.

A rather nice development of this program has been to 'charge' for each test that is made: using litmus paper costs a penny or so, but recording an infra - red spectrum may cost several pounds. This introduces a marking scheme in which student performance is measured in terms of the lowest overall cost to identify the compounds.

Discovering Physics (Open University, UCSD Pascal with OASIS authoring system)

The Open University uses a wide range of independent and distance-learning methods for its many thousands of students. This particular course 'S271-Discovering Physics' is described as a second-level general physics course. An important element is the summer school, at which students can use a range of programs that includes both tutorials and simulations. The particular programs described here were developed for the TERAK 8510:a microcomputer which is particularly strong on graphics and animation. The programs were written in UCSD Pascal with the aid of the OASIS authoring system to simplify text layout, graphics and answer matching. The programs included:

* (CPE is based in The Department of Computing, The Polytechnic, Wolverhampton, WV1 1LY)

ORBIT: a simulation of orbital motion.
FIELD: field and equipotential lines in electrostatics.
HOVER: a one-dimensional model of the motion of a helicopter.
A tutorial on mechanical equilibrium.
Tracks in a bubble chamber.
Gas simulation.
Magnetic Field between two coils.
Least-squares fitting of curves.

Taking just one example, ORBIT simulates the motion of a space vehicle around a planet. The user can specify the initial position and velocity of the vehicle and must carry out various orbital manoeuvres in order, for example, to dock with a command module. The user can fire rockets on the vehicle in one of 4 directions with various thrusts, and give various other commands. Users are encouraged to try placing the vehicle into orbits of specific shapes, and to explain the results in terms of kinetic energy and the like. The orbits are displayed on the TERAK as the simulation proceeds, as shown in Fig 2.9.

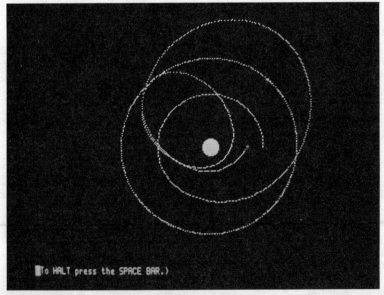

(To HALT press the SPACE BAR.)

Figure 2.9 ORBIT in progress

In Figures 2.10 and 2.11 we reproduce 'snapshots' from two other OU lessons. The first one is a plot of field potentials, which shows off the TERAK very well. The second is a representation of a physics problem, which shows both the graphics and text matching facilities in operation.

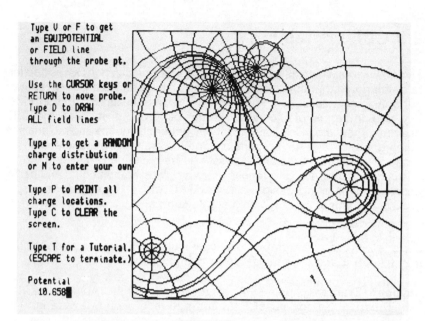

Figure 2.10 The Open University FIELD program.

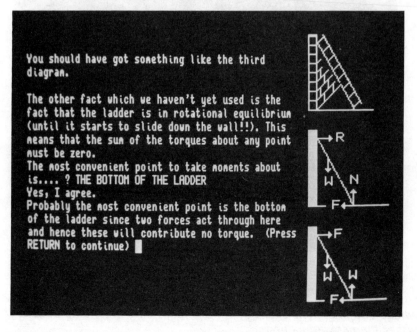

Figure 2.11 A tutorial on mechanical equilibrium (Open University)

2.3 CBL in Training

This is the area which has the most tangible benefits. When CBL is applied to training in either commerce or industry, the effects can be measured not only in cost savings (compared with traditional classroom methods) but also in terms of increased employee productivity. For the CBL designer, there are also advantages: it is generally much easier to analyse training topics and to prepare acceptable training materials than to produce educational materials to satisfy the teaching profession. Partly this is due to inherent differences in training and education (*) and partly because the training designer is working with a more uniform target audience in mind, often within a single company.

So, let's look at some examples of successful CBL in training, and see how they live up to the claims that we've made:

Keyboard Trainers (Apple-by-Apple for Apple II (or IIe), Apple Computer Inc.; Touch 'n' Go, for most CP/M computers, Caxton Software Ltd.)

Figure 2.12

* If you're not sure of the difference, imagine the reactions of parents whose daughter tells them that she's just had sex training at school, rather than sex education.

38

Firstly, let's see a very simple program, but one that makes you say "That's Nice!". It is one of the oldest applications of CBL: keyboard training. Packages to teach this vary from those that teach users how to find particular keys on the keyboard, all the way up to sophisticated Touch Typing courses. This particular package is modest in its aims, but it is nicely presented with colourful graphics and animation. The first part of the package introduces the QWERTY keyboard and requires the user to use the editing features of the keyboard. An example of a typical screen is shown in Figure 2.12.

Later in the program, the CTRL key is introduced as a 'helper' key to the other keys. All of this is done in an entertaining fashion, for example, one combination of keys must be used to stop a yo-yo on the screen. There is a useful section in the program, for first time users, which demonstrates 'user friendliness'- a concept that is always difficult to describe in words. If every Apple dealer gave away a copy of this program with each computer sold, there would be fewer customers asking silly questions.

We could spend the whole book discussing the many other keyboard training packages available. These range from the much-needed cassette package for the Sinclair Spectrum's tortuous keyboard, through to a minicomputer system used by Speedwriting/ Speedtyping Ltd which presents typists with on-screen exercises and keeps a record of their performance. Also, there is a program which teaches touch typing to a beginner, running on the BBC micro, available from the National Extension College of Cambridge. Yet another package that falls between these two extremes is Touch 'n' Go from Caxton Software. This is a 24 hour touch-typing course supplied on floppy disk for many popular CP/M business microcomputers such as the Superbrain and Osborne. The course contains some 74 CAL lessons which progress in difficulty, teaching you to use first the left hand and then the right. Each lesson has an exercise that you have to complete at the correct speed and with a minimum number of errors. A nice feature is that the package keeps track of the last lesson you completed, so you can start from that point when you return to the computer. (This book was typed on the Apple II using a word processor, and it might have been completed more quickly if I had used such a touch typing course!)

Ice Making at ICI Organics Division (Apple II, South Yorkshire Systems for Training, Education and Management Ltd).

Ice is required in large quantities in a chemical factory, and ICI's Huddersfield Works produces about 100 tons a day. It was decided to investigate the use of a CBL package in order to improve operator competence both in the routine operation of ice-making equipment and in the diagnosis and rectification of faults.

The designers of the CBL package firstly identified the objectives that were required of the package. Briefly, these were found to be:

i) Describe the refrigeration cycle.

ii) Relate the components of the cycle to physical equipment.

iii) Acquire detailed operating knowledge of temperatures and pressures.

iv) Describe the function of the evaporator, part of the ice maker.

v) Interpret simple faults such as loss of cooling water or loss of refrigerant.

The package developed to satisfy these objectives consisted of a booklet and a BASIC program written for the Apple II microcomputer. The program firstly assesses the student's basic knowledge of refrigeration and how they relate to the particular plant used by ICI. The program records the performance of the student on a disk file for the instructor. Various text materials are used to support the student, depending on a pass or failure in any particular section. The program includes realistic and animated representations of the ice plant on the screen, similar to the schematic in Figure 2.13

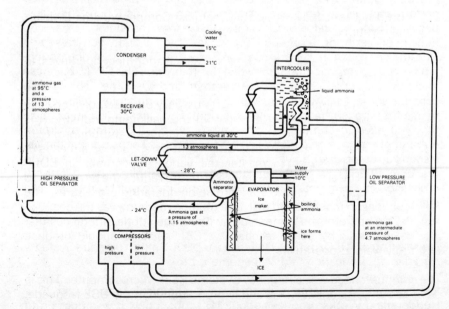

Figure 2.13 The "South AZO" Ice Plant

After eventual successful completion of a test, the student is presented with a computer based fault diagnosis exercise. A situation is presented which may be caused by one of three possible faults:

(a) Inadequate cooling of the condenser.

(b) Low suction pressure in the evaporator.

(c) Loss of oil pressure in the lubrication system.

As each situation is presented, the problem solving ability of the student is monitored. Failure to recognise the cause of a particular symptom (such as a 'high pressure alarm') requires the student to take some simulated corrective action. He may be required, for example, to increase the flow of coolant or to set some particular switches in order to correct the fault. At all stages, the correctness of his action are reported to the student and the number of incorrect actions and time taken to correct the fault are recorded on disk.

A package such as this enables a company to assess the competence of its employees or, alternatively, provides the opportunity to try 'what if' experiments without damage to valuable equipment.

Plastic Film Manufacture (Mobil Chemical Company, Films Division, Regency Systems RC-1 Microcomputer)

Like the preceding example, this one is aimed at shop-floor operatives, to show the practical importanve of CBL.

Mobil Chemical's Films Division produces biaxially oriented polypropylene film (BOPP) which is extensively used in the packaging industry. It is necessary to produce BOPP to very close tolerances and uniformity of thickness, and it was thought that CBL might be chosen as a means of training plant operatives to master the various operations in BOPP manufacture. The aim of the CBL package was to reduce the time required to train new operators and to standardise on operating procedures. The foremost reason for selecting CBL as a training medium was the desire to teach every operator the same things without the subtle differences that can be imparted by some teachers. A CBL package should produce uniformly trained operatives.

The computer used was a Regency Systems RC-1 Microcomputer. This is designed for CBL applications and is programmed in the USE language, which is very similar to PLATO's TUTOR language; in fact the RC-1 and USE have many of the features of PLATO, such as the touch-screen, special keyboard and graphics editors, but it is independent of any telecommunications requirements (as are other microcomputer derivatives of PLATO). The RC-1 is more expensive than, say, an Apple II but not prohibitively so.

Mobil's package consisted of three major parts. The first part was a set of tutorial lessons using text and animated graphics which covered the basics of fluid flow of molten material and the fundamentals of the equipment.

The second part was a test concerning the sorts of problems that crop up on the plant: all quite straightforward.

Figure 2.14 One of Mobil Chemical's operators, Willie Lee Clay, using a lesson on the RC-1.

But, the final part is the most interesting, since it uses a process simulator program, written in USE for the RC-1. With this program, the operator is put in charge of a simulated film manufacturing plant and is required to produce film to given standards. Whilst using the simulator, any one of nine problems can be chosen. These are the ones that most commonly arise in the operation of the real plant. In each case, the situation is that the plant is producing unacceptable film; time is passing and the operator must try to correct the faults that arise. As time progresses, a simulated roll of film is being produced and the operator can get cumulative gauge uniformity profiles. The various indicators and control settings are reproduced realistically on the screen, even down to random 'blips' in the gauge measurements which, whilst having nothing to do with any real variation in thickness, also arise in real life.

At the heart of the process simulator is a set of complicated mathematical equations which describe how the process reacts to the various settings available to the operator. Changes in the setting are all time dependent. For example, a change in temperature of the molten polyproplene may be selected, but the change will occur slowly, just as in the real case. The equations used in the simulator cause the process to respond in just the same time-scales as the real film making plant. Similarly, simulated mechanical adjustments can be made but, like temperature changes, they are not instantaneous in their effects. So, as the operator uses the simulator he learns that it is often necessary to wait, to see the cumulative effect of any changes made. Sometimes, the simulator is programmed with random and transient effects in film thickness which the experienced operator would ignore in real life. So, on the simulator, these transients are programmed to disappear after a time.

A thorough evaluation was made of this project. The results showed that the development costs of the CBL program were recovered in one year taking into account savings on normal training costs alone. There were also similar savings in terms of reduced wastage of scrap polymer and increased productivity. One rather nice idea introduced by Mobil has been to include a league table of the three employees who can solve the simulator problems in the shortest times, thus increasing competition.

2.3.4 Processing Travellers' Cheques (American Express, Wicat Systems Inc.)

Before we describe this application, it will be useful to define what is meant by 'simulation' as the word means different things to different people. The previous section was an example of what most people think of when they hear about 'Computer Simulations'. The computer is being used to simulated, through a set of mathematical equations, the behaviour of something tangible - in the case of Mobil it was a film manufacturing plant. The aim of the simulation was to provide an environment that was as close as possible to reality. In a similar fashion, one can simulate the complex interactions that take place between users of computer systems, such as the operators of mainframe computers, computer programmers, bank staff who make changes to customer accounts, or airline staff who book people onto aircraft.

These are all responsible jobs, and any errors made in real life will be potentially:

> Annoying (the computer operator who turns the power off at the wrong time).

> Time-wasting (the programmer whose programs are always full of bugs)

> Embarassing (the bank customer whose gas bill is £9,999,999 when it's usually £50)

> Inconvenient (the passenger who is sent tickets for the wrong destination).

The airlines were the first to recognise the benefits of simulation techniques, simply because they had installed a network of online booking terminals for travel agents. It was then an easy matter to sling in some cheap 'n' cheerful training materials to make sure that people occasionally got on to the right flight. Typically, the training materials would present, on the screen, a replica of the form that the agent would fill in when booking a real passenger to a real destination. A situation was posed to the trainee and he was required to complete the form, on the screen, correctly. After each passenger had been booked on to the flight, or when a simulated booking was cancelled, a make-believe passenger list was updated. All of this was surprisingly successful, and the approach has been followed by banks, building societies, credit card companies and the like. In all cases, there is an underlying model (e.g. a passenger list) which is updated with every simulated transaction. To distinguish this type of simulation from the numerical variety, it is often referred to as a 'DECISION TREE' since trainees are constantly required to make a decision (e.g. 'What do you type in the DESTINATION section?) as a result of which the model is updated.

Figure 2.15 demonstrates the 'trees' nature of the problem. More information on decision trees is in Section 3.1. In almost every case, users of such simulations have been mainframe owners (e.g. Barclaycard use an IBM mainframe, British Airways use Amdahl) which makes the one that

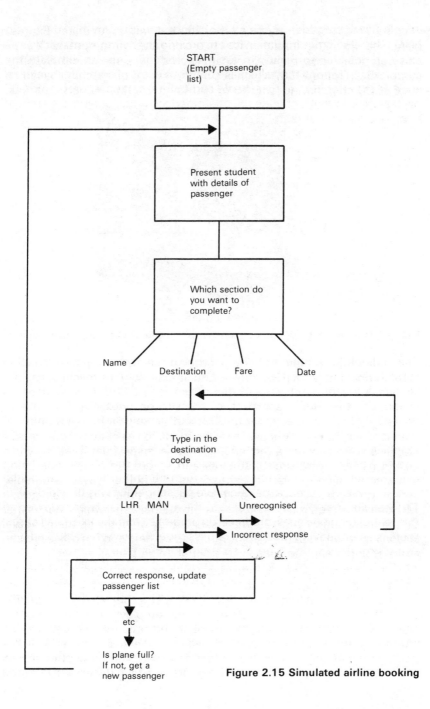

Figure 2.15 Simulated airline booking

we are now going to describe a little different, in that American Express have used a microcomputer with an exciting authoring system.

The computer chosen by American Express was the Wicat Systems model 150 (Figure 2.16) which is a multi-user 16 bit machine based on the 68000 chip, having 256 kB of RAM and a 10MB Winchester disk.

Figure 2.16 A Wicat 150 Computer similar to the one used by American Express.

This powerful machine was equipped with the authoring system called WISE (Wicat Interactive System for Education). Both the machine and the system are very much state-of-the-art so far as CBL is concerned. In contrast to the coding approach of most langauages, WISE is 'menu-driven'. By this, we mean that the CBL author selects from a number of menus. Thus, he could choose from the menu to select text or graphics. If graphics were chosen, a further selection is made from a menu which includes lines, dots, circles, squares and so on. If a question is being constructed, a choice would be made as to whether it was a multiple-choice question, true-false, or free-text. No programming language whatsoever is required of a menu system such as this, which means that CBL authors simply DESIGN the lessons, they do not code them. Actual lesson input can be performed by more junior staff, such as office typists, and this is the approach taken by several WISE users.

American Express selected individuals with no programming experience and minimal exposure to the computer itself. In a matter of days, they were producing 30 to 50 frames of WISE per day. The simulation package that they produced was for the training of new employees in the extensive amounts of information required to clear and process cheques moving among American Express and its selling outlets. By the end of the package, students were able to understand the work flow of their new department and, most important, they were able to perform each required

46

job task. The package used high-resolution graphics to represent "trays of work" which contain, in real life, the documents that they are required to process. On the computer, they used the actual procedures of American Express to process the documents - on the screen they saw realistic representations of the screens that they would see when processing real documents in real life. For American Express, the advantages were that, not only were the procedures being learnt safely, without mis-processing of actual accounts or tying up expensive equipment, the training was actualy shorter than before, by around 50 per cent.

Flushed with their success, American Express invested in a larger Wicat system 200 with 30 student terminals, and added three more courses to the Wicat system. One of these covered the American Express ALARMS system (Automatic Loss and Refund Monitoring System) which allows claims to be entered on-line without a separate data entry stage. The training was condensed to one day in which students learned to perform a dozen different functions. In just 4 months, 300 employees used the system, with a total of 3000 hours of training logged to date. It is the intention that CBL will be the primary delivery method of training at American Express.

2.3.5 Flight Simulation (British Airways, PLATO system)

In the preceding sections, we have been talking about simulation in various ways - the idea that you can simulate a physical process (as with the Mobil film making) or a business system (as with American Express). But the one aspect of simulation that most people have heard about - even if they know nothing about CBL - is the use of cockpit simulators by airlines and aircraft manufacturers. These amazing pieces of machinery (see Figure) are 'flown' by a trainee pilot and, in response to his directions, a combination of audio-visual devices, servomechanisms and hydraulic jacks simulate the behaviour of a real aircraft so realistically that it is difficult not to believe that you are in the real thing. Added realism is achieved by projecting computer-generated graphics onto screens facing the pilot.

Simulators of this sort have become so widely accepted by the entire airline industry that their use is now mandatory in flight-crew training: a commercial airline pilot must log a certain number of simulator hours just as he must maintain a statutory number of actual flying hours in the real aircraft.

But, there are aspects of pilot training that do not need the use of a full simulator. For example, acquiring an overall knowledge of some aspects of navigation or a fairly detailed knowledge of how to operate one particular piece of specialised equipment. In these cases, it may be advantageous to train pilots in such tasks while they are waiting to use the full simulator and, by transferring such training tasks to a microcomputer, it has proved possible to make substantial economies as compared with either classroom instruction or the use of the actual equipment (both real aircraft and simulators are expensive beasts!).

The resultant CBL packages are called 'part-task simulators' and they usually comprise a computer terminal which can display a high-resolution representation of part of the display seen by the pilot, and an underlying CBL package which will interpret and respond to the trainee's actions.

Some of the pioneering work in this area was started in 1975 by American Airlines, using the PLATO system, to train pilots on aspects of the Boeing 727. At about the same time, United Airlines began using PLATO in a slightly different way, exploiting its CML package (PLM- PLATO Learning

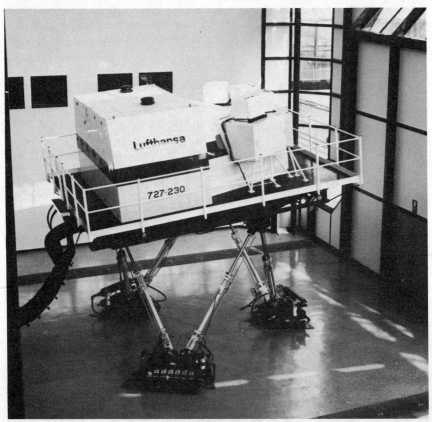

Figure 2.17 Reproduced by permission, Redifon Simulation

Management) to manage the use of instructional materials and to control tests and record keeping. Both American and United went on to construct part task simulators for new aircraft, including the Boeing 767 which lends itself very well to CBL because its cockpit contains computer screens and push-type square buttons, which are easier to represent than the dials and levers of older aircraft.

A lot of work has been done in this area and if you want to read more about it, there is a reference, below *. We would now like to describe just one use of PLATO, this time at British Airways.

This application uses a stand-alone PLATO system for delivering lessons originally developed by the Boeing company for the flight management system of a 747 aircraft. The stand alone system is simply a normal PLATO terminal connected to a disk drive which can process the lessons held on floppy disk. Figure 1.2 shows a photograph of such a system. The lessons can either be supplied, ready to run, on the disks or can be downloaded from a PLATO mainframe. This gives some economy (reduced telephone charges) with flexibility since the terminals can be used to edit the lessons on the mainframe and modified copies can then be re-loaded onto the disks. This is British Airways' intention, since the equipment on their 747 aircraft is not exactly the same as that referred to in the training package supplied by Boeing.

A flight management system (FMS) is used for many purposes, for example to set the engines for maximum economy, to read navigational data from radio beacons, and to do the dozens of tasks that were previously done by aircrew inspecting dials, flipping switches and turning knobs. The FMS is, in fact, a computer which has to be programmed before take off with data such as:

> Route to be followed
> Fuel load
> Number of passengers
> Amount of freight

During a flight, the FMS may have to be re-programmed if, for example, the destination airport is closed. To become adept at programming this equipment, pilots can use a simulator but this limits the number of trainees and it allows them to make mistakes. A preferred method is the partial PLATO simulation which presents a realistic picture of the FMS

* *(Journal of Computer Based Instruction, Vol.8, No. 3, Feb. 1982, Special Avaition Issue.)*

control and display unit. A diagram of the display is shown in Figure 2.18, exactly as it appears on the PLATO screen.

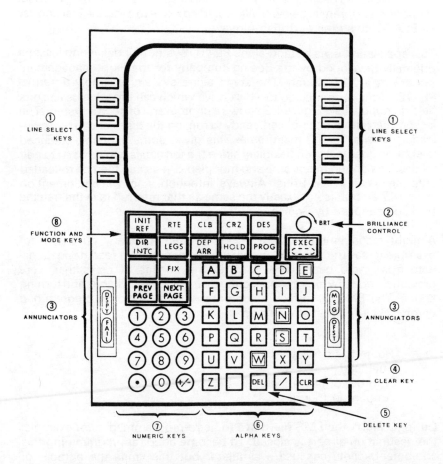

Figure 2.18 The control and display unit of a flight management system, as it would be seen on the PLATO screen.

The PLATO simulation enables the trainee to touch the screen just as the FMS control buttons are pressed. For example, to enter the cruising altitude, the figures are 'typed' on the numeric keys, and changes or deletions are made just as on the real thing. Having entered the data (which appears on the bottom line of the display area) it is entered into the correct part of the display by pressing the line-select keys on the right hand side. An interesting feature of the FMS display is that it is not static.

The display area will show one set of data for entering passenger and freight data, another for navigational data and so on. The different parts of these variable displays are accessed through the same line select keys, which can be thought of as 'soft' keys (i.e. their functions depend on the screen display).

The PLATO simulation gives pilots practice in completing FMS data entry and, unlike a full simulator, gives feedback for wrong answers and help if the student is stuck. An excerpt from the instructions for a typical lesson is shown below - no apologies are made for the FMS jargon, although the following does contain more explicit information than the pilot would be shown, since he would be familiar with the terms.

BRITISH AIRWAYS 747 FMS - PLATO LESSON 2

(The instructions begin by explaining what is going to happen, and that L/S is an abbreviation for Line Select.)

This flight is from Toronto International to Montreal Mirabel on April 15, 1982. It uses a standard company route stored in the data base. Stored company route "01/135" is from waypoint YYZ, via airway Y98 to waypoint MSS, then on to V203 to YUL.

Your ATC (Air Traffic Control) clearance is:

"CLEARED TO MONTREAL, MIRABEL AIRPORT IS FILED, MAINTAIN FL370"

Use the following sequence to complete this lesson:

FMS PREFLIGHT

FMS .... INITIALIZE

Data Base- CHECK
Observe- IDENT page
Observe- MODEL and ENGINE types correct (747-200 and RB211)
Observe- NAV DATA ACTIVE (upper) dates current.

Position initialisation page- DISPLAY
Push-POS INIT L/S key.
Observe- POS INIT page.
(This gives the start position of the aircraft for this particular mission)

IRS (INS) Position- ENTER
Push- LAST POS L/S key.
(LAST POS is the last position of the aircraft in latitude and longitude when the FMS was last switched off)
Push- SET IRS (INS) POS L/S key. (IRS is the Inertial Reference System)
Observe- latitude/longitude on selected line.

GMT- CHECK

..... and so on.

Remember that the trainee pilot has a PLATO screen facing him. The CHECK instruction means that he simply observes that the details in the data base- e.g. model number and engine type- are correct. Then, in the DISPLAY sequence, the POS/INIT line select key is pushed, to reveal the POS INIT page on the simulated display (showing the start position of the aircraft). Next, under the ENTER sequence, the LAST POS (last position) and SET IRS (Inertial Reference System) line select keys are pushed. As the lesson proceeds, data is typed in to the FMS using the calculator-like keyboard, all simulated on the PLATO screen.

This application represents the leading edge of CBL in its present form, and may be of some comfort the next time you are gripping the armrests! PLATO is not, of course, the only system to have been used in pilot training; for example, TICCIT from the Hazeltine Corporation and the RC-2 micro from Regency Systems have been widely used, and are both described in Chapter 18. The RC-2 is of great interest in that it emulates many features of PLATO in a completely stand-alone system, employing the USE language which is very similar to TUTOR.

Further progress is certainly possible, especially with such stand-alone training systems, and one direction that may be particularly profitable is in linking such a micro into the same model (the set of mathematical equations) that controls the mechanical simulator. At present, a subset of these equations is used on PLATO, Regency and other micros (re-programmed in an author language) to represent part of the model. This is necessary, in part, because such systems must be programmed in an author language (e.g. TUTOR or USE) to satisfy training requirements whilst the simulator is programmed in an engineer's language such as FORTRAN, Pascal or CORAL. What is NOT feasible at present is to use an author language to program a full replica simulator (the term applied to such comprehensive simulators as shown in the previous photograph) as these languages tend to be too slow for demanding real-time applications.

Sometime in the future, it may be possible for a training micro to access the FORTRAN program (for example) that is controlling the full simulator and for both the simulator and the micro to then run in parallel. At present, there are obstacles to this. For example, some languages do enable you to access a program written in an alien language (e.g. even SuperPILOT on the Apple lets you access any Pascal program) but, by so doing, you exit from the author language and lose all of its useful training attributes. Also, the training micro may let you down in the speed of its hardware, thus forever chasing the faster simulator. A compromise is to let the training micro access the same database of variables that is used by the simulator, so that the two can run independently whilst maintaining the advantages of each. This has, in fact, been demonstrated with a Regency Systems RC-2 stand-alone micro running under the USE author language and connected to a simulator running under FORTRAN (see Chapter 18 for details of Regency USE).

Clearly this type of problem can be solved, given some advances in the speeds and capabilities of both hardware and software, so that two or three people could be on the simulator flight deck, and many more could be 'flying' parts of the same simulated aircraft without the necessity of re-programming the model.

Part Two:

PLANNING -

The Key to Successful Lesson Design

Now that you've seen that CBL can and does succeed, you need to learn the correct techniques so that CBL will also succeed for you.

The next three chapters should help you in three different ways:

Chapter 3 helps you to choose a style of presentation to suit your topic. It also tries to help you in choosing the topic in the first place.

Chapter 4 gives a fairly comprehensive review of the stystems approach to training - basically, a way of making the best use of your time.
It shows you two powerful methods of course design.

Chapter 5 shows how to convert your course design into a form suitable for the computer. It concentrates on splitting a lesson down into frames, and then shows how to use a simple design sheet approach to plan how your lesson will appear to the student.

Chapter 3

Choosing What to do and Where to Start

We have already described (in Chapter 1) the way that CBL divides into computer managed learning (CML) and computer assisted learning (CAL). This chapter, indeed the rest of the book, concentrates on the CAL element. But, just as CBL could be divided, so can CAL, so we're going to explain what these divisions are. You should be able to relate them to the examples presented in Chapter 2 and, more importantly, it should help you to decide what sort of CAL is best for your application. So, the latter part of this chapter attempts to give some advice on the choice of topic and it contains some initial thoughts on the choice of hardware and software. Firstly, however, let's see how we can classify CAL.

3.1 Choosing a style

There have been many attempts to classify the various CAL styles. By a 'style' we mean 'How it appears to the student'. This is one possible breakdown:

SLIDE SHOW: this is also called 'demonstration' or 'exposition'. A CAL program of this sort presents a sequence of demonstration or illustration materials with little or no interaction with the student other than, perhaps, 'PRESS RETURN TO CONTINUE'. This style is sometimes used in a classroom situation where the teacher is using the computer as a visual aid.

TESTING: a program may be used to administer a test and store the results securely. The test may follow a slide show segment or a reading assignment, for example. You can regard testing as part of CML if you wish, but it is a common part of many CAL lessons. The important thing to remember is that a test is a test - it is not a lesson. Therefore, if your purpose really is to deliver a test, you must ensure that each question and answer is NOT followed by any feedback such as 'good' or 'NO - what a stupid mistake'. In either case, you would be distorting the purpose of the test by encouraging or discouraging the student. From the point at which you give any form of feedback you have either potentially improved or reduced the student's performance on the rest of the test.

DRILL AND PRACTICE: This is a repetive sequence of

> Question
> Answer
> Feedback

As you can see, it is simply testing plus feedback.

For example, in mathematics, you may devise a drill and practice sequence in which addition problems are posed to the student. After each student answer, the feedback is presented which might attempt to explain why any incorrect answer is wrong. For example, if you ask the question

> $35+26=?$

and the student replies

> 51

then the feedback might be

> 'You forgot the carry'

The drill would carry on until mastery was achieved which might be, in this case, getting 5 consecutive answers correct.

Drill and practice is a useful but a rather rudimentary form of CAL that has got the medium a bad name in some people's opinions.

TUTORIAL: This is a more sophisticated form of CAL in which the sequence is a series of connected (often branching) units which engage the student in an interactive dialogue of teaching and testing. Essentially, it is drill and practice, but with a teaching element and a more richly-branching structure. As shown in Figure 3.1, drill and practice is related to one very small area of knowledge, whereas a tutorial brings together many related facts and ideas. Very often, tutorials are used to teach CONCEPTS or PROCEDURES. For example, you could write a tutorial on recognising faults that may occur on a microcomputer. Each fault (e.g. faulty RAM chip) is characterised by a number of symptoms (e.g incorrect oscilloscope readings, characteristic error numbers displayed etc.) and the set of symptoms ,in total, defines the 'fault' concept. Your program would have to teach the recognition of each and every symptom before you could be sure that the student understood that particular fault. Similarly, a tutorial program to teach the procedure of correcting the fault would require that any possible incorrect actions of the repairman were corrected and explained.

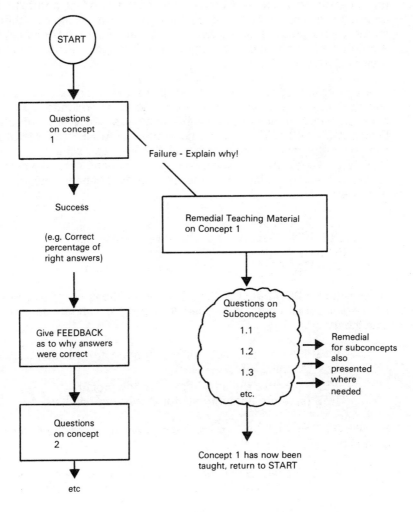

Figure 3.1 A simple tutorial sequence

The most important requirement of a good tutorial program is the quality of its feedback. Research has shown that student performance is maximised by giving feedback and then asking a further question to ensure that the feedback itself has been understood.

COMMAND MODE: most tutorials, though student-paced, are controlled by the designer of the program. By this, we mean that the designer (i.e. you!) have got a pretty fair idea of how most students are going to answer the questions that you ask. Most of your effort will, in fact, go into trying to anticipate what students might say (i.e. type) and in dealing with the small minority who get the answers wrong. It is you who will be directing them through the package and shunting them off through side roads to improve their performance.

In a few cases, people have tried to place the tutorials under student control. When this happens, the word 'tutorial' is no longer appropriate because of its connotations of teacher-control, so we refer to this style as COMMAND DRIVEN or as being under LEARNER CONTROL. For example, Tagg and his co-workers at Hatfield (see section 2.1 on the QUERY package) have devised a common command system which bolts on to all of their teaching programs. The set of commands includes such words as:

> HELP (give advice)
> EXPLAIN (description of the subject matter)
> GO (run the program)
> COMMANDS (what commands are available)

Having chosen COMMANDS, the following additional list may be available (these are actual commands used in a program about the motion of satellites):

> HEIGHT (set the height of a mountain from which a stone is
> > thrown)
> SPEED (choose the initial speed of the stone)
> TIME (sets the time interval for displaying results)

So, when using such a program, the student chooses the order of the commands which might be:

> :EXPLAIN (an explanation of the physics of satellite motion is
> > given)
> :HEIGHT 5000
> :SPEED 7000
> :TIME 5

:GO   (a table of results is displayed, including the height and
        speed of the projectile at 5 second intervals)
:SPEED 10000
:GO   (more results, with just the initial speed changed)
:FINISH

In contrast, a tutorial version of this program might ask you first for the height, then check the input against expected values, give suitable messages such as 'too high' or 'too low' and so on, and then proceed to the next input.

In the same vein, the TICCIT system (marketed by Hazeltine Corporation) has a special keyboard with keys marked, for example, EASY, HARD, PRACTICE and so on. Within TICCIT, the teacher can create a lesson which corresponds to a 'map'. The map is filled up (by the teacher) with examples, problems, and explanations. The student, when working through the lesson, uses the TICCIT keyboard to select, say, an explanation or to try an example. Having chosen the latter, an EASY, MEDIUM or HARD one can be chosen.

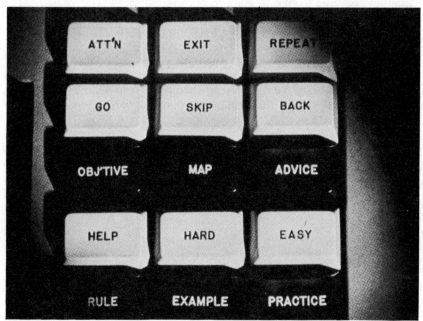

Figure 3.2 Through learner control keys on the TICCIT keyboard, the student can see displayed (by pressing "RULE") a statement of the rule to be mastered; (by pressing "EXAMPLE") examples of its application; and (by pressing "PRACTICE") practice problems. Instructional material level is controlled by the "EASY" and "HARD" keys.

In this way, the lesson is truly under learner control.

NUMERICAL SIMULATION: this is closely related to modelling, and people are often confused by the two terms. Modelling is the process of building a mathematical model (e.g. a set of equations that describe the flight of a rocket, or the economy of a country) whereas simulation is the use of such a model to simulate a real process. We gave some examples in Chapter 2, and a good one to recall is the use of PLATO in the simulation of part of a flight deck. Behind the movement of the meters and all of the other visual effects on the screen is a set of equations (the model). The example given in the previous section concerning orbital motion is also a simulation, but it is used within the framework of a command package.

DECISION TREE: Some people think of this as a simulation, though it tends not to use mathematical equations, so we will not confuse the issue by using the same name. In a decision tree, we are using a representation of some process, such as a database of airline passengers or bank customers, and making changes to it by, for example, adding passengers to the existing plane load, or altering a customer balance. In each case, the situation changes from one state to another:

STATE 'A' ⟶ New Passenger ⟶ STATE 'B'

The states are quite different; for example, state 'B' may be 'overbooked' or just '75% booked'. To this extent it is a simulation, and you should refer to section 2.3 which describes a typical program (American Express). This simulates very precisely the interactions that a clerk has with a computer when dealing with company transactions.

Another example of a decision tree which is much less of a simulation is the Action Maze. This presents a situation, asks the student to choose from one of several possible choices, and presents a new situation. The most well-known action maze is 'Joe Bailey', a management training maze, which goes something like this:

Joe is always late
for work. What are
you going to do:
1. Fire him
2. Interview him
3. Speak to his workmates.

1. The entire company goes on strike.

2. He says he'll try harder.

3. They snigger.

Each of these responses is followed by another list of possibilities for our aspiring manager to answer. The pathways rapidly multiply, but the object of the game is to find out why Joe is always late, and how best to deal with the problem - that is the end point of the 'maze'. Just as with the other examples, you are changing the state of the 'game' with each response given.

GAMES: many children have learnt more about computers by playing space invaders than by exposure to any number of traditional learning techniques. In a similar way, a game element can be added to many programs in the form of fantasies (see, for example, the Spellicopter idea in section 2.1).

Adventure Games

Another interesting aspect of gaming is the use of Adventure Games, which seem to have been little used in serious CAL as yet. The first Adventure game was written by Crowther and Woods of Stanford Research Institute. It was based on the game of Dungeons and Dragons, in which the players progress through the labyrinth of a 'dungeon' into various rooms. At the start of the game, the players do not know the layout of the dungeon but, as time progresses and they go from room to room, a map can be constructed. At each player's turn, a move is requested to enter a particular passage or room. An umpire, called the Dungeon Master, consults his map and tells the player what objects will be found - such as swords or treasure. At some points, a mythical battle will take place between the player and some beastie, the outcome typically being decided by a throw of the dice, the weapons that have been collected by the player and the outcome of previous batttles. What Crowther and Woods did was to replace the dungeon master with a computer program that stored the map and predicted the various fates that awaited the players.

The first such computer game was simply called Adventure, though hundreds of others have appeared including Dragonquest, Ghost Town, Zork and, appropriately, New York Subway! In most of these, the player is given some initial information about the immediate environment, and then can move around by typing commands such as Move Up, Move Down (or North, South etc.). There is usually a repertoire of other simple commands which might be, for example:

Climb Stairs

Open Door
Pay Taxidriver
Collect gun
Inspect Rock

The program responds appropriately to each command. For example, when you Open Door the program may say 'the door is locked, you must find the combination to unlock it' or, if you 'inspect Rock', you may get a lump of gold or a reply 'I see nothing unusual'. All games have some aim, such as rescuing trapped explorers or finding treasure, but the details of the game are limited only by the imagination of the designers.

Really good adventure games are very hungry in terms of memory consumption: the mazes themselves store large amounts of array space, and the verbose instructions may easily consume up to 100K of disk storage. Nevertheless, they are of considerable potential for learning and training applications. One, academic, reason is the dialogue required between the user and the machine. In most current games, only simple commands are permitted, so programs that understood natural language would represent a step forward. The drive towards natural language dialogues is also a major part of research in new Author Languages, so there is an obvious convergence. Another reason for being interested in Adventure games is that their few applications in training have been very succesful. Notable amongst these has been the surrogate travel project of the American CIA. In this, a CIA agent 'drives' a simulated car around an unknown town, in order to become familiar with its layout. At every road junction, the agent can turn left, right, go straight on and so on, whilst the scene is displayed on a videodisk player, in exact synchronisation with the agent's progress. In this way, learning takes place, and the similarity to an Adventure game is obvious.

Perhaps the lesson here is that really useful CAL adventures, requiring massive programming and high cost video technology, are best applied where costs are not too important.

3.2 Choosing a Topic

That concludes our classification. The next thing is that the real reason you have bought this book is surely that you have a problem to solve, and you suspect that CBL might be the answer. To that extent, you already have a topic in mind for CBL presentation, but in any event the following check-list may be helpful:

Make it Short

-- and make it simple. It is very easy to get too ambitious, especially after looking at the applications we've been talking about for the past couple of chapters. But, some of those represented man-years of effort, whereas you are probably at the feasibility study stage. As a first project, the program should represent no more than 5 or 10 minutes worth of instruction: that way, you'll produce a polished product.

Is there a Large Audience?

Like many other educational technology tools, CBL is expensive so far as the first 'master' copy is concerned, but become dramatically cheaper as more copies are made and more students use it. This is pretty obvious- traditional training typically costs £20 per hour, whilst CBL on a microcomputer is delivered for around £2 per hour.

Is it a Standard Topic?

It's no use choosing a topic that's taught differently by every teacher, because it is then certain that your package will be unacceptable to most people. Either choose a topic that can only be taught one way (e.g. every one agrees on how to fill in some type of form) or provide the CBL part as one element of a larger package that a teacher can customise locally with his own notes, or by adding his own personal examples in the program.

Can Standard Hardware and Software be used?

If the package is only for internal use, this presents no problem, but if you envisage national or international usage (or, even actual sales!), go for a widely available computer that uses software that either is 'free' with the computer (yes, even the dreaded BASIC if needs be) or which comes as an integral part of your package, or is likely to be purchased by your intended users (i.e. its price will not act as a deterrent).

Do you have the design skills?

Well, we hope so after you've read this book. You really also need some background in educational technology if you are to undertake Task Analysis and the design of behavioural objectives, a critical part of many training packages. You'll need graphic design skills to make sure that your lessons have the right impact, and you'll need to know about flowcharting and, possibly, coding in the language of your choice. Most of these are covered in this book, but we can't hope to make you an overnight expert.

Are there other people you can call on?

Think about the Media

For a first attempt, choose something which can be presented mainly through the computer- with documentation, of course, in the form of notes for students and teachers. Larger packages will almost certainly need the support of other media - work books, audio or video tapes. Make sure that the necessary skills exist to support the media preparation and delivery.

Consider the Audience

OK, you know to press RETURN after typing in a reply, but do the users? Do they know how to use the editing keys to correct errors? Is fast or accurate typing required? Are your instructions - both in lesson and the documentation - easy to read FOR YOUR AUDIENCE and are they unambiguous? And, if you're collecting student statistics, remember that the unions may give you a hard time unless you consult them and tell them why you need to collect the data. It may be data that's collected inefficiently already, or it may just be that it enables a student to re-start from where he left off. So TELL them!

Make it Fun

And we don't mean funny! There's nothing worse than seeing the same old joke every time you use a package, and your humour may not appeal to everyone. But you can make it enjoyable, and you can inject the 'video ethic' that has such universal appeal in video games. You should try to add these motivating components, or make sure there is someone on hand who can help you- probably someone with a bizarre sense of humour and a great imagination.

Make it Stick

There is no point in writing the best CBL package if nobody uses it. It is vitally important to ensure that they do so in advance before wasting a minute of your precious time. If you are a teacher, make sure that the use of the package will appear on the syllabus as a compulsory, not an optional item. If you are a trainer, make sure that this package will be the only way to learn a particular skill. If there's any disagreement, take up golf instead.

Management Backing

If you can involve your manager, head of department or whatever, so much the better. This is intimately related to the Make it Stick principle: once you have got everyone to agree, from the boss downwards, it makes subsequent shilly-shallying that much more difficult.

Project Management

Set up a timetable for the project, showing who'll do what and by when. Use a year planner or some other device. You might like to construct a chart with headings such as:

Task; Responsibility; Start Time; Duration; Finish Time; Completed On.

Make sure everyone involved has a copy, and have regular progress meetings.

Test the Product

You may think that this only needs to be thought about after the program is completed, but you need to have ongoing advice and monitoring as the package develops. Do you have a colleague who understands the subject area as well as you do? Does he have the time and inclination to play the part of the dumb student?

3.3 Choosing Hardware and Software

We've already talked about this at several points, and we'll keep bringing the subject up throughout the book, but we'll end this chapter with a summary of the issues as far as we can at the moment.

First of all, if you intend to use the in-house mainframe, think carefully. Very few of the major manufacturers have the sort of CBL software languages that you will need to produce exciting, graphical, colourful and motivating CBL lessons. A few, for example IBM, do have a well-supported authoring system and we suggest that you make a careful assessment of such a product against your lesson needs. It could be a useful route. You must remember, however, that most DP managers tend to give training a lower priority than, for example, the payroll program so there may be times when response times are poor. Also, there are often weekly maintenance afternoons when the computer will not be available and, even worse, when the mainframe keels over at an unscheduled time; when this happens, kiss goodbye to your training.

If your organisation uses a particular breed of microcomputer, try to use it and equip it with a suitable authoring system. An increasing number of micros have such software, for example the Apple II with SuperPILOT, the Commodore range with Microtext and the IBM computer with COMBAT.

In a small number of cases, it may be worth investing in dedicated training micros. For example, you may feel happier in having the support of a professional training organisation such as Control Data with their PLATO system. A further potential advantage, if you are embarking on a large CBL project, is that PLATO and a few other systems have a library of existing courseware that MAY be useable by your organisation while you are preparing your own package. Also, if a detailed costing justifies it (see Chapter 18) you may find that the higher productivity of such a system may offset the generally higher apparent costs. Or, you may require to control videodisks which might not be feasible with your present micros. In either case, it is always advisable to try leaning on your present supplier to get you out of the mess. For example, some manufacturers already have translators for PLATO lessons, whilst others may be able to patch their software for video adaptation.

In other words, our advice to you is to follow the simplest and easiest path, especially in the early days. Prove yourself with a popular micro and some inexpensive software in the feasibility stage. Multi-million pound or dollar investments come later!

Chapter 4:

DRAWING UP A PLAN

Before you touch the computer, it is necessary to do quite a bit of pre-planning so that the lesson is as succesful as possible. We'll be having a lot to say about this later on, but we have already indicated that CBL is a labour intensive medium with a high development ratio: we saw in the previous chapters that ratios of 100:1 to 200:1 are not uncommon. Of course, we also know that the medium is one of the most effective yet developed, so the investment of your time is well worth while.

Through these next three chapters, you will be shown how to set about designing your lessons in a systematic way. To begin with, we will look at the overall problem of designing educational materials, regardless of the whether a computer or some other medium is being used. After that, we'll face the problem of implementing the lesson on a computer using a straightforward visual method that will get you from the ideas stage to using the computer in the shortest possible time.

4.1 Why did Henry Fail?

You are probably itching to get to the keyboard to type in your first CBL program, but beware! The microcomputer is a seductive machine, and it is tempting to use it as the sole means of instruction. Let me illustrate this problem: you have decided to use a computer as the central tool in your instructional repertoire. Because of this decision, your subsequent decisions become polarised into using the computer as the ONLY means of instruction. Because of this polarisation, you produce screen after screen of text, each screen ending with 'press RETURN to continue'. Is that good instruction? Is it cost effective? Probably not and, more than likely, you would not do this, but many CBL packages are of this style.

Instead, let's presume that you write perfectly good CAL lessons that are motivating, interesting, and fun to use. And yet, Henry Jones, a fairly average student, always gets a 'fail' grade in the tests at the end of your lessons. Why is this? is it because-

He is dim?

He is inadequately prepared?

Henry does not learn well from a computer?

Your lessons are badly designed?

The first two reasons are largely Henry's problem. The third problem is rarely recognised by CBL enthusiasts - they just re-present the lesson time and time again until Henry passes. It's an interesting idea - it means that the method is guaranteed to be 100% effective - in time! But, it might be much more effective and a better use of Henry's time, to let him have just two attempts, then to use some other medium instead, like a book or videotape. As Henry progresses through a course, the computer might even learn what is the BEST medium for Henry- this is not an admission of failure for CBL.

The fourth reason in the list is what these three chapters are all about- the possibility that the lesson was badly designed in the first place. The subject of educational design is, of course, vast and there is little space to summarise the subject in three short chapters. Professional trainers are probably already aware of the main techniques - in which case these chapters are just a reminder - but others may find this quick overview of interest.

4.2 "I want that course ready by tomorrow........"

Much of what we are going to talk about is derived from Systems Analysis, a subject that has its roots mainly in the design of large business systems. As such, systems analysis is beloved by COBOL programmers and the like, and there is a strong temptation to transfer these old-ish ideas to CBL. But, do they work? The answer is a cautious 'Yes' for a small project but maybe not for very large and vague ones which CBL often tends to be. But, they are applicable in some cases, and it will do you no harm to find out about them now, even if you only make use of some of the ideas.

Many producers of CBL lessons want quick results- either to be first in the market place or because they have been instructed to get a quick result. Systems analysis is not necessarily conducive to this 'fast buck' approach, so it is more often the case that CBL materials are designed by the enthusiast, whose approach is to spot a likely application, code it and offer it to the potential audience. This approach is as shown below:

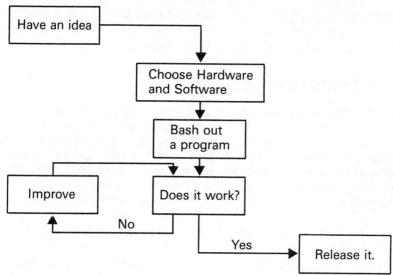

Figure 4.1 CAL for the Enthusiast

"......Five Good Reasons Why it Won't be"

The approach in the previous section is the one that many have used - myself included - when trying to persuade colleagues that CBL is worthwhile. We jump in, coding feet first, with little regard for the finer points of design. This can be very successful, but there are possible pitfalls for the over-enthusiastic amateur, as highlighted by Selden *:

HAS ANYONE SEEN MY GOAL? Often, little market research is done into what training is actually needed.

PEOPLE AREN'T LEARNING WHAT I WANTED THEM TO! Do the intended audience have the prerequisite skills? Are the questions ambiguous?

THERE'S A BUG IN MY COURSE! CAL lessons are always complex, requiring very careful planning with flowcharts, for example.

* P.H. Selden 'How to Avoid the Predictable Headaches of CBI', Training/HRD, September 1981, pp26-32.

THE PROGRAM BUT NO ONE IS USING IT! Maybe it's just boring, but did you ensure in advance that it would be prescribed for all who would benefit from it? Really, your audience should be given no choice as to whether they use it because students and other teachers will argue endlessly about what makes a good lesson.

SOMEONE REJECTED IT AT THE LAST MINUTE! Make sure that every manager, headmaster or other politician approves your project at each critical point. Involve everybody who matters.

4.3 A Systematic Approach

Now, all of this is not intended to deter you- the CAL entrepreneur. You should just be aware of what can go wrong and who is waiting to trip you up. To make sure that things go right, one method is to use the 'Systems Approach to Training'. This is beloved by the military, banks and other organisations who are using somebody else's money. When 'properly' done, a full systems study is a vast and expensive operation. But, you- the enthusiast who wants to do things properly - can still make use of parts of it.

Firstly, let's look at Fig.4.2 which summarises the Systems Approach.

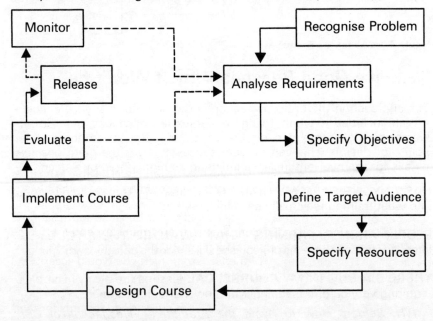

Figure 4.2 A Systems Approach

70

Let's look at each step in this diagram:

ANALYSE REQUIREMENTS.

The first stage of this process is often called 'job analysis'. It simply means that you write down the main components of the problem that you intend to put on to the computer. If you are training someone to learn a new skill, you could do this by observing a skilled person and writing down the jobs that they do. For example, if you wished to train a TV maintenance engineer, you might observe that his jobs include: diagnosing faults with the aid of various instruments; replacing faulty components; adjusting the controls; filling in a repair sheet. If you were teaching organic chemistry, your jobs would include: teaching about chemical structures; getting the students to be able to predict the outcome of certain reactions; demonstrating safe laboratory techniques and so on.

There is also a second phase of analysis, often necessary because the job analysis has produced quite large learning problems - too large to fit comfortably into one CBL lesson. In training parlance, this is often called 'Task Analysis'. It is a thorough analysis of each of the smaller jobs that we have already identified. The objective of this analysis is to produce quite small topics that will require about 15-20 minutes of interaction for the average student. There are several ways of performing a task analysis, for example:

> Continuing to observe a skilled person.

> Issuing a questionnaire to skilled people.

> Or, just talking to someone who is good at the particular job

SPECIFY OBJECTIVES

An objective is some statement of what the student will be able to do after using your lesson. You may specify that he should be able to 'identify any of 5 different faults in a vertical hold circuit of a TV set' for example. But you would not say 'Appreciate vertical hold faults' because appreciating is not the same as doing! Of course, there are many exceptions to the requirement for rigid objectives: you might be writing 'nice-to-know' lessons such as 'the history of the firm' for which you would accept less than complete matery of the subject matter.

Some educationalists dislike objectives, but some good reasons for their use include:

1. How do you know what you are teaching if you can not describe it?

2. Much of teaching is actually training, for which objectives were developed. For example, numeracy, literacy and computer programming.

   Here are some examples of objectives:

   "Translate a given sample of English prose into French, with the aid of a dictionary, to 90% accuracy."

   "Repair a random vehicle electrical fault using a standard tool kit within 20 minutes."

Such objectives all contain action verbs (e.g. translate, repair) and have a common pattern:

PERFORMANCE	CONDITIONS	STANDARDS
e.g. Repair a random fault...	using a tool kit.....	within 20 minutes.

If your statement does not fit into this category, you have not written an objective!

Objectives are not only handy for focussing the mind on what you want to teach, they also help you to construct the test questions that you are bound to need, to ensure that your students understand the lesson. For example, in the above example, you could generate 10 faults and provide the tool kit. Of course, you might decide to pass the repairman if he gets 8 out of the faults fixed. If so, modify the objective so that it reads:

Within 20 minutes for 80% of the cases.

Or, to be more subtle, there may be easy and hard faults - in which case you could devise tests for novices or for experts - again modifying the objective - and hence the test questions accordingly.

Test Questions - and how to write them

One item that deserves a special mention right now is the use of test questions. As we indicated earlier, test questions pop out of our objectives, but they can take several forms, and it is useful that you know about them now. One reason for this is that most experts agree that test questions must be designed concurrently with the objectives. Here is a classification of each major type of question:

Multiple Choice

For example:

"Which of the following is a valid PILOT statement:

     a. M:RED OR BLUE
     b. M:RED!BLUE
     c. M RED!BLUE

Write your answer (a,b, or c) in this box ☐

The incorrect answers are called distractors, and they must appear to be plausible. There are points for and against this type of question:

FOR	AGAINST
Easy to check.	Students might guess the correct answer
Produces reliable results.	Distractors may reinforce incorrect ideas.

A variation on this theme is the 'concealed multiple choice'. In this case, one answer is shown at a time, and the student is asked if it is the correct answer. This minimises guesswork.

True/False

For example:

"This is a valid PILOT match instruction

     M:RED!BLUE

Is this True or False?"

For and against, we have:

FOR	AGAINST
Easy to construct	50% chance of guesswork
Easy to check	Questions may not seem unequivocal
Easier when distractors are difficult to concoct.	to some students.

Matching Lists

For example

"Match the PILOT command letters to their descriptions:

A. Display Text	1. A
B. Accept input	2. M
C. Match input	3. D
D. Calculate value	4. U
E. Call subroutine	5. C
	6. V
	7. T

Write your answers in the grid below:

```
┌─────────┐
│A B C D E│
├─────────┤
│         │
└─────────┘
```

Enter 1 under A if you think that 'Display Text' is denoted by 'D' for example.

Notice that D and V are thrown in as plausible distractors for those who might think that D means display and that V means value (they don't!)

The good and bad points are:

FOR	AGAINST
Easy to check. Assesses several points in one question.	Difficult to construct.

Short Answer

For example:

"Write a PILOT statement that will match against the keywords RED, AMBER or GREEN"

This is the nicest but most awkward sort of question. Answers are usually allowed to include extra words, perhaps spelling mistakes or just phonetic matching. Although BASIC and the like perform badly when asked to match answers to such questions, author languages such as PILOT perform very well. Taking the above example, we could write a PILOT command to do the job for us in one line. The equivalent in BASIC would be many lines.

The major drawback to short answers is trying to anticipate what the student might say. You can grow a long grey beard trying to work this out, so an alternative is the 'completion' type of question:

"A valid PILOT statement that will match against RED, AMBER or GREEN is ...."

This limits the possible answers, and you can even give a clue by matching the number of spaces to the correct number of characters in the answer.

Now we'll return to the steps in our systems diagram (figure 4.2).

DEFINE TARGET AUDIENCE

Who is going to use your package? If they do not all have the same level of PREREQUISITE knowledge, you may have to provide extra teaching materials. For example, can they all use a keyboard? If not, would a Typing Tutor package be useful? Remember that you will not be there to answer the student's questions- the computer can be thought of as an interface between you and the student.

SPECIFY THE RESOURCES

It may be that the computer lesson is the only resource that the student will need, but it is unlikely. More often than not he will need such things as:

> Paper and pencil for note taking.

> Printed instructions, diagrams and so on to be referred to during the lesson.

> Books, audio cassettes, video player and any of the other multi-media echniques that he may need to use.

> Special 'hands-on' equipment. Like a faulty TV set, for example.

This may all sound very obvious, but CBL exponents seem to have a blind spot in this direction. I think that the effort of producing the CBL lesson was just all too much for them! The easiest way round the problem is to make a check list which you hand out with the disk or whatever before your student starts work. That way, it is his responsibility to get his own act together. Even better is to be sure that the teacher or trainer uses the check list.

DESIGN THE COURSE

Let's presume that you chosen your training problem and that you've followed the above prescription. If you've not, don't worry, since we'll be using an actual example later on.

So far as the course generally is concerned, we may now have to lay down a design for the CML component, stating the test questions to be used, the lessons to be presented depending on the results of tests, and the media to be allocated to each student.

For the CAL part of the lesson we need to plan the sequence of presentation. What we need is some sort of graphical method that will help us in designing our final lesson. A familiar tool is the flow chart, beloved of programmers for many years. A simple flow chart might look like this:

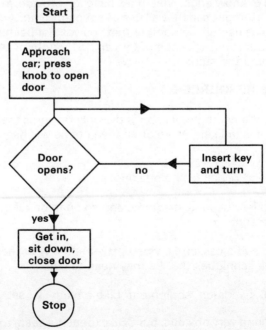

Figure 4.3 A simple flow chart

76

Just as for a process like this, a flow chart can be drawn to represent a complete CBL course or lesson. It can also be used as a detailed design aid for coding any language statements, but this is to be discouraged because such flowcharts are invariably produced after the program has been made to work.

In chapter 8, we show how to use a particular type of flow chart.

IMPLEMENT COURSE

With the aid of a flowchart and a suitable CBL system, we now convert the course into a program. At this stage, it is important to document and test the programs.

EVALUATE

This means different things to different people. I take it to be a 2-stage process of:

Internal Validation: a small group of representative users test the program and changes are made as needed.

External Validation: the program is released for wider usage under scrutiny. For example, the users may be required to complete questionnaires.

At any stage it may be necessary to back-track and repeat or refine some stages. Notice the dashed line in Fig. 4.2 connecting 'evaluate' and 'analyse': evaluation may reveal a change in working practices necessitating a new task analysis.

Finally, the package is released for routine usage. Notice that a 'monitor' stage is included to ensure that a package always works as intended.

As we said at the start of this section, you may need only a flavour of this approach - but don't dismiss the idea. It does help you to develop your ideas and enables you to present a well-structured plan of your intentions.

4.4 Designing for Real: some practical methods

So far, we have taken a broad look at the systems approach - or those parts that are most useful to CBL designers - in the broadest possible context. We have also examined some aspects of objective testing, but we have not specified how to design a lesson in such a way that the objectives are likely to be specified. Naturally, there is no way that we can guarantee that a particular student will master a particular subject, but what we are after is some sort of design method that will make it most likely that mastery will be achieved.

Who do you believe?

Educational design is the province of educational psychologists, who write learned papers and lengthy books on the subject of design techniques. For the CBL entrepreneur, life is not long enough to indulge in the luxury of extensive research. Also, these experts never seem to agree and - particularly worrying - they are mostly unable to explain their theories clearly to the layman. For these reasons, we are going to present - in the next two chapters- just two theories very briefly; each of them is useful in certain applications, but if you wish to apply them fully, you will almost certainly have to do a little more reading. Firstly, we will describe 'Stimulus Response' models of learning - these are useful when the learning task is a fairly straightforward series of linear steps. Next, we describe Component Display Theory, which is more applicable to complex situations.

Chapter 5

Stimulus - Response Models

Imagine that you wish to teach a simple task, such as repairing a vehicle electrical fault or filling in a standard form. You have written down the objectives and, thanks to a thorough task analysis, you find that you can write down a sequence of small instructional steps that will enable the learner to achieve mastery. Each small step is of the form:

$$STIMULUS \longrightarrow RESPONSE$$

The stimulus is provided on the computer screen. For example, we may present a picture of a distributor with a question alongside it, such as 'identify the low tension terminal'. This is the stimulus. The learner identifies the cable by, for example, typing a letter (the components could have letters A,B,C etc. alongside them). This is the response.

To make this crystal clear, and to avoid any misunderstandings in the future, it is worth differentiating between response, which we have been talking about so far, and feedback. The response is what the student does, having been presented with the stimulus. For example, typing an answer, touching the screen and using a lightpen are all responses. Feedback is what you give to the student after the feedback.

A lot of research has gone into the nature of feedback, of which there are two types:

PASSIVE FEEDBACK: the message is simply displayed and the learner progresses to the next learning point.

ACTIVE FEEDBACK: the message is given in the form of a question to which the learner must respond before proceeding.

For example, using the above stimulus, the correct response might be 'B' (i.e. the component marked with a B on the screen) and the feedback might be:

PASSIVE: That's right- let's carry on.

ACTIVE: That's right - how did you know?

In the latter case, a short answer might be called for, such as 'because it is connected to the thinnest cable". This time we've caught out the student who guesses the answer. As would be expected, active feedback is more successful, especially with less able learners (curiously, with above average learners it makes little difference) simply because the learner is more actively involved in the learning process. The snag is, of course, that it means more work for you!

A compromise is to explain why a response is correct or not, rather than a bland yes/no. On this point, beware of what feedback you give. For example, you might think it acceptable to have your program choose randomly from a pool of messages such as:

        Yes
        Correct
        Great!
        Fantastic!
        OK
        Fine

Although YOU know that the messages are equivalent, the student does not, so which would he prefer? Think carefully about feedback!

A response often leads to a further stimulus. For example, in the above case, the next stimulus might be:

'A voltmeter is now attached to the LOW TENSION TERMINAL. Please type in the voltage shown on the meter:...............'

In this case, the screen will show a simulated meter with the needle located on a scale. The response is the voltage typed in by the student. Then we might give a further stimulus, such as 'Is this the expected voltage?' and so on. In this simple form of teaching, we have a stimulus-response chain:

$$S \longrightarrow (R,S) \longrightarrow (R,S) \longrightarrow \quad \ldots \ldots \quad \longrightarrow (R,S) \longrightarrow R$$

5.1 Learning Points

Where appropriate, this so-called 'chain' type of learning is very effective. The main reason is that the student is actively involved at each tiny step, building success upon success; indeed, progress from one S-R pair to another is only possible after mastery of that step has been demonstrated.

Each tiny S-R step is sometimes called a rule or learning-point. If we examine the learning points in the above example, we find an interesting relationship:

1. Identify low tension terminal.

                      Related TERMINAL

2. Read voltage on low tension terminal.

                      Related by VOLTAGE

3. Ask if voltage is correct.

5.2 Matrices

As you can see, what we term a learning point is actually comprised of a stimulus-response pair; for example, point 3 would have the question 'Is this voltage correct?' as its stimulus, and the (correct) student reply as the response. If we were to continue to add more points, we would find that each learning point is related to its predecessor, and vice-versa. Hence, the reason for calling this 'chain-learning'. We can represent a chain pictorially by a simple table, or matrix, with the identifying numbers of the learning points running across and down the side of the matrix, as shown in Figure 5.1. This figure only uses 5 learning points, though in reality there will usually be many more. For each pair of points that are related to each other, we put a tick in the appropriate box, except on the main diagonal where each point MUST be related to itself!

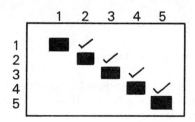

Figure 5.1 A simple 'Chain Learning' Matrix.

81

Since the matrix is symmetrical, it is only strictly necessary to fill in the upper half of the matrix, though it's sometimes a useful check to complete the whole matrix. The interesting thing about such a matrix is that, if you had been building it up as the learning points were written down, you would immediately recognise the pattern as being characteristic of chain-learning. And, chain-learning is very common when we are trying to teach a procedure such as form filling or simple repair methods. So, the matrix would help you by verifying that you are indeed teaching what you thought was intended.

Many other matrix patterns may emerge. For example, consider the following learning points, which relate to a chemistry topic:

1. An aromatic compound contains a 6-membered carbon ring.

2. Benzene is aromatic and 6-membered.

3. Toluene is aromatic and 6-membered.

4. Xylene is aromatic and 6-membered.

etc.

This time, we find that 1 is related to 2 by the word aromatic and that 1 is related to 3, 4 etc. Also, 2 is related to 3 and to 4. In fact every point is related to every other, because 2, 3, 4 etc are examples of 1. What we are teaching is a definition or CONCEPT of 'aromatic compound'. Whenever this occurs, a cluster of ticks is seen on the matrix, as shown in Figure 5.2.

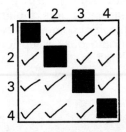

Figure 5.2 Concept Formation in a Learning Point Matrix.

In reality, a matrix may contain several clusters and chains. Another type of cluster arises when teaching discrimination between different items. For example, we might be designing a lesson on the use of a computer keyboard, producing the following learning points:

1. The keys on a computer keyboard are located in groups.

2. The numeric keys are on the top row.

3. The letter keys are on the bottom three rows.

4. The function keys are located on the right hand side.

Each of these points could have an associated question - for example, requiring the student to press certain keys. Each of these four points are associated by the word 'keys'. But, points 2 and 3 differ from each other since they indicate the different parts of the keyboard where the keys are to be found. Similarly, points 3 and 4 are each related to point 1 but differ from each other. Wherever differences appear, we put a cross rather than a tick, so our matrix is now a cluster of ticks and crosses, as shown in Fig 5.3

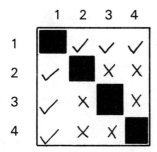

Figure 5.3 Learning Point Matrix with Similarities and Differences.

Having found a learning matrix of this type, we can see that it will be necessary to include questions that test a student's understanding of the critical differences. A lesson that only asked questions about similarities would not be adequate. Again, the matrix has helped us to check our teaching strategy.

Some other standard patterns arise in matrices. One common one is where a tick occurs only between certain pairs of learning points. For example, between 1 and 2 and between 3 and 4, but not between 2 and 3. This characterises 'Signal Learning' in which the student must learn definitions. For example:

Learning Point 1: What is the capital of France?

Learning Point 2: Paris is the capital of France.

The two points are connected by 'capital of France'. But, the next learning point may be 'What is the capital of Holland?' which is unrelated to any preceding point.

5.3 Optimisation of Learning Sequences

A further use of a matrix is to reveal faulty lesson design. Consider the following learning points that might emerge in 'booting' an Apple II computer:

1. Take the diskette from its outer cover.

2. Hold the diskette with the notch on the left.

3. Open the disk drive door.

4. Insert the disk into the disk drive.

5. Close the disk drive door to securely lock the diskette.

6. Press the re-set key.

7. Whilst removing it from its outer cover, do not touch the diskette surface.

You should be able to verify that the matrix now looks like Figure 5.4

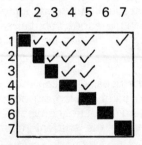

Figure 5.4 Mis-placed Learning Points (Only the top half needs to be completed, as the matrix is symmetrical)

Points 1 to 5 are linked through the word diskette and other associations. The lone tick between 1 and 7 indicates that point number 7 is misplaced. Putting it between 1 and 2 yields a tidier matrix with all of the ticks grouped about the main diagonal. Althought this example is very obvious, a larger lesson can easily demonstrate this phenomenon, as extra learning points are often added as afterthoughts. Therefore, our matrix can help, not only in detecting what type of learning is to take place, but also in determining where planning errors have arisen.

Chapter 6:

Component Display Theory

In the preceding sections, we have emphasised the need for a logical ordering of material without, it is admitted, a lot of thought as to how the teaching material is to be presented. Students can, of course, learn a given topic in a variety of ways and from a variety of media. We happen to be concerned with CBL as the main medium but it may be surprising to learn that WHATEVER THE MEDIUM the most critical factor is the presentation strategy. This means, for our present purposes, the sequencing of the CBL materials and the ways in which they relate to each other. For a pure CAL lesson, it is WHAT is presented and WHEN. If these are inappropriate, no amount of investment in expensive technology will improve the effectiveness of the lesson.

Component Display Theory has been developed, by Professor M. David Merrill, to provide answers to these what and when questions. In this chapter, we present one of the first summaries of CDT to appear in a general publication.

6.1 The Performance-Content Matrix

CDT evolved from the observation that different types of learning outcomes require different types of teaching procedures. For example, simple facts can be 'learned' by recitation whereas a more esoteric subject such as the Theory of Relativity demands a more subtle approach.

Fundamental to CDT is the recognition that any cognitive topic has two characteristics:
  . its content
  . the type of performance required of the learner.
This is shown in Fig 6.1

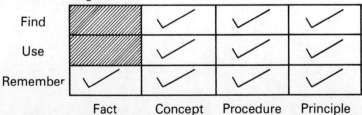

Figure 6.1 Content/Performance Matrix (performance runs vertically, content horizontally)

This matrix is simple to understand - for example, you may require someone to

  remember a fact
  use a procedure
  find a principle

and so on. There are two impossible things - finding or using facts. For example, you can't 'find' the colour of a live wire, instead you remember it. You can't 'use' your birthday either. This leaves us with 10 possible learner outcomes and it is worthwhile to define what we mean by each of the terms in the matrix.

For the performance level:

FIND: derive or invent something
USE: apply knowledge to a particular case
REMEMBER: recall some item(s) of stored knowledge.

And for the content level:

FACT:	an item of information associating symbols, events or objects and so on e.g. Red is a primary colour
CONCEPT:	a group of items sharing a group of common characteristics e.g. Acids turn litmus paper red and cause sodium bicarbonate to effervesce. (An acid must possess each of these properties)
PROCEDURE:	a sequence of steps e.g. a flowchart for a computer program
PRINCIPLE:	an explanation or prediction e.g. Ohm's law

6.2 Using the P-C Matrix

To demonstrate the apparent validity of the matrix, here are examples of some test questions correctly identified for their performance and content categories.

REMEMBER - FACT

1. What is the morse code for the letter L?
2. How many legs has a centipede?

REMEMBER - CONCEPT

1. Define the term "Super Nova"
2. List the characteristics of edible fungi

FIND - CONCEPT

1. From the given data, describe how you would identify a Super Nova
2. Sort these plants into two different groups, and explain how you did it

REMEMBER - PROCEDURE

1. How do you make a sponge cake?
2. List the steps involved in merging two files

USE - PROCEDURE

1. From the given ingredients, make a sponge cake.
2. Write a program that will merge files "A" and "B" into file "C" using the method described to you.

FIND - PROCEDURE

1. With the aid of the given ingredients, find a way to make a successful sponge cake.
2. You are given two files, "A" and "B". Devise a means of merging the two into a third file, "C".

REMEMBER - PRINCIPLE

1. Explain Ohm's Law.
2. Explain Archimedes' Principle.

USE - PRINCIPLE

1. Predict the voltage at point "B" in the circuit.
2. Using the balance and beaker of water provided, determine the density of the brass block.

FIND - PRINCIPLE

1. For various voltages, V, applied across the resistor, R, measure the current I, that flows and devise a relationship between V, I and R.
2. You are provided with a chemical balance, various objects and liquids of different densities. Weigh the objects immersed in the liquids and explain your results.

You may wish to try out the above ideas for yourself. Either analyse your own test questions, or try to categorise the following into their correct P-C combination:

1. Is this an example of a cumulus cloud?
2. What is the symbol for a church?
3. What are the characteristics of a mammal?
4. Write a behavioural objective for this task.
5. Explain why the engine will not start.
6. Start the engine.
7. Sort these shells into shoreline types.
8. What will happen to the voltage at "A" if Resistor "B" is short circuited?
9. De-bug this program.
10. List the symptoms of a patient suffering from pneumonia.
11. Reassemble the SRA2 within 10 minutes, blindfolded.
12. Explain the test procedure for measuring the efficacy of an anti-histamine drug.
13. Devise a means of testing a new anti-histamine.
14. Explain how a microwave cooker cooks food.
15. Fill in a sick-leave certificate.
16. Write down an example of a FOR.....NEXT loop.
17. With a FOR.....NEXT loop, find the largest number the computer can store.
18. Explain how to fly a light aircraft on a course visually between the three points shown on the map provided.
19. Show how a vector diagram is used to compute mid-course corrections.
20. Show how a sodium discharge lamp produces yellow light, making reference to any related phenomena if you wish.

The answers are on the next page.

Answers to Questions:

For brevity we use U=Use, R=Remember, F=Find for performance, and F=Fact, C=Concept, Proc=Procedure, Prin=Principle.

1. U-C	2. R-F	3. R-C	4. U-Prin	5. F-Prin
6. U-Proc	7. U-C	8. F-Prin	9. U-Proc	10. R-C
11. R-Proc	12. R-Proc	13. F-Proc	14. R-Prin	15. U-Proc
16. U-C	17. U-Proc	18. U-Proc	19. R-Proc	20. U-Prin

So, at least on the face of it, the classification does appear to work: it categorises knowledge into suitable small areas. This is important because it means that we can now state what sort of knowledge we are trying to teach. And, if we know that, we have narrowed down our options as to how to teach:
there seem to be just ten possible teaching strategies corresponding to each cell in the P-C matrix.

We have seen how any subject matter could be categorised in terms of its content and the performance required. Also, we've taken some existing test questions and categorised them according the content and performance. Therefore, you can use this fundamental technique either in the analysis of existing materials or in the design of new instruction.

6.3 Task Analysis and the P-C Matrix

Being a CBL designer, you will are often in the business of designing new lessons. Therefore, your first task is to analyse what you wish to teach in terms of content and performance so that you can be sure of which P-C combination you are actually teaching, as shown in Fig 6.2

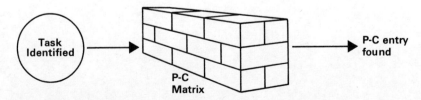

Fig 6.2 P-C Entries Identified

For any reasonable task analysis, there will be several tasks and several P-C entries to identify. You can think of a P-C chart as a look-up table that helps to focus your mind on the nature of each task.

For example, as a result of a task analysis for a radar operator, we might have:

Task 1:

> Recognise radar patterns.
> Because radar patterns have definite characteristics, this is "Use-Concept"

Task 2:

> Estimate speed of aircraft.
>
> Some mental algorithm is used, so this is an example of "Use-Procedure"

As another example, perhaps you are teaching organic chemistry:

Task 1:

> Recall the chemical formulae of various common isomers of benzene.
>
> Simple recall is needed, so this is "Remember-Fact"

Task 2:

> Describe the benzene nitration process.
>
> An example of Remember-Procedure

Task 3:

> Predict the results of chemical reactions based on known laws.
>
> This is an example of Use-Principle

Most of training and a lot of teaching is in fact at the Use and Remember levels. You are unlikely to be designing CBL lessons at the "Find" level.

6.4 Writing Objectives the easy way

You should now be able to correctly classify each task. You next write your objectives. Because there are only ten P-C categories, there are only 10 kinds of objectives. Therefore, a table of formulae can be drawn up similar to that in Table 6.1. To use this, you simply identify your P-C category and find its entry on the left hand side of Table 6.1. Reading across the particular row you find the conditions, performance and standards necessary for the particular objective. Thus, each row is a formula for an objective. To get the objective you actually require, you simply insert the necessary subject matter. Since we are not concerned with the "Find" level, Table 6.1 only has Remember and Use entries.

Each heading in the table is divided into a fixed and a variable column. By "fixed" we mean that part which is necessary, and by "variable" we mean those alternatives which do not affect the P-C category. For example, in "Remember Concept", the name of the concept must be present but it may be accompanied by words, pictures, symbols or other stimuli. Some examples are given for each case. Try your own examples, but don't worry if they don't quite fall into the suggested wording: it is only a guide, albeit an important one.

For your particular applications, it may be necessary to design objectives relating to either verbatim or paraphrase responses. In some cases - for example, knowledge of legal procedures - a fairly exact word-for-word knowledge of the subject is needed. In most other cases, a paraphrase version is acceptable.

Now that we have specified the objectives, we have also specified the test questions. In fact, when filling in the spaces in a row of Table 6.1, it is often difficult not to produce a test question. The difference from an objective is that an objective should be a general task statement, whereas the test questions are examples or applications of the objective.

Most educationalists consider that both the objectives and the test questions should be written before producing the accompanying instructional material. If this is not done, there is a danger of adapting the objectives to the lesson, thus distorting its purpose.

6.5 HOW THE THEORY HELPS IN CORRECT SEQUENCING

Having identified the objectives, it is now necessary to design a sequence of learning that will achieve the objectives. CDT identifies various types of "display" that can contribute to a lesson:

TABLE 6.1 Prescriptive formulae for objectives

	PERFORMANCE		CONDITIONS		STANDARDS	
	WILL BE ABLE TO (Fixed)	BY (Variable)	GIVEN (variable)	OF/FOR/ BY etc (fixed)	WITH (fixed)	MEASURED BY (Variable)
Remember Fact	Recall Information	Writing, Drawing, Ticking etc	Objects, Descriptions Drawings etc	Associated Inform- ation	No errors No delay	1 point for each correct answer
e.g.	Recall the parts of a micro- computer	Writing their correct names	The block diagram of a	Micro- computer with its unlabelled parts	No errors No delay	1 for each part
Remember Concept	Define or list charact- eristics	Writing, drawing etc	Words, pictures etc	Named Concept	Few Errors Short Delay	1 for each correct charact- eristic
e.g.	State the def- inition	Writing in the space provided	The term	"Fatty Acid"	At least 3 charac- istics within 60 seconds	1 point each
Remember Procedure	State the steps involved	Flowchart Writing etc	Aim, Goal	Named Procedure	Few Errors Short Delay	1 for each step
e.g	Show (i.e. state the steps)	by means of a flow- chart	how to sort an unsorted list	by the "Exchange" Method	As precisely as possible, within 5 minutes	1 point each section
Remember Principle	State the Relation- ship	Writing, Calculating Drawing etc	Words, Pictures etc	Named Principle	Few Errors Short Delay	1 for each part of relation

6.1 continued

e.g.	Explain	with suitable equations	how to calculate currents, voltages & resistances in the circuit diagram provided	by using Ohm's Law	As many as possible to be calculated within 10 minutes	1 for each correct answer
Use Concept	Classify	Writing, Sorting, Pointing etc	Objects, Pictures Descriptions	Examples	Some Errors Short Delay	1 mark for each correctly classified
e.g.	Classify	by writing "E" for evergreen, or "D" for deciduous	against the pictures	of 20 trees provided	90% right in 5 minutes	
Use Procedure	Demonstrate	Calculation Measurement Manipulation etc.	Situation, Materials Equipment etc.	Named Task	Some Errors Agreed Time	
e.g	Show	by measuring the positions & heights of the peaks in	the spectroscopic recordings provided	how to classify the compounds as amines or acids	Can be completed over the weekend	80% correct
Use Principle	Explain or Predict	Calculation, graph, reasoned argument etc	Data, Pictures, Descriptions etc	Named Problem	Some Errors Untimed	
e.g.	Predict	by means of a graph	how the voltage at point "P"	will decay when the battery is disconnected		

Primary Displays: these form the strategic backbone of the lesson.

Secondary Displays: each primary display is elaborated upon with material to help the student.

Process Displays: how the student should use or process the secondary
<u>_____</u> displays e.g. "Make a note of this diagram for
future reference".

Procedure Displays: how to use the medium. e.g. "Press NEXT to
<u>_____</u> continue"

Before you design any of these displays, you have to decide if you want to
teach the general or specific aspects of a topic. To make a distinction, we
will define "generalities" and "instances" A generality is simply the
general case or statement that covers a range of specific examples. Thus,
the generality of a concept is a definition and the generality of a procedure
is a process (i.e. a statement of a procedure). An instance is the particular
case of, say, a concept. In this case, the instance would be an example
having all of the attributes required by the definition.

So, we have two possibilities- generality or instance- to combine with one
of two possible performance levels- remember or use (we are excluding
the 'find' level). This gives four possible outcomes, of which 'Use Instance'
has no practical applications, leaving just three:

Outcome	Meaning	Example
Remember Generality	Recall existing general knowledge	Describe the XYZ procedure for separating acids and amines (Process)
Use Generality	Apply knowledge to a new case	Demonstrate how to use the XYZ procedure to separate acid A and amine B. (Process)
Remember Instance	Recall a specific case	When was the Treaty of Rome signed? (Fact)

Of course, you only have partial control over the situation. Some learners
may solve a problem by a Use Generality strategy when you expected
them to Remember an Instance. This can be circumvented, of course, by
restricting the time allowed to answer the question. The important thing is

that you have recognised what outcome you intend to teach. You must now devise a strategy that will achieve that outcome.

6.6 Primary Displays

CDT suggests that, regardless of the teaching medium, there are four primary strategies or displays corresponding to the combinations of:

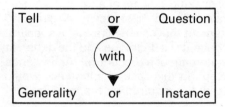

We've already met instances and generalities. By "Tell" we mean a passive imparting of information. In CBL, this corresponds to the "Slide Show" sequence mentioned at the beginning of this book. By "Question" we mean the interactive participation of the student. In CBL this may include Drill & Practice or tutorial modes. The four primary displays are shown pictorially in Table 6.2

	Tell	Question	
Generality	TG	G-Practice(IG) G-Test(QG)	T=Tell G=Generality I=Inquisitory
Instance	Teg	eg-Practice(Ieg) (Drill & Practice) eg-Test(Qeg) (Test)	Q=Question eg=example (instance)

Table 6.2 The Four Primary Displays relevant to CBL

As to HOW we tell a generality, this depends on the content of a lesson. It may help to refer to Table 6.3 which clarifies what is meant by the generality and instance levels of the various content types, when applied

96

to the primary displays. For example, the generality of a concept is a definition, whereas the instance of a concept is an example. To use or obtain practice in the use of instances, we classify and to practice a generality we state the definition in some form.

	EG (Tell Generality)	Eeg(Tell Instance)	Ieg(Instance Practice)	IG(Generality Practice
FACT	--	A --> B	A --> ?	--
CONCEPT	Definition	Example	Classify	State Definition
PROCEDURE	Process or Algorithm	Demonstr- ation	Demonstrate	Describe process or algorithm

Table 6.3 Generalities, Instances and Concept Types in Primary Displays

As can be seen from the previous tables, the Question dimension is sometimes referred to as "Inquisitory". By this we mean that we ask a question and then give feedback - we are inquiring in an informal and helpful way. This helps us to define Drill & Practice as a sequence that can be represented as

Ieg_1 --> Ieg_2 --> ......--> Ieg_n

i.e. one enquiry after another.

Similarly, a test uses a series of "no-help" questions in the form
Qeg_1 --> Qeg_2 --> .....--> Qeg_n

And, a tutorial may take the form:

TG--> Teg_1, Teg_2 ...Teg_n --> Ieg_1 ,Ieg_2, ... Ieg_n,--> Qeg_1, Qeg_2, ..., Qeg_n

In other words, a generality is told, followed by some examples. Then the student is involved in an inquisitory sequence followed by a test.

Sometimes a general rule is introduced after presenting a number of examples:

Teg_1 --> Teg_2 ..... Teg_n --> TG

Therefore, most common teaching strategies can be accommodated by this form of shorthand. This enalbles you - if you want to do - to jot down a skeleton description of lessons you teach at the moment. This exercise will, as you see, have its uses.

Far more important is the selection of the correct sequence of primary displays in order to achieve a given outcome in a new lesson. For example, you have analysed the task you wish to present in a CBL lesson and have decided that it is concerned with using a generality. It might involve applying a general procedure. Component Display Theory claims that the best sequence for your CBL lesson should be:

Presentation   **Practice**   **Performance**
EG--Eeg_1, Eeg_2,...., Eeg_n --> Ieg_1, Ieg_2...Ieg_n --> Qeg_1, Qeg_2 ...Qeg_n

That is:

Tell the general procedure (for example)
Tell a number of examples
Inquire about new examples, with feedback.
Test with yet more new examples.

CDT claims that similar sequences are necessary to teach at any performance level. These are shown in Table 6.4. Notice that a distinction is made between verbatim and paraphrase performance. By paraphrase, we mean a summary or alternate acceptable words or pictures as a student response.

Table 6.4: Consistency of Primary Presentations with Teaching Outcomes

Read from left to right for the correct sequence consistent with any desired performance. Notes: IG.P is a paraphrase versions. Iegs and Eegs means 2 or more examples. Ieg.r means an alternate representation (see text).

	PRESENTATION	PRACTICE	PERFORMANCE
FIND		Iegs, IG	Iegs, IG
USE	EG, Eegs	Iegs	Iegs
REMEMBER GENERALITY PARAPHRASE	EG, Eeg	IG.P	IG.P

98

REMEMBER GENERALITY VERBATIM	EG	IG	IG
REMEMBER INSTANCE PARAPHRASE	Eeg	legs.r	legs.r
REMEMBER INSTANCE VERBATIM	Eeg	leg	leg

The use of paraphrase is shown as IGp in Table 6.4 at the Remember Generality level. This use of a subscript might also be used at the Remember Instance Paraphrase level. But, it is more usual to accept mastery at this level if the student can respond to the example presented in a slightly different form denoted as legs.r in the table. For example, if he is required to remember a chemical reaction, it may help if it is represented by:

an equation
or, a demonstration
or, various forms of words.

Each of these could take the form of an enquiry or of a test question. For example:
Complete the equation
Tell me what will happen next
Is one of the products sulphuric acid?
and so on.

By following the above procedure, CDT has helped us to generate the main flow or backbone of our CBL lesson. CDT is not of course, specific to CBL and you may find it equally useful for other media. The difficult stage is always in relating what you want to teach to the performance level. Having identified this, the rest is straightforward.

6.7 Secondary Displays

Now that the main flow of the lesson is defined, CDT highlights the secondary presentation forms which are simply the various components of the primary forms. For example, a topic may be elaborated by various techniques that include:

Human interest, historical background and the like, called context.
Information as to the correctness of an answer referred to as
feedback.

Rhymes, nonsense words, pictorial devices and other aids generally
called **mnemonics.**

Attention-focusing aids such as highlighting, capital letters, flashing,
arrow, all called **mathemagenic help** or just help.

Notification of information needed before the particular topic can
be grasped is called **prerequisite help.**

and so on. They are all presentation aids that help in understanding the
particular topic that forms the primary presentation. One can recommend
the use of particular secondary presentations for any given primary
presentation, as shown in Table 6.5. Notice that Qeg and QG test
questions are omitted since test items must not provide any form of help,
other than clarifying ambiguities.

	EG (Tell Generality)	Eeg (Tell Instance)	Ieg (Instance Practice)	IG (Generality Practice)
Use	H,P,R	H,R	R,FB	FB
Remember Generality Paraphrase	Mn	H	--	FB
Remember Generality Verbatim	Mn	--	--	FB
Remember Instance Paraphrase	--	R	R,FB	--
Remember Instance Verbatim	--	H	FB	--

Table 6.5 R=Alternative Represenation; Mn=Mnemonic; F=Feedback;
H=Mathemagemic Help; P=Paraphrase

As can be seen, the critical and dominant feature is the use of feedback at
the practice level. Although RIGHT and WRONG may be acceptable
feedbacks, research has demonstrated that the best form of feedback is a
more interactive one:

On giving a correct answer, the student is told why it is correct and must
respond in some way to continue.

On giving an incorrect answer, the feedback should involve the student to demonstrate how to obtain the correct answer. At an extreme level, this feedback is tantamount to a further leg or IG question.

As a minimum, the feedback should explain why the answer is correct or incorrect - Remember that, in a CBL environment, you will not be present as an instructor.

This is a very brief look at CDT. By way of conclusion, the theory has some things to say about test items and their relationship to objectives:

1. Feedback

Because of the danger of influencing subsequent performance, test questions should not be followed by feedback until completion of the whole test.

2. Objectives

Enough test items should be included to adequately measure objectives. For example:

	Verbatim Test Items	Paraphrase Test Items
Remember-Fact	1 per fact	
Remember-Concept (Definitions)	1 per definition	2 or more
Remember-Procedure	1 per element of procedure	
Remember-Principle	1 per principle	
Use-Concept	Samples of new instances	
Use-Procedure	Number depends on complexity of task	

3. Divergence

All situations or questions should not refer to the same situation. They should relate to the same spread as in the objective (e.g. in classifying items)

4. Difficulty

If there is more than 1 test item, use a range of easy to hard questions. This helps to identify experts and novices.

5. Criterion (Performance Standard)

Verbatim items must be 100% correct. Paraphrase recall items are usually accepted at about the 90% correct level. At the use level, around 80% of the test questions correct, perhaps setting 90% for expert and 70% for novice.

6.8 An Example

Suppose that you were designing a CBL lesson to teach people how to fill in a form. Perhaps it is a form to claim an Income Tax refund or social security. This lesson is intended to be equally useful to Government departments or members of the public.

Step 1: Identify Performance & Content

Pretty clearly, this is a Use-Procedure

Step 2: Define the Objective & Test Questions

Referring to Table 6.1, how about:

"Be able to demonstrate, by transferring information from a letter to a computer terminal, how to fill in Form IR29 as measured by at least 9 out of 10 examples being correctly filled in."

Note that this is a CBL exercise: the filling in is done on the screen, not on paper, so as to provide for interaction.

Step 3: Sequence the Primary Displays

First of all, we recognise that we are teaching a generality: how to fill in lots of IR29 forms, not just a specific case.

So referring to Table 4.3, a suitable sequence should be:

Primary Display Content

EG   Show the form and explain what each part is for,
                    suitably highlighted.

Eeg$_1$ ..... Eeg$_n$ Show a suitable range of examples being completed
                    The letters could be provided as student notes and the
                    forms on the screen could be completed step by step.

Ieg$_1$ .... Ieg$_n$ Provide correct answer feedback as the user fills in the
                    form. Feedback should be immediate but Ieg may be
                    decreased as more forms are filled in correctly.

Qeg$_1$ .... Qeg$_n$ A suitable range of 10 forms is presented. No feedback
                    is provided until the end of the test. In case of failure, a
                    remedial lesson should be available.

Step 4: Add the Secondary Displays

To the presentation parts (the EG and Eeg sequences), we might add:

Help: some highlighting or flashing of the various fields on the form,
perhaps.

Paraphrase: explaining parts of the form in different ways, say.

Representation: the various problems that arise in the letters could be
represented in different ways, even though they are the same problem.
You would need to embellish each of the remaining steps, but the
important fact is that this design should achieve the original aims. You can
try a similar approach on one of your own problems.

Reference

Those wishing to delve deeper into component display theory can contact:

M David Merrill, School of Education, Department of Educational
Psychology and Technology, Waite Phillips Hall 801, University of
Southern California, Los Angeles, California 90089.

103

Chapter 7

It Works for Pigeons But......

7.1 Arguments against the systems approach.

Despite the obvious appeal of the Systems Approach, you may have the uneasy feeling that it is all too inhuman- fine for the computer, but not for you or your students. This is a failing of the rigid application of such a method which, if carried to its logical conclusion, prescribes one learning method for all learners. This may be OK in military training, but in other areas we may be making the mistake of requiring students to adapt to a particlar teaching design. This is not, however, a fault of the systems approach. It simply means that you should design your lessons flexibly, so that they can be used by a range of students.

Given the constraints of contemporary software, we should aim to offer:

> Flexible help, feedback and tutoring sequences.

> Different media or different CAL lessons that achieve the same aim.

One should also be cautious about interpreting tests too literally. Invariably, these are completed on paper or at a keyboard, whereas the real job may require actual equipment. Just because someone scored 90% on fixing simulated fuel faults in a computer program is no guarantee that he can mend your car. A child who can recite an 8 times table may well have difficulty in working out the price of 9 packets of sweets at 8 pence each (if you don't believe it, try it on some 6 or 7 year olds).

The only problem is that we are stuck with what we have got. To test understanding, there are many styles of test, but these do not test understanding. For example, I can calculate standard deviations, but so can my computer. Which understands it better?

7.2 The Deadly Combination

The most important question is: do system methods such as these work? The answer is, yes if the training project is either very small OR is very static and well-understood. In most other cases, it is like chasing a moving target: the nature of the training problem is constantly changing. So, no matter how thorough the systems analysis, by the time the implementation is presented to the trainer, it is inadequate. This is not peculiar to training, but to any large software project. Thus, many people are now arguing the case for 'exploratory programming'- a class of interactive software that encourages changes as the circumstances change. If you wish to read about this radical approach, try "Power Tools for Programmers" by Beau Sheil, in DATAMATION, February 1983, pp131-144. To quote from the article: ".... a large programming project with uncertain or changing specifications is a particularly deadly combination for conventional programming techniques". So, a rigid adherence to systems methods may just be the kiss of death to successful CBL!

7.3 All is Not Lost!

The next point is that all of the theory presented so far relates to 'behaviourist' methods. This is fair enough, since in training- and a lot of education- we are trying to change behaviour into a specific trained pattern. The older, stimulus-response model is very linear in its approach. This is understandable because, to the untrained observer, humans do seem to communicate in a linear manner as, for example, by the words on this page. But, although communication may be linear, the way that the mind works is not. For example, Tony Buzan in such books as 'Use Your Head' (BBC Publications) shows that patterns such as the one shown in Figure 7.1 are more useful that the usual neat lists for note-taking, preparing speeches and the like.

Networks such as this are more appropriate for serious CBL, although they are more difficult to implement on present-day personal computers using languages such as PILOT. The computer is required to store a representation of the student's present state of knowledge- and this implies some form of network. One reason that this is necessary is that some students learn by mastering one thing after another (serialists) whilst others skip from point-to-point over a wide subject area (holists). Therefore, the system should ideally be able to adapt to either style or any intermediate one. When we get into the subject of knowledge networks,

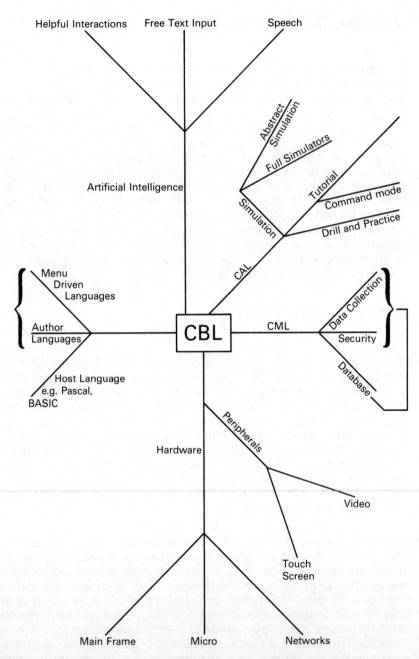

Fig 7.1 A 'Brain-Pattern' for the Subject of Computer Based Learning.

we begin to need the techniques of Artificial Intelligence and, in particular, Expert Systems. Many of the newer CBL systems (including the 'exploratory programming' environments) are being written in LISP - long beloved by AI workers.

To get a good grasp of the general area of CBL design, its psychological issues, and how these new systems impact on CBL, you might enjoy reading "Myth of the Learning Machine" by John Heaford, Sigma Technical Press, 1983.

If you want to get started in AI, you might like to read 'Build your own Expert System' (by C Naylor, published by Sigma Technical Press, 1983) as a simple introduction. One of the most comprehensive books on this subject is by Gordon Pask (Conversation Theory, Elsevier, Amsterdam,1976) and you may also find of interest the paper by P. David Mitchell ('Can CAL Link the Theory and Practice of Instruction', in COMPUTERS AND EDUCATION, vol.3, pp295-307.). A more recent book that covers most aspects of Artificial Intelligence as applied to CBL is: INTELLIGENT TUTORING SYSTEMS, ed. D Sleeman and J S Brown, Academic Press, New York, 1981.

Chapter 8

Preparing Your Plan for the Computer

In the previous chapters, we saw how to analyse a problem, and begin to plan a solution. We now want to plan the actual lesson, so that it can be input into the computer, using the language of our choice.

Again, we suggest the use of planning aids, and the first one is a HIERARCHY to help in analysing the structure of our course.

8.1 Hierarchies and CBL

A hierarchy aims to break down a course into a collection of individual lessons, and then to break each lesson down into separate topics that will ultimately become CBL programs.

Let us presume that you have a fairly substantial course that you wish to convert into CBL form. Perhaps its a course on organic chemistry, or mathematics or a foreign language. In order to form a hierarchy, we describe the aims of the course. These are more global statements than objectives and a suitable aim might be:

> 'To teach the main points of the BASIC language to non-programmers.'

We then divide the course into MODULES and this division will be maintained into the CBL coding, such that there will be one program for each module of the course. There are several advantages:

1. It leads us into the idea of identifying smaller and smaller chunks of instruction.

2. It is a good programming discipline, since it allows the development of different parts of the course to proceed independently.

3. It can permit some freedom of choice for the learner. If some modules can be studied in any order, you can present a menu from which to make a choice. This increases the acceptability of CBL to first time users. Interestingly, the existence of this visual represent-ation gives a 'road-map' to the student which actually helps in building up a picture in the mind of how the different pieces fit together.

4. If some modules must be completed and mastered before some others, it is a simple matter to set up a management system which checks to see if the student has completed the necessary pre-requisites. We will illustrate this shortly with an example.

This is how our hierarchy looks so far:

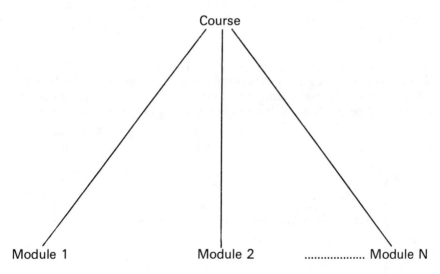

Each module is usually concerned with a small number of related objectives, normally no more than about 10. It is a good idea to have the CBL program keep track of the learner's progress through each module, and a suitable format of a screen for display to a student is shown in Figure 8.1.

```
Course Title: Modern European History
Student Name: John Roberts


Module        Average        Prerequisite      Your progress
title         completion     modules           to date
              time


M1            20             none              pass
M2            15             M1                pass
M3            25             none              incomplete
M4            15             M2,M3             not attempted
M5            20             M2,M4             not attempted
```

Your overall progress: completed=2; incomplete=1; not attempted=2

Figure 8.1

A further visual aid to the student is to show him, on the screen, a route map which is simply a graphical representation of the same information. This is a very valuable aid to learning, since it shows how additional practice or help modules fit into the hierarchy (see Fig. 8.2).

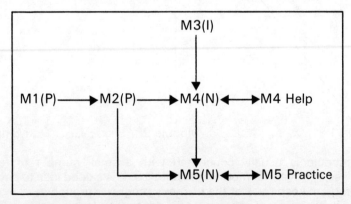

Figure 8.2. A Module Route Map (M1..M5 are the module names. P, I and N signify Pass, Incomplete and Not attempted).

Obviously, this involves quite a bit more work to get a good representation on the screen, and it tends to be more of a feature of more complex systems such as TICCIT.

Getting back to our example of the BASIC course, we might have such modules as:

    Using the keyboard
    The PRINT statements
    Arithmetic Statements
    IF....THEN statements
    FOR...NEXT loops
    Alphanumeric strings
    READ...DATA
    Arrays

If you have gone to the trouble of keeping track of the student's progress, it would also be a good idea to present a MENU on the screen to enable a choice to be made, subject to the constraints of having to do some modules in a particular order. In fact, you could even add one line to the progress screen (Fig. 8.1) which says 'Which Module do you want to try next?'.

Each module is divided into one or more INSTRUCTIONAL UNITS, or IU. Each IU deals with just one or two small topics or objectives. Again, just as for the modules, some rules for moving between IU's are needed but they are kept simple. Just as for a module, some IU's within a module may be studied independently, in other cases there may be a required sequence. In the simplest case, we will just have a number of independent IU's:

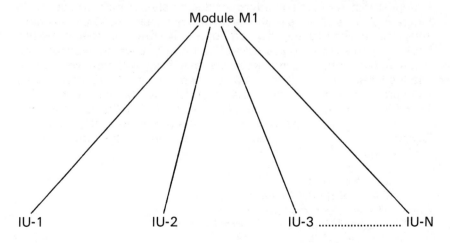

Module M1

IU-1   IU-2   IU-3 .... IU-N

Taking the 'PRINT statement' module in our example, we may have the following IU's:

IU-1: Printing simple numbers
IU-2: Printing numeric variables
IU-3: Printing string variables
IU-4: Using data separators in PRINT statements
IU-5: Using the TAB command

The first 3 IU's could be studied independently, but IU-4 would certainly need IU-1, IU-2 and IU-3 to be completed. A similar progress sheet can be constructed on the screen for the student and, again, a choice can be made, 'menu-style' from the allowed choices.

8.2 Planning an Instructional Unit

There are quite a few points to remember that will make the design process easier for you. The next few pages give some hints and tips.

Using design sheets

If you are trying to produce screens of text or graphics, the actual design of the screen that will be presented to the learner may easily become haphazard and messy. This is because you are having to imagine just where the text and graphics will finally end up. It is very much easier if you have a graphics editor package on your computer, although this always involves some experimentation and, in any case, it is usual to add extra text or graphics as an overlay to some pre-stored picture.

I suggest that you use some form of design sheet similar to the one in Figure 8.3. (This sheet is based on an original design by Wicat Systems, and is adapted here for the Apple computer). There are several advantages in using such sheets: you can sketch out how you want the picture and text to appear and you can discuss it with colleagues before you start to use the computer. Also, there is a school of thought that suggests that fairly professional screen design is essential to get the most out of CBL. Therefore, design sheets like these can be used by both the course author and the graphic artist alike. As a final advantage, there is a lot to be said for having standard screen formats with pre-set areas in which you can place such things as:

Name of the IU
Name of the frame within a IU
The learner's response
Feedback, hints or the correct answer

```
      0  1  2  3  4  5  6  7  8  9 10 11 12 13 14 15 16 17 18 19 20 21 22 23 24 25 26 27 28 29 30 31 32 33 34 35 36 37 38 39        511
   0 |                                                                                                                              |
   1 | IU                                                                            FR                                            |  ▲
   2 |                                                                                                                              |
   3 |                                                                                                                              |
   4 |                                                                                                                              |
   5 |                                                                                                                              |
   6 |                                                                                                                              |
   7 |                                                                                                                              |
   8 |                                                                                                                              |
   9 |                                                                                                                              |
  10 |                                                                                                                              |
  11 |                                                                                                                              |  Hi
  12 |                                                                                                                              |  Res
  13 |                                                                                                                              |
  14 |                                                                                                                              |
  15 |                                                                                                                              |
  16 |                                                                                                                              |
  17 |                                                                                                                              |
  18 |                                                                                                                              |
  19 |                                                                                                                              |
  20 |                                                                                                                              |
  21 |                                                                                                                              |
  22 |                                                                                                                              |
  23 |                                                                                                                              |  0
      0 ────────────────────────────────── Hi-Res ──────────────────────────────────▶ 560
```

PRESENTATION: Delay____or Key-Press_____Next_____

MENU:　　Choice_____
　　　　　Destination
　　　　　Feedback on error _____

QUESTION: Multiple Choice_____T/F_____Match List_____Short Answer_____
　　　　　　MC Type_____　　　　　　　　　　　Num Range_____

Answer	R/W/N	Score	Feedback	Next
Time Out				
XS Tries				

CALCULATION:　Input Variable_____
　　　　　　　　Validation _____

　　　　　　　　Equations _____

　　　　　　　　Next

SPECIAL OPTIONS: e.g. NEXT, HELP with destinations

There are various entries to be made on the forms, and we'll describe these as we go along. One small point: the forms are marked out for the Apple II screen, so you may have to modify them for your computer. Although we will explain the forms carefully here, we will NOT be making great use of them in later chapters, as we do not have the space to illustrate lesson planning in great detail. But, the general techniques for translating the forms into language code WILL become clear later, whilst these notes should help you to use the forms to the best possible advantage in your situation.

The Four Frame Types

It is useful to construct most lessons from a small number of types of frame. The 4 most important ones are:

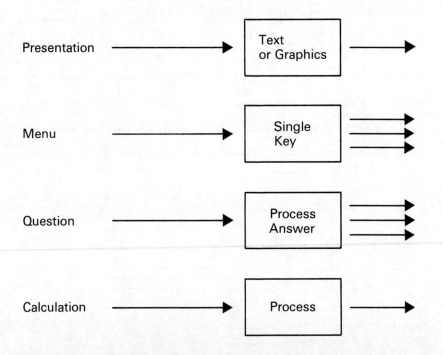

For each frame type, a single form can be used to design both the image on the screen AND the interactions between the student and your program. BUT, note that a frame is not necessarily one screenful of information. You may need a combination of design sheets to represent one frame (see Fig. 8.4).

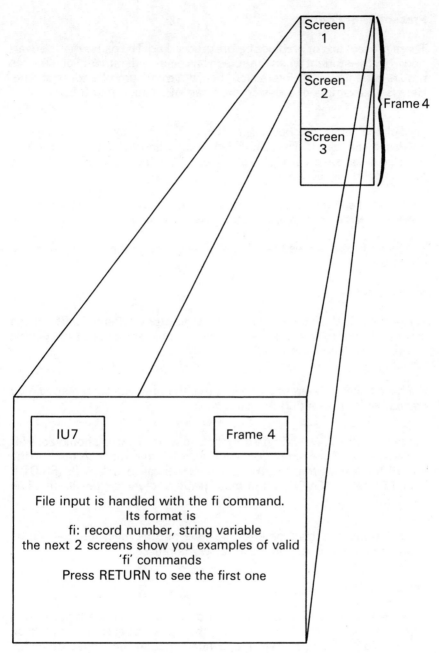

Screen 1

Screen 2

Screen 3

Frame 4

IU7

Frame 4

File input is handled with the fi command.
Its format is
fi: record number, string variable
the next 2 screens show you examples of valid
'fi' commands
Press RETURN to see the first one

Figure 8.4 One screenful of information. This is part of frame 4.

Presentation Frames

These present text or graphics before proceeding. The pause may be over-ridden by the student when the screen has been understood. Such frames require a minimum of interaction, hence a minimum of understanding. Here is an example of a design for a part of a circuit (Fig 8.5).

We tick the 'retain' box because further parts of the circuit are going to be overlaid on top of this. The IU is called Circuits, and we've called this frame Start, so these are entered into the boxes to remind the student where he has got to in the lesson.

We have ticked 'Key-Press' so that the student will press a key to continue. If the next part were to appear automatically, we could tick 'delay' instead.

The 'next' box indicates that 'diode' is the name of the next frame to be displayed.

Menu Frames

These provide the student with options to study different parts of the course. Normally, this is achieved with a single key-press. An example menu form is shown in Fig. 8.6:

We have ticked 'pre-erase', meaning that the previous screen should be erased before presenting this one.

In the MENU box, we indicate the labels to which control should pass for each key press. For example, on pressing key A, the student is taken to the part of the lesson that begins with the label called OVER. (In PILOT it would be called *OVER, but in most BASICs it would have to be a line number.)

Notice, in the 'feedback on error' box, we put the message that will be shown to the student if an incorrect key is pressed.

Question Frames

These are used for the various types of question that we discussed in section 4.3. The form allows for any of the types we described, in addition to Numerical Range answer (i.e. a numerical answer must be within prescribed limits).

```
0  1  2  3  4  5  6  7  8  9 10 11 12 13 14 15 16 17 18 19 20 21 22 23 24 25 26 27 28 29 30 31 32 33 34 35 36 37 38 39
0                                                                                                                        511
1   IU  CIRCUITS                                                        FR   START
2
3
4
5          Here  is  the  first  part  of  the
6          circuit:
7
8
9
10
11           R1                              ↓                                                                          Hi
12                                                                                                                       Res
13
14
15
16
17
18
19          PRESS  ANY  KEY  TO  CONTINUE
20
21
22
23                                                                                                                       0
0 ──────────────────────────── Hi-Res ──────────────────────────────→ 560
```

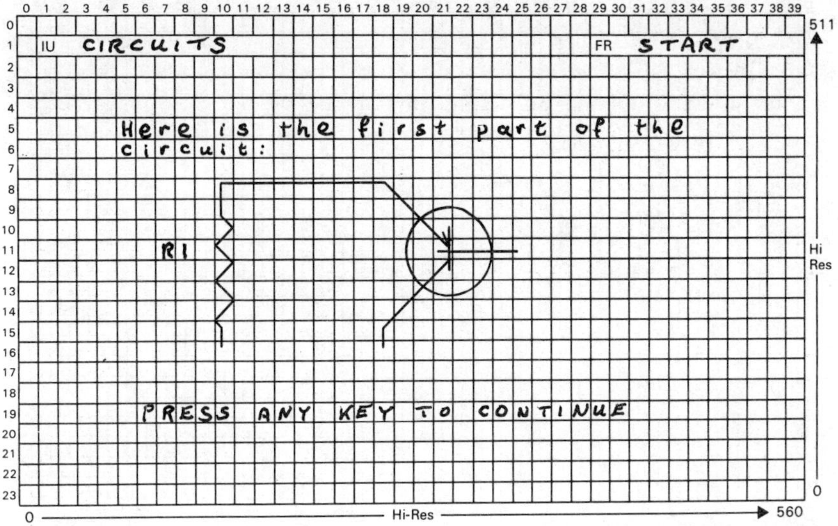

PRESENTATION: Delay____ or Key-Press ✓ Next DIODE _____

MENU: Choice _____
           Destination
           Feedback on error _____

QUESTION: Multiple Choice ____ T/F ____ Match List ____ Short Answer _____

           MC Type _____   Num Range _____

Answer	R/W/N	Score	Feedback	Next
Time Out	W			
XS Tries	W			

CALCULATION: Input Variable _____

                Validation _____

                Equations _____

                Next

SPECIAL OPTIONS: e.g. NEXT, HELP with destinations

Figure 8.5

117

```
0  1  2  3  4  5  6  7  8  9 10 11 12 13 14 15 16 17 18 19 20 21 22 23 24 25 26 27 28 29 30 31 32 33 34 35 36 37 38 39
```

Row	Content
1	IU START .... FR OPTIONS
4	Please choose one of these:
6	A. Overview
8	B. Start-up procedure
10	C. Practice
12	-or TYPE Q to quit-
15	-->

(grid rows numbered 0–23, columns 0–39; markers 511, Hi Res, 0; Hi-Res axis 0 — 560)

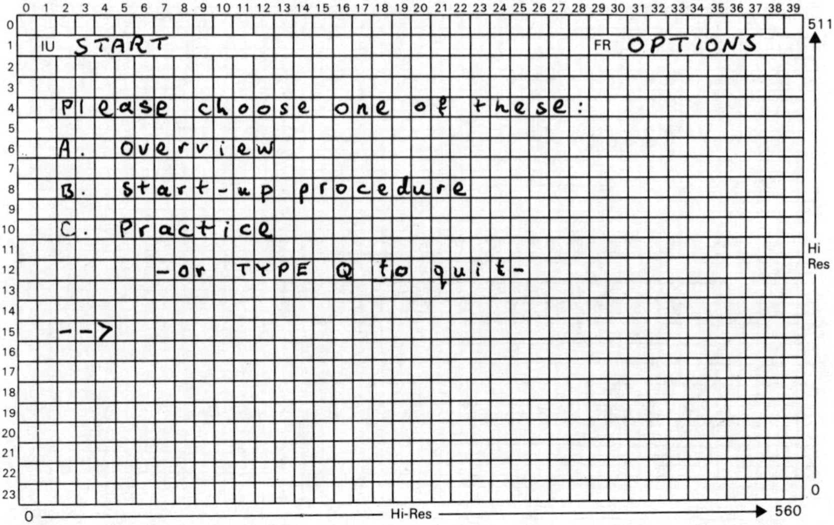

PRESENTATION: Delay____or Key-Press_____ Next _____

MENU: Choice ____A____B____C____Q_____
 Destination Over   Supp   Prac   Quit
 Feedback on error Please type A, B, C or Q

QUESTION: Multiple Choice____T/F____Match List____Short Answer_____
 MC Type _____ Num Range _____

Answer	R/W/N	Score	Feedback	Next
Time Out	W			
XS Tries	W			

CALCULATION: Input Variable_____
 Validation _____

 Equations

 Next
SPECIAL OPTIONS: e.g. NEXT, HELP with destinations

Figure 8.6

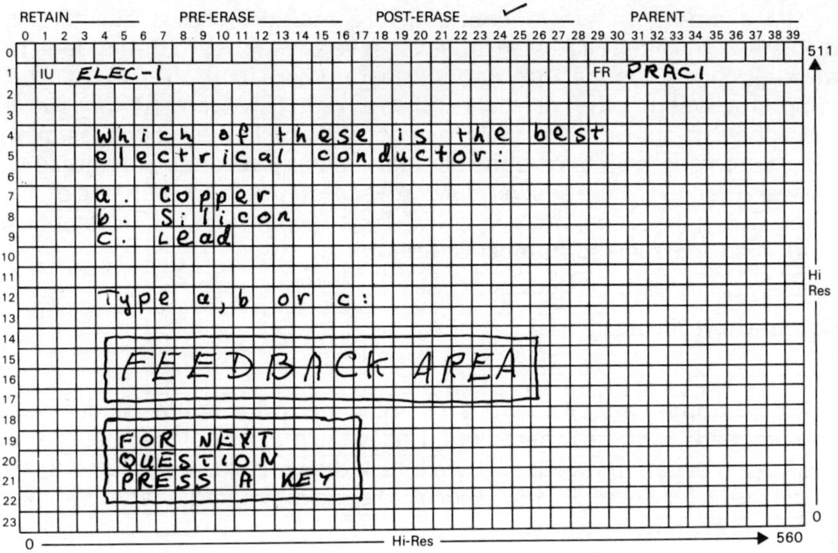

```
  0 1 2 3 4 5 6 7 8 9 10 11 12 13 14 15 16 17 18 19 20 21 22 23 24 25 26 27 28 29 30 31 32 33 34 35 36 37 38 39
0                                                                                                        511
1  IU  ELEC-1                                                         FR  PRAC1
2
3
4        Which of these is the best
5        electrical conductor:
6
7        a.  Copper
8        b.  Silicon
9        c.  Lead
10                                                                                                        Hi
11                                                                                                        Res
12        Type a, b or c:
13
14        ┌──────────────────────────────┐
15        │   FEEDBACK AREA              │
16        │                              │
17        └──────────────────────────────┘
18
19        ┌──────────────┐
20        │ FOR NEXT     │
21        │ QUESTION     │
22        │ PRESS A KEY  │
23        └──────────────┘                                                                               0
  0 ─────────────────────────── Hi-Res ───────────────────────────────► 560
```

PRESENTATION: Delay_____or Key-Press_____ Next _____

MENU: Choice _____
         Destination
         Feedback on error _____

QUESTION: Multiple Choice ✓__T/F____Match List____Short Answer_____
          MC Type_____   Num Range_____

Answer		R/W/N	Score	Feedback	Next
	a	R	2	That's right	PRAC2
	b	W	0	No - that's a semiconductor	PRAC3
	c	W	1	No, Copper is a better one	PRAC3
other		N	—	(Repeat Screen)	PRAC1
Time Out		W	0	The answer is COPPER	PRAC3
XS Tries		W	0	" " " "	PRAC3

CALCULATION: Input Variable_____
              Validation _____

              Equations _____

              Next
SPECIAL OPTIONS: e.g. NEXT, HELP with destinations

Figure 8.7

In the example shown in Figure 8.7, a multiple choice question is displayed. The 'feedback' area is used to give a response to the student. In the question box on the form, we indicate the score for each answer and, if important, whether the answer is judged as right (R), wrong (W) or neutral (N). A neutral answer is one which is not allowed in the list of possibles. Also, we might wish to give the student so many seconds or minutes to answer, then to tell the answer (for zero) score); this is the purpose of the 'Time Out' entry. Also, there is an XS Tries response, if the student has more than the allowed number of attempts.

Calculation frames

The final frame type takes input variables, performs some calculations, and proceeds to some other frame. This is the purpose of the final part of the form. Validation means that we check the variables before doing the calculation; for example, the student may have entered a letter when a number was requested.

8.3 On to the computer!

You can now design each unit as a sequence of frames, interlinked to represent the logic of your instructional strategy. Whilst the interlinking will generally be complex, the sequence of IUs will often consist of a mainline sequence to be followed by successful students, with numerous 'sidings' or 'branch lines' for remedial assistance. This is shown in Fig 8.8 for part of a BASIC course.

It is now a fairly simple task to convert the large pile of design sheets in front of you into code for the computer. The important thing is that you have designed how the program should look as it runs, and you can check this against its actual appearance on the screen. Throughout this book you will see how easy it is to translate forms such as these into program statements and you can, if you wish, develop fairly standard procedures for rapidly coding them, or standard program skeletons to deal with routine problems, such as coding up menu forms.

It is even possible to dispense with coding altogether, but we'll leave that topic until almost the end of this book. Right now, we're going to presume that you WILL need to learn a programming language! To give you an idea of what is involved, we conclude this chapter by taking a birds's eye view of what is involved in coding a program for the flow-chart shown in Fig 8.8

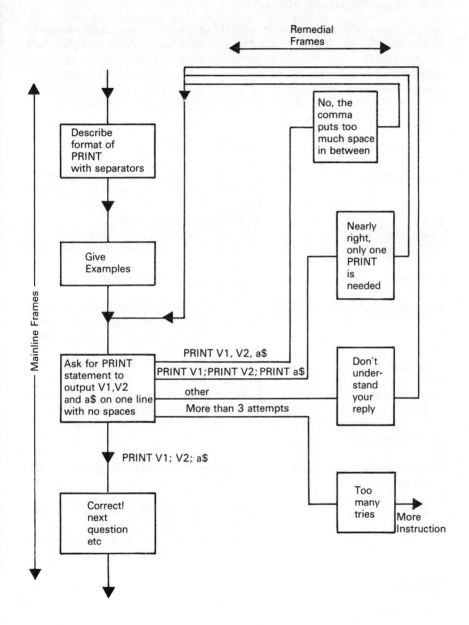

Remedial Frames

Describe format of PRINT with separators

Give Examples

Mainline Frames

Ask for PRINT statement to output V1,V2 and a$ on one line with no spaces

PRINT V1, V2, a$

PRINT V1;PRINT V2; PRINT a$

other

More than 3 attempts

No, the comma puts too much space in between

Nearly right, only one PRINT is needed

Don't understand your reply

PRINT V1; V2; a$

Correct! next question etc

Too many tries

More Instruction

Figure 8.8 Part of a frame sequence for IU-4 (using data separators in BASIC PRINT statements

121

8.4 A Simple Program

Very soon, you'll be able to write a PILOT program but, since all authoring languages share similar principles, we can translate Figure 8.8 into "pseudo-code". This will not be a real program and it will not run on a real computer. But it will resemble PILOT and quite a few more languages, so it gives you the feel of what it's like to write a program. Let's presume that we have the following list of available "pseudo-code" commands:

Command	Meaning
frame (label)	Identifies section of lesson and gives an identifying label to which control can be passed
text	Starts a sequence of text
input (response)	Waits for user to type an answer
if (Q) then (F)	If condition Q is true then pass control to frame label (F)
keypress	Proceed to next frame when any key is pressed.
match (response,/{string})	If "string" occurs anywhere within "response", the computer sets an internal variable "test" to "true", otherwise leave it at "false".
calc (expression)	Do a calculation
goto (frame)	Transfer control to a particular frame
use (frame)	Execute a particular frame, then return to the beginning of the present frame

frame (description)

Here is how our flowchart will look, when we translate it into pseudo-code commands

text	A PRINT statement of the form < line number > PRINT List of contants and / or variables > The list is separated by commas or semicolons
Key-press	
frame (ex1)	
text	For example to print a numeric constant

122

30 PRINT 20
And if V had been assigned the value 20,
30 PRINT V
would have the same effect.

keypress

frame (ex2)

text   To print a message, just enclose the text
                                  in quotation marks:
                                  90 PRINT "This is a message"

More example frames

frame ex20

text   As a final example, this statement
                                  25 PRINT "The values are; X,Y
                                  This prints the message, immediately
                                  followed by X, but the value of Y will
                                  appear in the text zone, like this:
                                  The values are 20.7   36.4

keypress

frame ques 1

calc tries = 0

text   Now it's your turn. Write a PRINT
                                  statement that will output V1, V2 and a$
                                  on one line with no spaces between
                                  them.

keypress

frame ques1a

calc tries = tries + 1
If tries > 3 **then** ques 1x
input (response,)
match (response, <PRINT V1; V2; a$>
if test-is-true **then** ques 2
frame help 1   (this frame tests for first alternative)
text   No, the comma puts too much space
goto ques 1a
frame help 2   (this frame tests for second alternative)
text   Nearly right, only one PRINT is needed

123

```
goto ques 1a
frame ques 1x
text                        Too many tries! The answer is
                            Print V1; V2; a$
                            Try the next one

goto ques 2
```

~~~~~~
rest of program
~~~~~~

```
frame query
text                        Sorry, I don't understand your reply
```

We don't pretend that this even begins to approach a "good" language, but it is interesting to see how the branching nature of the flowchart is preserved in the necessarily linear program. Notice how we have used meaningful names for each frame, and how the frame that poses the question is split into "quesl" and "quesla". The reason for this is so that the welcome message "Now it's your turn" is not repeated when (or if) the student has to have more than one attempt.

You should be able to see how the program works. What other commands would you add to our "pseudo-code" list?

Part Three:

PILOT as an Example Authoring Language, and Apple SuperPILOT as an Authoring System

We could choose to talk in general terms about author languages, some books even discuss hypothetical languages. Instead, we take the view that you may wish to use an actual product. PILOT is one such product, and Apple SuperPILOT is a particularly good example. In fact, SuperPILOT is more than a language, and qualifies for the term 'Authoring System'.

The next seven chapters cover most of the things you need to know about PILOT, and also cover SuperPILOT more concisely than its accompanying manuals, thus providing a useful reference.

Even if you never use PILOT, you'll still find the many hints, tips and techniques useful for whatever language you finally use.

Chapter 9

LET'S START PROGRAMMING!

If you've got this far, you probably are wondering if you'd ever get to using a computer at all. That is, if you're the practical type who isn't afraid of a keyboard. On the other hand, if you're convinced that you'll never be able to use a microcomputer, DO NOT READ THIS CHAPTER. Because you're just about to be proven wrong: you'll see that it's much easier to write programs than to design lessons!

If you are the user of a personal microcomputer, it is almost certain that you already have BASIC for 'free'. This chapter examines the usefulness of such a general purpose language for writers of CBL lessons. Also, it attempts to make out the case for using an author language such as PILOT, and an author system such as Apple SuperPILOT. All of these terms will now be defined.

9.1 General Purpose Languages and CBL

The quickest and cheapest way to get started in CBL is to use the native language of your computer. For many this will be BASIC, although some will prefer other general purpose languages such as Pascal. By 'general purpose' we mean that neither of these languages was necessarily intended for CBL, although they can be quite suitable.

As an example, a group of teachers in the Isle of Man have written a program called TT Race (available at many teachers' centres in the UK). This is a simulation of a motor cycle race, making use of various parameters such as engine size, type of tyre, throttle setting and gear ratio. These dictate the simulated speed of a motor bike around a circuit. The interaction between the user and the computer is mainly numeric, such as choosing a setting from 0 to 9 for the throttle; there is no requirement to examine text answers, so BASIC was an adequate choice in this case.

A further reason for choosing BASIC for this program, and many others intended for school use, is that the users could only be assumed to have certain types of inexpensive computers equiped with BASIC. When we look at more elaborate CBL applications, we find that other general purpose languages are used. For example, Alfred Bork of the University of California has used the Pascal language to develop an entire physics course- something far more ambitious than has been attempted in the UK. Advanced concepts such as vector algebra are taught by computer, using high-quality graphic displays. In these CBL lessons, Bork does use some text input from the users. His Pascal programs examine word stems to determine what the users are trying to say. This simple strategy is remarkably effective and has led naive observers to conclude that his programs must be using some sophisticated Artificial Intelligence methods. In fact, the word stem matching involves nothing more than a Pascal procedure to search the user input for the particular stem.

This second example is perhaps more representative of 'big CBL' as opposed to the relatively small self-contained project. It led Bork to dismiss 'cutesy authoring languages' in favour of professional programmer's languages such as Pascal or Ada. In his environment, Bork is correct. He has very able programmers and powerful computers to support his work. Much of it is very mathematical, requiring rapid calculations on very complex equations in physics and high-resolution graphics. For different reasons, the choice of BASIC for 'TT Race' was correct: the need for the program to run on inexpensive machines only equipped with BASIC and programmers in the shape of teachers willing to burn the midnight oil for little financial reward. And, the fact that it could be assumed that the users were also conversant with BASIC meant that local modifications could be made to make the package locally acceptable. (This is known as the 'add an egg' syndrome: cake mixes are thought by some housewives to be more home made if the instructions call for them to add an egg!)

Outside of the two scenarios we have presented for the use of BASIC or Pascal, the justification for the use of general purpose languages in CBL becomes more tenuous. Once even modest amounts of text input are called for, the programmer is tempted to write subroutines or procedures to examine the input. He will write subroutines to examine text for:

Keywords in isolation.

Combinations of keywords.

Mis-spelt words

and so on. Unknown to him, he is writing his own author language. For example the calls to the appropriate subroutines, might include this

127

sequence to examine if one of three colours had been typed:

```
LET a$='blue'
LET b$='red'
LET c$='white'
GOSUB 9000
```

where subroutine 9000 is the 'keyword matcher' consisting of a dozen or so more lines. But this is equivalent to one line of PILOT:

```
m:blue!red!white
```

The lines of BASIC are just as much part of an author language as the line of PILOT. They require a strict order of input and have added nothing to the creative process- they are just more cumbersome. So, it is likely that the general purpose language will produce a program that is much longer, with the added problems of having to remember which variable names to use, keeping track of line numbers and so on.

For the first time programmer, the problem is much worse. You need to have a lot of experience before you can write good CBL programs in BASIC and even more for Pascal. There are so many tricks of the trade to learn, so many subroutines to design and test. With any decent authoring language or system, there is less learning to be done before successful programs are written. Beginners can make a start with only half a dozen commands and, in PILOT, there are only about 15 in total- each having a simpler syntax than BASIC. In other words, the use of an author language lets you, the teacher, concentrate more on what is to be taught and to bother less about the foibles of a complicated language. (I have regularly taught PILOT to novices in one day and then watched them complete quite complex projects).

Having made the argument for an author language, it must be said that there are several applications for which they are unsuited. We would accept that enquiry-type CBL involving the use of databases is best suited to a specialised package such as dBase II which gives optimum ways of storing and retrieving data. Similarly, PROLOG is a good choice when teaching logic as a programming language, whilst giving a natural way of interrogating large amounts of data. And, LOGO is an excellent vehicle for teaching about programming or for letting students formulate their own theories of geometry and the like.

What we are trying to suggest is that an author language is especially well suited to those appllcations where you wish to involve the student in some dialogue approaching the one that you would have with him in real life.

There is little truth in the arguments of those who disregard authoring languages as 'cutesy'. The better types of authoring language operate on at least two different levels. For example,with Control Data's PLATO you can design lessons by a simple screen dialogue, or by writing actual TUTOR commands. With Apple SUPERPILOT, you can use a graphics editor, or write PILOT statements, or use Pascal- and you can mix all 3 methods of use as you wish. Similarly, the Wicat WISE system has an easy-to-use menu driven system, but also you can dive into Pascal or other languages as you wish. With one of these better authoring systems, you are gaining flexibility with no loss of computing power.

9.2 Why Choose PILOT (and why not to)

There is a very good reason for you to agree with our choice of PILOT, and that is because most of the rest of the book uses PILOT to illustrate the uses of an author language. So why is it a sensible choice?

There are literally hundreds of possible languages that you can use in the writing of CBL lessons. They range from the general purpose BASIC, through author languages such as PILOT all the way up to PLATO and other sophisticated systems. As you saw in the Chapter 2, you get what you pay for, broadly speaking, when it comes to computer based learning. The more exotic the software, the easier and faster it is to produce the finished lessons. But, also, the price goes up in direct proportion to the sophistication of the software. Bearing in mind that you are interested in using a microcomputer for CBL, it is alarmingly easy to find that you can easily spend far more on the CBL authoring software than you did on the entire collection of hardware.

I don't know how you feel about this, but to me it all seems a bit crazy. Most microcomputer software is relatively cheap, even for its most sophisticated variants. A spreadsheet planner package costs about a hundred pounds, and a decent Pascal compiler about two hundred pounds. And yet, a CBL authoring system (as opposed to just a language) can set you back up to ten thousand pounds. Now, if you are a training manager in a nationalised industry, or in some other fortunate position that you are able to spend large amounts of someone else's money, you may be able to afford the luxury of such expensive software. But most of us have to be a bit more frugal, if only for the reason that we may mish to experiment with CBL to see if it is appropriate. Then after finding that it really is useful, you will be all the more able to make convincing arguments as to why you should invest in a more expensive system.

Requirements

So, what we require is a language that is well-suited to CBL. We will immediately dismiss BASIC for most applications because it was never intended to be used for CBL. It is well suited to numerical calculations, but the aspects that are particularly important to us as prospective producers of CBL include:

The ability to match student's answers for the expected answers in a number of ways (e.g. single keypress, individual words, sequences of words, and allowing for spelling errors)

Editing the student response for extra spaces, upper and lower case.

Good error detection: for example, determining if a number was input when a string was expected, and giving a warning message.

Answer counting: the ability to easily give different feedback messages, depending on how many times the student has answered incorrectly.

A full range of mathematical and string handling features.

Easy and effective graphics commands to enliven lessons.

File commands that enable you to keep student records with a minimum of fuss.

A simple syntax: simple enough for a non-computerate person to start using quickly and effectively, yet powerful enough to avoid frustrations for the experienced programmer.

Possibly, the ability to control peripherals such as videotape or disk.

In some cases, the ability to use other languages or packages already written in some other language.

Above all, what you will be happy with is a language that is simple to use for simple applications, something that you get to grips with in an hour or so. It should not be so complex that it gets in the way of the lesson you are trying to create. As you think up more and more complicated problems, you will accept that the programming effort increases in proportion. Also, it should be representative of the general class of author languages so that, if you do decide to move on to a more expensive system, your experience will not have been wasted.

Possible Contenders

Given these arguments, there are very few contenders that can be considered at the moment; especially if you are looking for something that will work on a range of microcomputer hardware.

One strong contender must be Microtext for the BBC and PET computers which satisfies most of the above conditions and is, on the face of it, very easy to use. However, once you get beyond the production of simple lessons, many of the features of Microtext resemble those in BASIC or PILOT and require the same level of sophistication. The major attraction of Microtext is that it is 'frame oriented' rather than 'line oriented' (as are PILOT or BASIC) so that the text edited on the screen is laid out in the same way that it will be presented to the student. As an example of how Microtext can be used, here is a complete frame, more or less as it would be seen on the screen by the programmer:

*10   (header)

What is the capital city of   (text)
Spain?
?   (prompt)
madrid ->40, barcelona->50,   (responses)
tarragona ->60
.... (terminator)

In this frame, a question is asked of the user. A response MADRID sends the user to frame 40, and so on.

Microtext is a sophisticated representative of a what is termed 'Frame Handling' software. Such systems require you to plan your lessons as a sequence of frames and you then input your information into each frame in a fairly predetermined sequence. They work particularly well for very simple lessons.

The PETCAI package for the PET works in a similar fashion, being able to match simple answers and branch to a new frame. Like Microtext, an author can store and retrieve frames to and from disk, and each frame is

131

designed on the screen. The possible responses are filled in on a protected area of the screen, with routeing instructions in the form of 3-digit frame index. The PETCAI author can specify the number of attempts allowed on a given frame, the allowed time and the type of matching (e.g. phonetic) to be performed.

On a personal note, a frame generator that I once designed for the TRS-80 required that you input, for each frame:

> The text or graphics for the frame
> The question to be asked
> The anticipated answers
> The destination frames for each answer

This worked very well for simple applications, especially if there were very few alterations to be made subsequently. But, the problem with all of these frame generators is that, whilst they are excellent for simple applications, they soon run out of steam when you ask them to do complicated or interesting things. For example, most of them have great difficulty in handling expected answers that consist of sequences of keywords, perhaps containing alternative words or mis-spellings. Answer counting is awkward or impossible for many of them, they have limited record keeping abilities and even their calculation features are limited (e.g. integer only) or non-existent. As you can imagine, such factors are serious limitations when it comes to producing exciting and stimulating CBL.

For all of these reasons, this book will concentrate on the use of an author language. Whilst we could have taken the stance of using a hypothetical language, it was decided to be pragmatic and to introduce the PILOT language. It is representative of author languages, it is sufficiently flexible and powerful for most applications in the home, school, college or industry, and it is reasonably priced: currently between £50 and £200, depending on the implementation. Also, it is available on a wide range of microcomputers which means that you can, if you wish, purchase a copy of PILOT and start to write your own lessons. Note that what I am not saying is that PILOT is the best language, nor necessarily the best chice for you. It is simply a reasonable compromise that will enable you to make a good start in CBL.

9.3 Which Version of PILOT?

This clearly depends on the hardware that you already own. Some versions of PILOT are quite terrible; I can't tell you (here) which ones they are, but before you buy, ask these questions of the salesman:

Does it have a graphics editor to facilitate graphical work?

If you need them, does it have character and sound editors?

Does the version being offered include all the features of COMMON PILOT as a minimum? These features are described fully in this book, and a checklist summary is given later.

Does it include graphics instructions?

Does it have floating point arithmetic?

If you have any special requirements, such as the control of videotape or disk, or linking to other languages, will the version satisfy these requirements?

What major extensions have been added to take advantage of the hardware?

Can you access other languages, such as Pascal or BASIC?

You might also find it entertaining to ask if you can see a demonstration of a sample program- see how fast it runs, what the graphics are like and so on. It is useful if the version is able to run lessons immediately without saving them to disk: only a very few do, and this is perhaps a minor point. One thing that will make life easy for you is if the version has got good text and graphics editors as these speed up the production of lessons quite dramatically. A useful frill would be the existence of an alternative frame generator mode, so that you could write lessons in frames, or PILOT code, or in a general purpose language such as Pascal. (See Chapter 17 for a prototype PILOT generator)

Apple SuperPILOT

Some people think of PILOT as being just like BASIC, but with the addition of the match (m:) command. Some poor versions may be like that but, in any event, we suggest that you want more than just a language- you need an authoring system that includes a good version of PILOT together with lots of other useful software.

A version of PILOT that is a particularly good implementation is SuperPILOT for the Apple II computer. It satisfies most of my criteria except for not being able to run programs until they have been written to disk. Given the other good features, I can overlook this one drawback. (You can execute single lines in 'immediate' mode, which is better than nothing!)

SuperPILOT is provided as a package of two manuals (one for the language, the other for the system editors), an Author disk, sample lessons, and two 'Co-Pilot' disks containing a complete CAL course in PILOT. SuperPILOT is centred around the 'lesson text editor'. You access this from the main menu page, as shown in Figure 9.1.

```
                  SUPERPILOT


     Lesson Text editor ----------- L
     Character Set editor -------- C
     Graphics editor ------------- G
     Sound effects editor --------- S
     Initialize a diskette ---------- I
     Diskette copy utility --------- D


   Type option letter and press RETURN
   Press CTRL-C to return to this menu
```

Figure 9.1 Main SuperPILOT menu

Having selected the lesson option, the screen clears, to be replaced with a list of the lessons currently stored on the lesson disk (in drive 2) and a new list of options:

```
   New, Edit, Run, Print, Delete, Quit
   --->
```

You then type the initial letter of the option. For example, type R for run, and the system asks which program you want to run. One neat feature is that if, instead, you respond with CTRL-I (i.e. hold down the control key at the same time as pressing the I key), you are put into 'immediate mode' which enables you to type in PILOT statements one at a time, and see their effect.

Presuming you want to type in a program, choose N for new, follow this by the name of your program and the system responds with a line of prompts, as shown below:

```
   > Edit: Cpy Del Find Ins Jmp Rep Xch Quit
```

This looks a bit cryptic, but it is modelled on the UCSD Pascal Text Editor (not surprisingly, since SuperPILOT is written in Pascal). For example, you would select 'I' to start inserting the lines of your program, 'D' to delete parts of it, and 'X' to exchange characters for other characters. It is just like using a word processor, even down to the level of automatic wrap-around and formatting to make your program look pretty.

It is usual, having created the bulk of your program this way, to interact with the other editors in the system. These are:

THE GRAPHICS EDITOR. This enables you to draw complex pictures without writing any PILOT statements.

THE SOUND EDITOR. Sounds or music can be created and re-played at any point in a program.

THE CHARACTER SET EDITOR. This enables new alphabets (e.g. Greek or Cyrillic) to be created or special shapes such as little men that can chase around the screen.

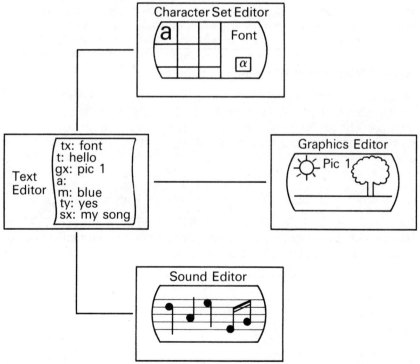

Figure 9.2 Different Editors in SuperPILOT.

We'll be having a lot more to say about SuperPILOT in the sense that it is simply a good implementation of the language.

SuperPILOT, Pascal, and UCSD

This section is included solely for those interested in technical details of SuperPILOT. If you'd rather stay practical, skip to the next section.

Those of you in the know may be interested in how Apple SuperPILOT (and its predecessor, Apple PILOT) relate to Pascal. Firstly, the most common implementation of Pascal for the Apple is UCSD Pascal. The UCSD part is an abbreviation for University College of San Diego, and it indicates the OPERATING SYSTEM in particular, not just the dialect of Pascal. To be correct, we should talk about the UCSD p-system. The p-system is a hypothetical computer, termed a 'software emulation' of an ideal machine. It uses an intermediate medium-level language called 'p' (for pseudo) code and this serves as a link between the programmer and an actual computer, in that one side of the p-system link is specific to some particular computer, but its other side looks exactly the same to the programmer, regardless of the hardware. So, programming in UCSD Pascal on the Apple is exactly the same (well, very nearly the same) as when using a DEC, or an IBM or whatever. Although there are, in fact, small differences, they pale into insignificance when you think of programming in BASIC on a Spectrum, Tandy, PET.........etc!

At the heart of UCSD is its operating system which is almost pleasant to use (again, compared with the traumas of some others which the libel laws prevent us from mentioning) in that it is menu-driven, with the available options displayed across the top of the screen. So, to take an example, obtain a copy of Apple UCSD Pascal (which is supplied on 4 disks!) and 'boot' the Apple (jargon for starting it up) which is done simply by switching on the Apple with the disk labelled Apple1 in drive 1. After the Welcome screen, you'll see a blank screen with the top line:

```
Command: E(dit, R(un, F(ile, C(omp, L(ink, X(ecute, A(ssem, D(ebug ?
```

You choose from the commands by pressing just one letter. If E is chosen, the top line changes to

```
Edit: A(djst C(py D(lete F(ind J(mp R(place Q(uit X(chng Z(ap
```

And so on, each letter taking you further down the hierarchy of menu commands. Nice, isn't it? Because it's so nice, Apple PILOT and

SuperPILOT are also pleasant to use because they are based on UCSD Pascal; for example, the editor commands shown above are almost identical. Also, with the Filer command selected from within Apple Pascal,followed by 'L' to list the directory, this is what you will see if you put the SuperPILOT Author disk in Drive 2:

AUTHOR/DISK LISTING

```
AUTHOR:
SYSTEM. APPLE        32  27-Apr-82
SYSTEM. PASCAL       27  27-Apr-82
SYSTEM. CHARSET       2  27-Apr-82
SYSTEM. MISCINFO      1  27-Apr-82
SYSTEM. LIBRARY      21  27-Apr-82
SYSTEM. STARTUP      15  27-Apr-82
INTERP. CODE         47  27-Apr-82
PILOT. FONT           2  27-Apr-82
MUSIC. FONT           2  27-Apr-82
EDITOR. CODE         35  27-Apr-82
PRINTER. CODE         4  27-Apr-82
FORMATTER. DATA       4  27-Apr-82
FORMATTER. CODE       8  27-Apr-82
DUPLICATE. CODE       8  27-Apr-82
GRAFEDIT. CODE       21  27-Apr-82
CHAREDIT. CODE       17  27-Apr-82
SONGEDIT. CODE       21  27-Apr-82
17/17 files, 7 unused, 7 in largest
```

As you can see, the author disk contains a number of standard Pascal files, and a much larger number of files that each do a special job in SuperPILOT. For example, INTERP.CODE is the interpreter to run your PILOT program. GRAFEDIT.CODE is the graphics editor. Any file ending in .CODE is an executable Pascal program in compiled form. This means that you modify the Author disk to your own liking by adding new files, or modifying old ones. You may need to do this if you want to link the Apple to Video equipment, as this almost always requires the user to modify that part of the interpreter which processes the V: command. It might also mean that the unscrupulous could make pirate copies of SuperPILOT.

SuperPILOT is used to produce lessons on a second disk, appropriately called a LESSONS disk. A typical directory listing obtained using the Pascal filer is shown below:

137

LESSON DIRECTORY

```
%
LESSONS:
SYSTEM.APPLE       32 27-Apr-82
SYSTEM.PASCAL      27 27-Apr-82
SYSTEM.LIBRARY     21 27-Apr-82
SYSTEM.CHARSET      2 27-Apr-82
SYSTEM.MISCINFO     1 27-Apr-82
SYSTEM.STARTUP     47 27-Apr-82
FILECOPY.TEXT       6 27-Apr-82
GENERATOR.TEXT     10 27-Apr-82
COPY.CODE           3  4-Aug-83
DOODLE!.FOTO       16 27-Apr-82
DOODLE!.GRAF        2 27-Apr-82
TEST.DATA          51 27-Apr-82
TEST.TEXT           4 27-Apr-82
BALLOON.FONT        2 27-Apr-82
LAFBIRD!.FOTO      16 27-Apr-82
LAFBIRD!.GRAF       4 27-Apr-82
BEETHOVEN.SONG      1 27-Apr-82
17/17 files, 29 unused, 29 in largest
```

This still contains some Pascal bits and pieces, but lesson files can be identified since they end in .TEXT. Graphics files end in either .GRAF (normal graphics) or .FOTO (quick-draw graphics). Character set files end in .CHAR, sound files in .SONG and data files in .DATA. So what? Well, it can just be useful to know about these things. For example, much later on in this book, there is an example program that outputs data into a .DATA file, then converts it into a .TEXT file. This makes the system think that the file is now a PILOT lesson, which it can run, rather than a data file, which it can't. The conversion is done with a Pascal program called COPY.CODE which is NOT a normal part of SuperPILOT, but I produced it under Apple Pascal, then copied it across to my PILOT disk as part of my very own customised system. Which all makes the compatibility of Pascal and Apple PILOT a very fortunate situation.

Now you can see what I mean when I say that SuperPILOT, like Apple PILOT before it, is an authoring SYSTEM, not just a language. What about the competition?

138

Other Versions of PILOT

Most of the major manufacturers supply versions of PILOT. Some examples are:

Commodore PILOT. This disk-based version is available for the model 64. Although it does not have a graphics editor, it does make good use of Commodore graphics including 'sprites'.

Atari PILOT. Also disk-based, this provides Turtle Graphics as a motivator for children.

Sinclair PILOT. This is offered by ourselves, Sigma Technical Press, as a cassette version. It makes extensive and novel use of Sinclair software and hardware features.

Tandy Color Computer PILOT. This is supplied as a plug-in cartridge implementation of COMMON PILOT.

Obviously, there will be several differences between the different versions and we will point some of these out as we progress through the language features. As it is not possible to elaborate on all the differences, we will be content to present:

The so-called standard features of COMMON PILOT, as proposed by Micropi Inc , and as used as the basis of all implementations.

Extensions found in Apple SuperPILOT, representing the most enhanced version of PILOT available.

By adhering to this approach, it is hoped to cover most eventualities for present and future implementations. Again I would urge you to 'try before you buy'- there are some very poor PILOTs about!

9.4 Making a Start in PILOT

We've been at pains to emphasise the simplicity of PILOT, so let's try to justify our claim. A PILOT instruction consists of up to 7 parts, but it is usually much simpler than that. For example, to make the computer PRINT a message, you can type:

t:This is your PILOT speaking!

The 't' is an 'operation code', or op-code. There are about 15 such one or two-letter op-codes, depending on the version you have. The colon is obligatory, and separates the op-code from the 'field' which is the message in our example.

In between the op-code and the colon, you can put a number of useful things. For example, after displaying the message in the field, this instruction will leave the cursor at the end of the line:

th:Good Heavens.

The 'h' is called a modifier; it modifies the 't' and can only modify the 't'.

To go a little further, here is a very simple PILOT program. Its purpose is to ask somebody what kind of language they are using on the computer, and to give them two attempts at getting the answer correct:

```
*jiffy t:What language are you using?
a:
m:pilot
ty:That's right.
ey:
ms:english
ty:No, I meant what kind of computer language!
t1:Try again.
t2:It begins with P and ends with T. Try again.
j3:abandon
j:jiffy
*abandon t:The answer is PILOT.
```

The first thing you'll notice is that PILOT does not have line numbers, unlike BASIC. To refer to a line, you give it a name or 'label' and prefix it with an asterisk, as for 'jiffy' and 'abandon'. The program begins with asking a question and pausing for the student to input an answer, using the 'a' (short for accept) op-code. In the next line, we match (with the m op-code) against the expected answer, which is PILOT contained anywhere in the answer(i.e. PILOT is the field of this instruction). If the match is successful, we type the message "That's Right". The 'ty' means 'Type if Yes' and the 'y' part of the instruction is known as a conditioner. Since the answer is correct, we stop at this point, and the 'ey' combination of op-code and conditioner can be thought of as 'End if Yes'. Like the 'a': instruction, 'ey': does not need a field.

The next thing we do is to check to see if some joker has included 'english' in an answer. Also, we will accept incorrect spellings such as ANGLISH,

EGNLISH and so on. We do this by modifying the match op-code with the 's' modifier. So, ms:english looks for the word 'english' even with slight mis-spellings. The next line advises the student that we are looking for something to do with computers.

The t1: means 'type if this is the first time an incorrect answer has been given'. The '1' is another example of a conditioner- just like the 'y' conditioner, it causes the instruction to be obeyed only if some codition is true. The next line gives a broad hint if a second error is made, whilst the following line (j3:abandon) causes a jump to be made to the end of the program if and only if a third incorrect reply is made.

If less than 3 errors have been made, the line j:jiffy is obeyed, which returns us to the beginning of the program to ask the question again.

If you have a PILOT system by your side, try typing in the above program. So far, you can see that the most complicated statement seen so far is of the form:

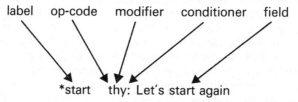

It is possible to get slightly more complicated, but I hope you'll agree that the syntax of the language is simple, brief and easy to learn. We'll see lots more in the next chapter.

Chapter 10

PILOT Text and Graphics

It is perfectly possible to write a program- in PILOT or some other language- that simply presents text or graphics to the user. This might seem a strange thing to do, especially when we are concerned with interactive teaching.

However, it is very important to be able to work effectively with words and pictures, as these provide the main stimulus from the computer to the person that is going to use the program that you have written. Such matters as the use of upper and lower case, bold characters and line spacing are obviously important to the ease of reading of text on the screen- which, after all, is not the most natural method of presentation. Also, the format of your screen design is important- where do you place questions, feedback or hints on the screen? If you are using graphics, you have a lot more opportunities for artistic flair and design- and also more opportunities to make mistakes! In fact, graphic design can be very time-consuming, so it is as well to expend your effort in the best possible way.

Occasionally, you may even find that you don't need any interaction in your lesson, in that all you wish to do is to present information. This mode of use is called 'exposition' or 'slide-show' for fairly obvious reasons. You might find it useful when devising a demonstration of some technique to accompany a traditional lesson. If you do have a computer available, this can be quite an attractive and cost-effective alternative to the overhead projector.

10.1 Displaying Text

As is the case for all PILOT statements, those required to present text must conform to the general syntax of the language that we introduced in Section 9.4. Like the majority of PILOT commands, a single letter is used for text display and this is the letter 't'. On most systems, it does not matter if upper or lower case is used for PILOT commands. In this book, you will see that we mainly use lower case because that is what the Apple, PET and

most other popular micros have adopted as their convention.
The most general form of the 't' statement is:

> <*label> t<modifiers> <conditioners> <relational expression>:<text field>

where each item enclosed in brackets <.....> is optional.

Therefore, the simplest form of the 't' (standing for 'text' or 'type')is just:

> t:

All that this does is to print a blank line, so it is the equivalent of the BASIC:

100 PRINT

Anything that you wish to appear on the screen follows the colon:

> t:This is a message to appear on the screen!

An automatic 'line feed' takes place at the end of such a statement, leaving the cursor on the next line, ready to start the next line of text. So, these four lines will cause a poem to be displayed on separate lines:

> t:The fair breeze blew, the white foam flew
> t:The furrow followed free
> t:We were the first that ever burst
> t:Into that silent sea.

If instead, you do not want to skip automatically to a new line, you simply use the 'h' (for 'hang'- i.e. hang in mid-air) modifier. Like this:

> th:Here we are
> t: on the same line

And this would produce the output:
> Here we are on the same line

always presuming that you remembered to include the leading space before the word 'on' in the second line, otherwise you would get 'areon'.

Now, this might not seem to be much of an advantage, but it is useful when you want to ask a question and to have the student type his answer immediately afterwards, as in:

th:Please type your answer ->

It obviously looks more natural to have this happen than to have the typed answer appear underneath. In this case, it would look like this:

Please type your answer-> I haven't a clue

And that's the sort of answer you usually get, but don't blame the computer!

SuperPILOT Variations

In this, and all subsequent chapters, we will note the additional features of PILOT available to users of Apple SuperPILOT, whilst also indicating what you may need to do to achieve the same effect with some other implementations of PILOT. In this case, we deal with the variations on the Type command.

The main extensions are achieved with the 'ts:' (short for type-specify) command, the effects of which are described below. If you want a quick demonstration, try the program in Figure 10.1.

```
:
:
r:Examples of special cases of 't'
:instructions
:
th:This stays on one line, like ; in
:BASIC
:
t:You can use
ts:s2
t:DOUBLE SIZE CHARACTERS LIKE THIS
ts:s1
t:
t:And you can change the thicknes
ts:t2
t:So that the text is BOLDER.
ts:t1
t:
t:Another trick is to change the line
:spacing
ts:l3
```

```
t:So that we
t:now get 3
t:line spaces rather than one.
ts:ll
```

Figure 10.1 A partial demonstration program for SuperPILOT type-specification commands

Viewport. ts:vl,r,t,b (where l=left, r=right, t=top, b= bottom of screen; l and r can be from 0 to 39, t and b can be from 0 to 23)

This causes any subsequent text to be contained within a rectangular area, as shown in Figure 10.2. The main use of this is to isolate a part of the screen for a commentary, or for a student dialogue, whilst placing graphical material on the rest of the screen.

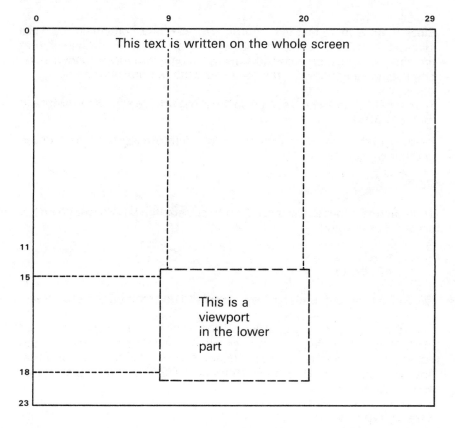

Figure 10.2

The text that appears in a text viewport is automatically re-formatted in SuperPILOT so that words are not chopped off. For example, if we had:

    ts:v10,20,15,20
    t:This is a very long line of text that we want to have displayed in
    :the text window, without losing any part of the words.

then the output would begin like this, starting at line 15 on the screen:

    This is a
    very long
    line of
    text that
    we want to
    have

Since there is more text to be output, the next line, containing the word 'displayed' will cause the text to 'scroll': i.e. the top line will disappear from the top of the viewport area and subsequent lines will all be pushed up by one line, making room for the new line at the bottom, and so on.

To re-establish the whole screen as the viewport, type ts:v as a shorthand for ts:v0,39,0,23.

Because of the formatting feature, it is difficult to imitate text viewporting in other dialects of PILOT.

Go To. ts:gx,y

This statement moves the text cursor to any column (x) and row (y) on the screen. For example:

    ts:g16,22
    t:Bullseye

will cause the word 'Bullseye' to be displayed in the middle of the screen.

This is easy to simulate in other dialects, either by including sufficient blank lines or by writing program lines that count the required rows and columns in a couple of loops before displaying the text. Another alternative is to output the required number of ASCII control characters, as shown in section 10.2

Size of Type. ts:sn

This enables you to write double size characters:

```
ts:s2
t:Aren't they big!
```

After this, you use ts:s1 to change back to normal-sized letters.

On some computers (e.g. the TRS-80) double sized characters can be invoked by transmitting a special ASCII character, otherwise you are stuck, as you are for the next two extensions.

Thickness of type. ts:tn

By using

```
ts:t2
```

the characters are displayed in bold type. Normal type is restored by ts:t1.

Modes of Type. ts:mn

This is less obviously useful;
ts:m2 causes new characters to overwrite existing characters, without erasing what is at present in that position.

ts:m3 enables you to temporarily overwrite some existing text or graphics with a t: statement. The trick is that when the new text is re-written in the same position, the previously-erased material reappears!

Transmit ASCII. ts:xn

This sends ASCII character number 'n' to the present text cursor position. For example, the following lines cause the cursor to be positioned at a particular place for the student to input an answer:

```
t:Fill in the blank.
th:2+ =6
ts:x8,8,8
```

As you'll see in the graphics section, this is almost equivalent to an alternative form using ASCII codes or character strings as part of a graphics statement which is available in most other dialects.

Line Spacing. ts:ln

This simply puts blank lines between text lines. You can simulate this either by including lots of t: lines, or you simply include additional line space characters as string variables at the end of each line.

Printer Output. ts:p

With this command in operation, all output is simultaneously sent to the printer. The command ts:q prevents further printer output.

Animation: ts:an$,ts:wl,r,u,d and ts:dn

These seem to be unique to SuperPILOT, and are used to give the appearance of animation by rapidly displaying character strings on the screen. They are dealt with fully in the Language Manual. Briefly, if the text cursor is positioned anywhere on the screen, we can write a command such as:

ts:aHello

and the characters are displayed instantly- leastways, very much faster than with a normal t: command. We can also fill a string variable with characters and print it equally rapidly. So, if y$ contains 'Hello' then this would have the same effect:

ts:ay$

Animation effects are caused by the use of the second command, ts:w, where the 'w' stands for 'walk'. So, we walk the string around the screen and rapidly display it with the ts:a command,as in:

ts:g10,10
ts:a Hello
ts:wr
ts:a Hello

The leading space will cause the 'H' to be erased as Hello walks to the right. As it could get tedious to do a lot of walking, SuperPILOT permits the use of a repeat factor, as in the following line which moves 'Hello' ten spaces to the right in a smoothly animated fashion:

ts:g10,10,*10(a Hello;wr)

To slow down the animation, or just to delay the lesson at some point, the ts:dn command can be used. In its simplest form, this might be:

ts:d10

A delay of, in this case, ten sixtieths of a second would occur before the next line is processed. Most other dialects will have a delay command that can be substituted, such as w:10. It is specifically used in animations in a form such as:

    ts:g10,10;*10(a Hello;wr;d20)

which causes the animation of 'Hello' to have extra one-third of a second delays between subsequent presentations.

Colour Commands

Background colour is selected with ts:bn where n is one of 21 possible colours.

Foreground colour is controlled by ts:fn, with the same colour range.

For the actual colours and for notes on intermixing them, read the manual.

You can exchange foreground and background colours with ts:i (for inverse) and restore them with ts:n (for normal).

Finally, the screen can be erased and repainted in a single instruction:

    ts:esn

where n is the re-painting colour.

Obviously, it is a bit of academic exercise to convert these statements for many other systems, it all depends how badly you want to implement them!

10.2 Variables and the Type Statement

As in every other computer language, PILOT permits you to use variables to represent numbers or alphabetic (string) data. Variables are used to represent anything which can change its value. We'll see, in later chapters, how they are used in detail but, for the moment, let us presume that we can either:

    Prompt a user to input the value for a variable

    or

    Calculate the value of a variable.

A numeric variable (i.e. a symbol used to represent a number) is denoted by either one letter or a letter followed by a digit. So, these are examples of valid numeric variables:

x   x1   w9   p   P

And these are invalid:

1x (letter must come first)   pp (only one letter allowed)

Let's assume that the variable called 'c7' has been used to store the result for a test. You can use this in a 't' statement like this:

t:You got a score of #c7 out of 20.

The actual value of c7 now replaces the variable name, so long as you precede it with a # symbol. You should also follow it with an extra trailing space, unless the variable is at the end of a t: line. If you follow these simple rules, and assuming c7 to be 15, your output should look like:

You got a score of 15 out of 20.

The other sort of variable is the alphanumeric or 'string' variable which is used to store a sequence of letters, such as JOHN SMITH or 'Lesson Five', or any other information that is useful in a CBL lesson. A string variable is represented by a letter or a letter and a digit, followed by a $ sign. So, these are valid string variable names:

x$ x1$ b9$ N$ N1$

As you'll see later, you must set the allowed maximum number of characters that can be stored in a particular string variable- this prevents PILOT from wasting space by assuming that all strings can be, say, 255 characters. In order to use a string in a t: statement, you follow the same rules as for a numeric varible, but precede the variable name with a second $ sign. Let's assume that you have correctly set up a string variable called n$.You can now write a type statement that will welcome someone to a lesson:

t:Welcome to lesson one, n .

Notice that there must be a trailing space after the variable. Now, if n$ contains the name 'John Smith', the above line will output:

Welcome to lesson one, John Smith.

150

You can include as many variables in a type statement as you wish, for example:

> t:Welcome back, m , to lesson #18 of module #m.

10.3 Remarks

Some people think that you should put plenty of commentary in your programs, which BASIC people do with REM statements. It can be useful to include comments at crucial points in your programs, if only to remind yourself how on earth that particular tricky piece of code worked. You do this with the 'r:' command:

> r:This is a reminder

It is ignored by the program, so remarks don't do much harm, and might even be useful. The only problem is that programmers tend to put remarks in to explain how a particular part of the program works, then change the code but not the remarks, leaving you with some pretty shoddy document-ation. For this reason, coupled with native laziness, you might like to minimise the use of this statment.

10.4 Graphics Commands

If PILOT only enabled you to display text, you could rightly query why you should consider using it. In fact, if the version of PILOT you've purchased is text-only (and/or if it is on cassette), you probably should not use it at all- you'll only be disappointed.

First of all, we'll deal with the graphics commands found in most versions of PILOT. These enable you to draw dots, lines and characters that can be combined into simple or complex drawings. After that, we'll mention the enhancements in SuperPILOT to the standard graphics commands, and finally show how a graphics editor can be used to produce pictures.

Standard PILOT Graphics Commands

PILOT graphics statements are of the form:

> g: list of commands

For example,

     g:es

erases the screen, ready for plotting. In COMMON PILOT, the picture is plotted in an area 512 units wide and 512 units high. This is shown in Figure 10.3: the x values run from 0 to 511, left to right, and the y values run from 0 to 511, bottom to top. So, the bottom left hand corner is at x=0, y=0 and the top right hand corner is at x=511, y=511. Actually, you may find that the version of PILOT you have does not conform to this standard. For example, the Apple uses x from 0 to 559, although y is from 0 to 511. Also, don't imagine that you necessarily have 511 individual plotting positions. For example, the Apple II has actually got only 280 by 192 screen positions. Just bear this in mind if you wish to convert someone else's program to suit your computer.

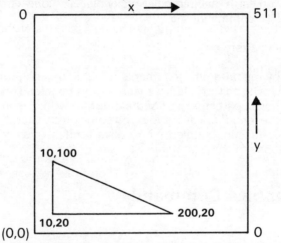

Figure 10.3 The PILOT Graphics Screen

Assuming that you've not done any special tricks, all graphics commands are taken to be relative to the origin at x=0, y=0 (i.e. the bottom left hand corner). As an example, these four statements will draw a triangle:

g:m10,20	(move to x=10, y=20 without drawing anything)
g:d200,20	(draw a line to x=200,y=20)
g:d10,100	(draw another line up to x=10,y=100)
g:d10,20	(draw a line back to where we started)

This used the m (for move) and d (for draw) commands. It can be expressed more compactly by a single g: statement, with the commands separated by semicolons:

     g:m10,20;d200,20;d10,100;d10,20

On most versions of PILOT, this also executes more rapidly. You can also 'undraw' or erase a line. Let's erase the horizontal line in the triangle that we just drew:

> g:r200,20

This simply re-drew the original line in black, to make it invisible.

You can also draw or erase dots on your picture. This places a dot at the centre of the screen (think of 'p' for 'point'):

> g:p256,256

And this erases it (q for quit):

> g:q256,256

Most versions let you draw lines and dots in different colours, though this depends on the particular computer. The command is of the form

> g:cn

where n is the number of the colour that is to be used. On the Apple II:

> g:c5

sets the drawing colour to orange.

Quite often, you will want to use just part of the screen for graphics. Rather than having to remember just where you are, it is easier to use an OFFSET, as shown in Figure 10.4. In the figure, we've chosen to do any and all drawing in the top right hand corner. Therefore, we use an offset of x=256, y=256, and draw all of our lines and points relative to this central point. So, if we now type:

> g:O256,256 ;d200,20;10,100;d10,20

the triangle will appear in the upper right, rather than the bottom left quadrant of the screen. In order to begin plotting from the normal (bottom

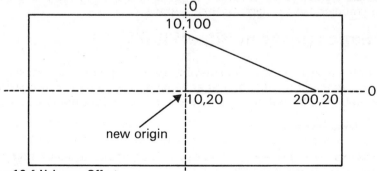

Figure 10.4 Using an Offset

153

left hand corner) you can either use:

> g:es   (erase screen and restore offset to 0,0)

or   g:o,0,0 (reset the origin)

One further feature of COMMON PILOT is that you can send ASCII characters (usually non-printing control characters) to the screen. This uses the x command. For example:

> g:x8,8,8

will cause (on the Apple) the current cursor to be back-spaced three times (since 8 is the ASCII backspace character). This might be handy if you were thinking in terms of character spaces. For example, perhaps you had drawn a picture of a triangle and wished to move the cursor to a particular place on the screen, prior to asking the student what picture you had drawn. One convenient place is the top left-hand (or 'home') position, for which your computer will have a particular ASCII character. On the Apple, we'd write:

> g:x25

A somewhat unlikely use of this command is to output printing characters. For example, this statement would type HELLO starting from the present cursor position:

> g:x72,69,76,76,79

But, fortunately, there are easier ways!

Often, it is easiest to get the text laid out correctly, and then to add any necessary graphics. In Chapter 8 (Fig 8.3) there is a useful design sheet that you can use or adapt for this purpose.

Enhancements in SuperPILOT

As for the type instruction, you may be able to add subroutines or sections of code that add these graphics enhancements to the version of PILOT that you have, though some are very specific to SuperPILOT.

Text Viewport g:vl,r,t,b

This is exactly equivalent to the use of a viewport in a ts: instruction (see section 10.1)). For example g:v10,30,20,23

causes all subsequent text to be output into a window running from column 10 to 30 and from row 20 to 23, inclusive. The full screen window is re-established either by

g:v0,39,0,23

or just

g:v

The viewport can be erased without erasing the rest of the screen by:

g:es

The viewport is actually 'painted' in the current background colour. This should be contrasted with

g:esn

where n is a graphics colour. This causes the entire screen to be erased, viewport and all. So, g:es0 would erase the entire screen in black.

Type on the Graphics Screen g:t(character string)

We mentioned that you could, just could write text on the screen by sending ASCII characters to it. A much more convenient method is to move the graphics cursor to wherever you wish, and then to write the text directly using the g:t command, like this:

g:m100,200   (move to x=100, y=200)
g:tHere we are!   (type the message)

These two commands can, of course, be combined:

g:m100,200;tHere we are!

Turtle Graphics

This is the most interesting enhencement, since it draws on the work of Seymour Papert, who developed the LOGO language (see section 2.1). The name arises from Papert's work in attaching a pen to a mechanical, computer controlled 'turtle'. The turtle is given commands to walk forwards, backwards, or turn whilst, at the same time, having the pen

155

either up or down. In this way, the person using the turtle can create pictures or designs on the floor, corresponding to the turtle's movements. More recently, Papert has invented 'screen turtles' which are simply the screen analogue of the floor-walking turtles. The LOGO language is a great favourite with children and the turtle-graphics feature is its most well-known and most visual feature. Apple SuperPILOT and Atari PILOT have incorporated Turtlegraphic commands which permit the easy construction of difficult geometric shapes. There are just two commands that are specific to Turtle Graphics:

Set Absolute Angle g:an

The 'turtle' is initially imagined to be pointing straight up, at an angle of 0 degrees. We can point in some other direction by typing, for example:

g:a45

It is now pointing North East, or at 45 degrees clockwise to the vertical.

Spin g:sn

The g:an command changes the 'absolute' angle, whilst this changes the relative angle. For example, whatever direction the turtle had been pointing, this command will rotate it by 30 degrees clockwise:

g:s30

The other turtle commands are similar to 'normal' graphics, except that they have just one argument (a number or a variable):

Moving and plotting g:mn, g:pn

Now that we have selected the angle, we can move along it and leave the graphics cursor there or plot a point. Refer to Figure 10.4 and you can see that the cursor (i.e. the turtle) starts at 0,0 the bottom left hand corner of the screen. Let's set the angle to 45 degrees, and move 100 units in that direction, at which distance we plot a point:

g:a45
g:p100

From this, you can see that this is easier to understand for children than the usual Cartesian system since it involves just an angle and a distance. The equivalent normal graphics command would be:

156

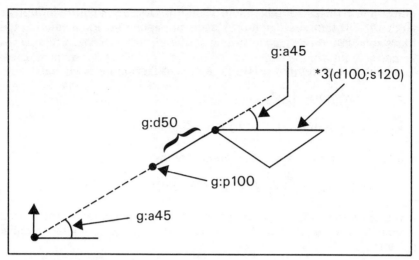

Figure 10.5 An example of Turtle Graphics. The turtle starts at 0,0.

g:p71,71

This looks simpler, until you realise that I had to compute the x and y distances as 100*cos(45), something that kids don't know about!

In Turtle Graphics, all plotting and drawing is done along the line set by the current angle. So, this draws a line of length 50 in the current direction

g:d50

And, of course, we can erase or 're-draw' a line or a point in much the same way:

g:d25   (erase for a distance of 25 units)
g:q10   (move 10 units along and erase one point at that location)

The main use of Turtle Graphics in PILOT is in the easy construction of figures, without having to worry about x,y coordinates. For example, this one-liner draws a triangle with sides all of length 100:

g:*3(d100;s120)

The * is a 'repeat factor' which, in this case, says that the part inside the brackets is to be repeated three times. Inside the bracket, we see that we

157

draw a line in the current direction, of length 100 and then turn through an angle of 120 degrees. Try it on a piece of paper, and you'll see that the triangle is drawn.

Similarly, this statement draws an approximately circular shape:

    g:*20(d20;s18)

It approximates the circle as 20 little segments.

And, if you want a really pretty effect, try this:

    g:o250,250;*12(*4(d100;s90);s30)

If you work this out, you'll see that it starts near the screen centre, then draws 12 squares, neatly daisy-chained into an approximately circular pattern.

Using Turtle Graphics on the Apple

There are two ways for you to experiment with turtle graphics:

1. In immediate mode

To get into immediate mode, read the language manual or section 9.3. of this book.

Reserve a portion of the screen for your commands by typing

    ts:v0,39,0,3

That gives you the top 4 lines of the screen so that you can see what you have typed. Then, you just type in any turtle command, remembering that the turtle starts life at the bottom left corner of the screen.

2. In lesson mode

A similar result is obtained if you type in and run the following program. Don't worry about how it works, all will be revealed later! Slight variations on the immediate version are that the bottom line is reserved for turtle commands, and the turtle begins its life at the screen centre.

    d:a$(40)
    g:o260,256;v0,39,23,23
    th:Command?

158

```
a:$a$
c:a$="g:"!!a$
xi:a$
j:@a
```

Graphics Exercises

Whether or not you have Turtle Graphics, you now know enough graphics instructions to create just about any pictures. Why not try these little brain teasers:

Draw the axes for a graph, like the one shown in Fig 10.6, and try to put the correct values on each axis:

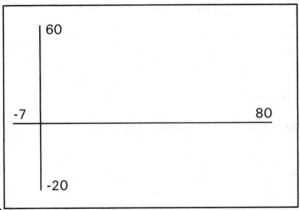

Figure 10.6

Draw the electrical circuit diagram in Fig 10.7, using graphics statements, as accurately as you can.

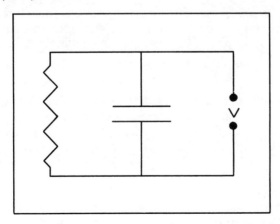

Figure 10.7

159

By way of a reward, and a final problem, here is a little program that uses Turtle Graphics to draw a spiral. It uses the c: (compute) statement, which we haven't met before, but it's pretty obvious how it works... just like the LET in BASIC. At the end of the program, there is a jump statement that causes the program to loop back to the label called STEP until the variable 't' reaches 100. Try to work out for yourself what it is doing and try thinking about how you would do the same thing if you did not have Turtle Graphics:

```
c:x=45
c:t=0
g:es
g:a45;m400
*step
g:dt;sx
c:t=t+1
j(t<100):step
```

You will find lots more examples of turtle graphics in Chapter 10.

10.5 Graphics the Easy Way

Apple SuperPILOT, and maybe other versions that I have not come across, have a really powerful device in the shape of a Graphics Editor. This enables you to create pictures interactively, and as I indicated in Chapter 9, it is the availability of editors for graphics, characters and sound, that distinguishes SuperPILOT from the rest and earns it the name of a development system, rather than just a language.

When you have created a picture with the graphics editor, you then SAVE it on disk with a file name, which might be 'example'. You can then call up that picture at any point in your program by a statment like:

```
gx:example
```

The gx: is an abbreviation for 'graphics execute'. By this means, you can build up a library of pictures and re-play them whenever you like. Without access to the editor, it is difficult to explain what it does. And, if you have got SuperPILOT or something similar with such an editor, it is so easy to use that an explanation is almost superfluous. But, basically, this is roughly what happens:

● You select the Graphics Editor, tell it you want to create a picture and give a name to the masterpiece you are going to work on.

● The editor replies by giving you a 'help' screen that you can refer to at any stage. This tells you what commands you can issue from the keyboard, and these include:

Move the cursor around the screen (either from the keyboard or with the games paddles)
Select a colour (type C, then a number from 0 to 8)
Draw a line
Draw a frame (rectangle) or a box (filled rectangle)
Draw a circle or oval
Fill an area with colour
Type text

Also, the whole picture can be moved around the screen, and the picture can be selectively edited. The latter is rather a nice feature, and a big improvement on the editor in the previous Apple PILOT, since you can move a marker to any component of the picture and erase it or insert extra parts. It's all so easy, and without a single graphics command. All of which makes one feel a bit apologetic for putting you through that previous section about individual graphics commands. Yes..... well.....sorry about that but, on the other hand, you might just not have SuperPILOT and, even if you have, very often you need to add extra bits and pieces to a picture that has been created with the editor.

The diagram in Fig. 10.8 could be created by the following sequence:

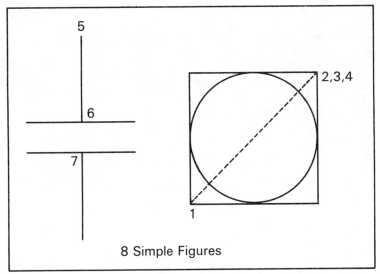

Figure 10.8 Simple usage of the graphics editor in SuperPILOT. The numbers 1 - 8 refer to the explanation in the text.

161

1. Move the cursor to the centre of the screen, either with the cursor-movement keys or with the joysticks.

2. Move the cursor diagonally towards the top right corner.

3. Press C for circle.

4. Press F for frame.

5. Move the cursor to the left.

6. Move it downwards, then press D to draw a line.

7. Draw the other lines in a similar way.

8. Move the cursor under the diagram, press T, then type the text.

To do much more than this, you'll have to read the manual and EXPERIMENT! Quite complex pictures can be drawn quickly and precisely.

Chapter 11

Principles of Answer Processing

One of the main reasons for using an author language is its ability to match against various types of answer. We may wish to match against an expected numerical answer, single keys, or whole words or phrases contained within a sentence. A language like PILOT lets you do all of this.

11.1 Getting a response

In PILOT, after presenting graphics or text, we can invite a response with the accept (a:) op-code. For example:

        t:Please type your name
        a:

The a: causes the computer to stop until a response is given, followed by the return key. The effect of this is to transfer whatever is typed into an internal buffer called %b. You can use %b (a 'system variable') directly if you wish, as in:

        t(%b="abracadabra"):That's Right

which might be useful if you required the student to type a password before your lesson could be used. And, you can display the current value of %b by typing:

        t:#(%b)

Note the compulsory # sign and the obligatory use of brackets, at least in Apple PILOT (try leaving them out and you'll see what we mean!). These rules also apply if you are printing out any other system variables. On other computers, you may find that the answer buffer is accessed in different ways- for example, on Commodore 64 PILOT, you type:

t:$%b

USING THE PR: CODE FOR AUTOMATIC EDITING

The contents of the answer buffer need not be identical to what was typed. Automatic editing is carried out by use of the pr: instruction. The editing options are:

pr:l   convert all input into lower case
pr:u   convert all input into upper case
pr:s   remove all spaces

For example, if we type

    pr:ls

then anything we type in at an accept (a:) line will have all spaces removed and will all be in lower case. Notice that the order of modifiers is immaterial- pr:sl is just as good. If you want to try this out, put your Apple in immediate mode (type CTRL-I during a lesson if you are in Author mode, or select RUN from the Lesson Text Editor page, then CTRL-I: see your manual or Section 9.3 of this book for more details) and type the following three lines.

    pr:s
    a:
    t:Buffer contains: #(%b)

Try experimenting with the pr: instruction. Notice that if pr:s is not used, all multiple spaces are condensed to single spaces, so

    APP   PLE COM   PUT   ER

becomes

    APPLE COMPUTER

OVER-RIDING AUTOMATIC EDITING

There are various modifiers for the simple a: op-code. It may be that you do not want any editing of an answer at certain points in the lesson, in which case you type ax:

which is short for Accept eXact. This over-rides any pr: instructions.

Care is needed when using the pr: command in some circumstances. Note that:

        A blank pr: (i.e. just pr: on its own) leaves any previous pr: options unchanged.

        If one option is changed, then any previous ones are cancelled. For example, pr:sl followed by pr:u will mean that spaces are no longer removed.

        Some dialects (NOT SuperPILOT) enable you to turn off all existing options (e.g. pr:z in Commodore 64 PILOT)

SINGLE KEY INPUT

Rather than accepting a sequence of characters, you may require a single key press, in which case, use:

        as:

this being an abbreviation for Accept Single. Whatever key was pressed is stored in the answer buffer. Notice that, after a normal accept instruction has been obeyed, the text cursor moves to the next line BUT after an accept single, the cursor stays on the same line.

Extensions in Apple SuperPILOT

There is an additional pr: option to limit the time for a response. By default, the a: will wait forever, but if you type:

        pr:t20

then the program will pause at the a: for only 20 seconds (you can choose any value from 1 to 32767) before carrying on. To make the best use of this option, you must use the TIM function also, as in the following short program:

        pr:t2
        t:You have 2 seconds to press the RETURN key....
        a:
        t(tim(1)=0):Too late!!!!

165

the function tim(x) contains the number of seconds before pressing the return key BUT if the time limit specified in the pr:tn instruction is exceeded, then tim(x) contains zero. You can use tim(x) to tell the student how long he took:

```
c:t=tim(x)
t:You took #t seconds.
```

The other goodie in SuperPILOT is the P (for Point) modifier:

```
ap:
```

When this instruction is used, a pair of cross-hairs (one vertical and one horizontal line) appears. Using the games-paddles or any other device, the cross hairs can be moved over the screen to select, for example, a correct answer. If you want to see this in action, try the program LEGENDS on the Apple SuperPILOT sample lesson disk, which uses the games paddles and cross-hairs to locate items on a map. On pressing the button of either games paddle, the horizontal and vertical coordinates of the cross hairs are stored in the system variables %x and %y, and the program then proceeds. It is also possible to modify the author SuperPILOT software so that the cross hairs are invisible and other pointing devices such as a touch screen (as on PLATO) are used.

11.2 Matching the response (non-numeric)

Having accepted the response, and possibly edited it, the next thing is to match it against your expected answer. This is done with the m: (match) op-code.

For example, this instruction will match for the word 'blue'

```
m:blue
```

And, any student response such as

```
    blue
or, it is blue
or, a blue,blue sea
```

will match successfully. PILOT signifies that the match is successful, by 'raising a flag'. The state of the flag can be tested with the 'y' and 'n' conditioners, these standing for 'yes' and 'no'. For example:

```
t:What colour is the sky?
a:
m:blue
ty:That's right
tn:No, it's blue
```

You can append the y or n to any op-code, although it is most commonly used as a type conditioner. For example, here is how to check that both 'black' and 'white' are both in the answer:

```
a:
m:black
my:white
ty:You got both of them!
```

Notice that the my: is esential in this case, since it says 'match against white only if the previous match was successful'. The order in the answer is immaterial, so either

        The black and white zebra
or,   The white car with black stripes

would match.

SEQUENCES

Frequently you want to match for words contained in a certain order in the student answer. You use the & symbol for this:

```
t:Put these into increasing order of size....
 :rhinoceros, squirrel, baboon
a:
m:squirrel&baboon&rhinoceros
```

Presuming that the student can spell, and that we're playing fair by talking about full grown examples, the following answer will match:

' First a squirrel, then a baboon, then biggest of all is the rhionoceros'

You can think of the '&' meaning 'any sequence of characters including blanks'.

ALTERNATIVES

The other thing you need to do is to check for one from a list of several possible answers (in computer jargon, using OR rather than AND logic). You do this with the '!' character:

```
pr:l
t:Name one country in the United Kingdom:
a:
m:england!ireland!wales!scotland
ty:Yes, you got at least one of them right.
```

This will match successfully with any one, or more than one of the words we specified. So, for example, 'Wales is one of them' would match and so would 'How about Wales or Scotland'. In other words, it is not an exclusive-or match. Notice that we preceded the matching with a conversion to lower case, so whilst one expected answer that would match successfully is 'England', so would 'england' or 'ENGLAND' or 'EnGlAnD'.

COMBINING & AND ! MATCHING

You can perform complex matching, so long as you are careful. For example,

```
m:blue!red&yellow
```

means that the match will be successful for either 'blue' or for 'red' followed by 'yellow'. What it does NOT mean is 'either blue or red followed by yellow', so this would match:

```
A blue hat
```

and so would this:

```
The red one's nice and so is the yellow one
```

But, this one would match, but for the wrong reason, if you expected that blue followed by yellow would be correct:

```
The blue hat with yellow flowers
```

It does, of course, match with 'blue' and disregards the yellow completely!

168

APPROXIMATE SPELLINGS

There are several ways of dealing with this problem. One useful method is just to match the word stem:

```
t:Name a 4-legged animal that likes mud....
a:
m:hippo
```

This recognises the fact that hippopotamus just might be mis-spelt. A similar trick is to use & for any sequence of characters within a word:

```
m:newcastle&tyne
```

will match 'Newcastle-on-Tyne' or 'Newcastle-upon-Tyne' presuming that you have used the pr:s instruction prior to the match.

If you suspect that particular characters may be incorrect, just insert an asterisk. This will match against 'byte', 'bite' (and, admittedly, 'bate', 'bste' etc):

```
t:What is the unit of storage in a microcomputer?
a:
m:b*te
```

Similarly, m:rec**ver would match any approximate spelling of the word 'receiver'.

For general mis-spellings, use the 's' modifier for the match command. Quite how this works depends on the computer you are using, but on the Apple, it permits one character to be incorrect anywhere in the answer. For example:

```
ms:apple
```

matches successfully with 'apple', 'apfle', 'arple' and so on. In some other versions, ms: allows an incorrect character, an omitted character or the exchange of adjacent characters. In Commodore 64 PILOT, matching is carried out by moving a 9-character wide 'window' across the answer so, whilst the ms: still only permits one wrong character within the window, it is a little less rigid (and a little more unpredictable). In all implementations, you can also insert a * for specific characters.

USING DELIMITERS

The simple m: is often too liberal in its matching. For example, m:yes

169

matches with 'yes' but also with 'yesterday' and 'dyes'. To avoid this problem, we put a % sign to mark the beginning or the end of a response, or a space. For example,

m:%yes%

will match 'yes it is' but not 'yesterday'. Use this with care as it can cause surprises. For example:

m:%disk%&%drive%

will not match 'disk drive', because the % means 'one space', and the way that we have written it means that a space is required after 'disk' and ANOTHER space before 'drive'. Even if the user typed 'disk drive' it would still not match because the automatic editing (pr: with no options converts multiple spaces to a single space). The correct form in this case would be

m:%disk%&drive%

which would match 'disk drive' but not 'disks drive'. Admittedly, it would also match the unlikely 'disk overdrive'.

A TEST PROGRAM

If you want to experiment with the m: op-code, and you have an Apple system, you will find that there is a short program called MATCH on the sample lesson disk in the old version of Apple PILOT. In SuperPILOT, it is on one of the CO-PILOT instructional diskettes. If you want to use your own program, try this:

```
d:m$(80);n$(80)
*start
t:Match string?
a:$m$
c:n$="m:"!!m$
t:Test string?
a:
xi:n$
ty:Success
tn:Failure
j:start
```

When you RUN the program, you are asked for the string to be matched

170

(the 'match string') and then for the string to test it against (the 'test string').

No apologies are made for the fact that most of this program uses commands that we have not yet explained- it is simply provided as a useful tool.

MATCH-JUMPING

If you have many matches to carry out, you can automatically skip to the next match if the present one has failed, by using the j modifier:

mj:red

.....

.....

mj:blue

.....

m:green

In this case, as soon as the match against 'red' has failed, PILOT jumps to the mj:blue, then, if this fails, to the final match, which does not need the j modifier. This avoids the necessity of explicit jump instructions and speeds up the program slightly.

11.3 Extracting information from responses

Most times, the normal accept, followed by a match statement is sufficient. But, on some occasions, it is useful to extract some valuable piece of data from the student answer and refer to it later. We have already seen one way of doing this, with the %b system variable. If this were stored in a string variable, by a computation (c:) statement such as

c:b$=#(%b)

then b$ is 'remembered' so that you can refer back to it or insult the student at some later point, as in:

t:Come on now! Last time you said it was b.

In this statement, whatever had been stored in the string variable b$ will replace the b in the type statement. Notice that WHENEVER you refer to a string variable in a t: statement, you must PREFIX IT WITH A $ SIGN and FOLLOW IT WITH AN EXTRA TRAILING SPACE. Similarly, if a numeric variable is used, it must be PREFIXED WITH A # SIGN and, of course, followed by a space. If you don't do this, PILOT won't substitute the present value of the variable, it will just type b or whatever, which is pretty but not very useful.

Knowing how to use variables helps us out when extracting data for real. To store the entire answer, an easier way than the tedious one we just described is simply to write:

    a:b

If the student types 'Good Morning' at this accept, then the variable b$ will contain 'Good Morning'. At least, it will if you remembered to DIMENSION the string b$ before it was used, with a statement such as:

    d:b$(80)

This tells PILOT to set aside 80 characters of storage space for the string b$. In SuperPILOT, a string can be up to 255 characters in length, and the total string space is 1600 characters- check with your manual if you are using some other dialect. Please don't write programs that do this sort of thing:

    t:Hi There! What's your name?
    a:a
    t:Sure is terrific to meet you, b, let's get started!
    t:Now then, b, what is 2+2
    etc
    etc
    .....

Boring after the first time, isn't it?

If the accept is written in the form:

    a:#p

then, the first number in the student answer will be stored in the numeric variable, p. So, if the student response is 'It might be 56, or maybe 57', the value of p is set to 56. If there is no number in the response, the error conditon is set without the program crashing, which is handy, since you

172

can test for the condition with the 'e' error conditioner:

> t: How old are you?
> a:#y
> te:Please type it as a number.
> je:@a

Only the first number can be extracted in this way, so if you have:

> a:#p #q

then the same number will be placed in both p and q. If you do use two or more such variables, note that you must put a space between them.

Finally, you can have both string and numeric variables in the accept line, in any order. For example:

> a:q #g

This stores the entire response in q$, and any number in the answer in g.

11.4 Matching numeric responses

Although the m: op-code can be used to match numbers (e.g m:5) a better method is to use a relational test. This has the advantage of being able to test for numeric ranges. For example:

> t:How many centimetres to an inch?
> a:#x
> te:Please type a number
> je:@a
> t(x=2.54):That's exactly right.
> ec:
> t(x<2.5 and x>2.6):That's very near.

The accept (a:) instruction finds the first numeric value in the student answer, and stores it in the numeric variable, x. We can use any letter or a letter and a digit for a variable - see section 10.2. The student can type just the raw number, or it can be contained in a string, such as 'There are about 2.5 centimetres' in which case, the accept statement finds the value of 2.5 and assign it to the variable, x.

The next line tests with the 'e' conditioner to see if there is a number in the response, otherwise the 'error flag' is raised and the message 'Please type a number is displayed'. The next line is a shorthand way of saying 'jump back to the previous accept statement if the error flag is raised'. In the next line, we test to see if the answer is exactly 2.54. The ec: means 'End if the previous Condition is true'. The condition is true if x equals 2.54, so the program will stop here if the user got the answer right. The final line checks to see if the value of x is between 2.5 and 2.6 . In SuperPILOT we can use the words 'and' and 'or' in relational expressions but, alternatively, and necessarily in some other versions you must use '&' for 'and' and '!' for 'or'.

11.5 Feedback messages

As you have seen, the match instruction is invariably followed by some form of feedback, which we have discussed in Chapter 4. One useful idea is to be consistent in where a feedback message is positioned. That way, a student will always know where to look and this improves the 'human engineering' of the program you are writing.

11.6 Tricky Matching

Although the match instruction has many variants, there are always some difficult situations. The first one arises in multiple choice tests, where you have asked the student to choose one AND ONLY ONE answer from a list of possibles. It would be inadvisable to write something like:

```
t:Please choose a,b or c
a:
m:b
ty:Yes, 'b' is the correct answer
```

The problem being that the crafty student will type 'abc' and still be judged correct. A better method is to use single key input:

```
t:Please choose a,b or c
as:
m:b
```

That way, only the single key entry of 'b' will be successful.

Sometimes, exact matching is required in the sense that we wish to compare the whole of the student answer with the expected answer. In this case, the simplest method is to use the answer buffer, as in:

```
t:For what is U.A.E an abbreviation?
a:
```

t(%b="United Arab Emirates"):Quite Correct.

Some things remain difficult. One particular problem is the trapping of alternative synonyms in a sequence. For example, if the correct answer to a question is

      9,10, jack

or   nine, ten, jack

or any other combination (e.g. 9, ten, jack) then this match will fail:

      m:9!nine&10!ten&jack

This is because the & 'binds together' the elements of an expression more tightly than a !. Therefore, the simple answer 9 would also be judged correct. We could solve this problem if PILOT would let us use brackets, to write an expression such as:

      m:(9!nine)&(10!ten)&jack

But it doesn't, so you can't.

We will return to the problem of matching techniques in Chapter 13.

Chapter 12

Keeping in Control

So far, we have been able to write our PILOT programs as a simple sequence of instructions- one thing just happened after the other. But, you often need to do more complicated things than this in a CBL program. It may be something as simple as going back to the beginning or, as we explained in Chapters 4 and 5, providing a complex network of remedial frames. Fortunately, you can do either of these very easily in PILOT.

12.1 Labels and the Jump command

In BASIC, we transfer control to a different part of the program by referring to the line numbers. For example,

200 GOTO 3100

This can be awkward, since we have to keep track of the line numbers and, also, a line number can't describe the meaning of a section of code. In PILOT, no line numbers are used, you just put a label anywhere in the program that you may wish to jump to. A label consists of an asterisk and a sequence of characters. For example,

*start

In SuperPILOT, a label can be up to 35 characters in length, though only the first 6 are significant. Normally, embedded spaces are not allowed, so you could not use '*the end' as a label. A label can stand on its own or it can precede an instruction, as in

*middle t:Now we're in the thick of it.

When used in this form, at least one space must separate the label from the instruction, otherwise PILOT will think that the whole line is a label. You can use labels according to preference, though some people find labels placed on separate lines easier to spot in a long listing. (Note that the SuperPILOT text editor has a Jump to a specified label option.) Most versions of PILOT treat upper and lower case as being equivalent in a program, so the labels *END, *end and *End are all equivalent.It is good programming practice to use labels that are meaningful, and to use similar labels for related sections of a lesson. So, you might use the labels *iu1, *iu2 and so on to refer to a set of related instructional units.

Conditional and Unconditional Jumps

Having labelled part of a program, we can now use the label as a destination, either for a Jump or a Use-Subroutine command. The jump is abbreviated by j: and, in its simplest form, has a label after the colon. For example:

```
*start t:This program goes on forever
j:start
```

This is an example of an UNCONDITIONAL jump- it will always be obeyed. More often, the jump is conditional on some event being true. For example, look at the simple flow chart in Figure 12.1

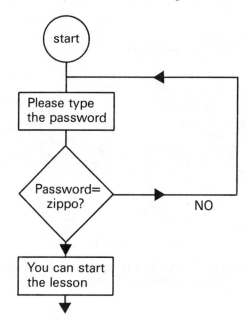

Figure 12.1

To code this into PILOT, you need something like:

```
t:Welcome to the start of this lesson
*access t:What is the Password?
```

```
a:
m:%zippo%
jn:access
ty:You can now start the lesson.
        (rest of program follows)
```

Just as you saw in the previous chapter, the yes (y) and no (n) conditioners are used, but this time they condition a jump command. The jn: is read as 'Jump if No', i.e. carry out the jump to the specified label only if the match is unsuccessful. In place of the ty: at the end of this program, you might want to send the user to some other destination, so you might use something like

```
jy:part1
```

A common use of labels is in providing access to different instructional units, as we discussed in the menu frame example in Section 5.2.2. To turn the design sheet in that example into PILOT code, you could write:

```
pr:l
*menu g:es
t:Please choose one of these:
t:
t: A. Overview
t: B. Start up procedure
t: C. Practice questions
t:    or type Q to quit
as:
m:a
jy:over
m:b
jy:start
m:c
jy:practice
m:q
ey:
r:If we get this far, the wrong key has been pressed.
t:You must choose from A,B, C or Q
j:menu
*over

(code for the overview unit here)

j:menu
*start
```

178

```
(code for start up procedure here)

j:menu

*practice

(code for practice questions here)

j:menu
```

This is a rather crude basis for a menu driven program, but it will work. Notice in particular the use of meaningful labels.

Jumps to labels can also be conditional on some relational expression being true. For example:

```
         j(x=8): label8
or
         j(x<5 & x>7):range
```

SPECIAL JUMP CONDITIONS- look, no labels!

The more labels you use, the slower your program will run, as PILOT has to keep track of them in a 'label-table'. To reduce the dependency on explicit labels, there are some special forms of the jump instruction:

last accept: j:@a

This transfers control to the last accept instruction that PILOT has executed. For example:

```
         t:Please type a number:
         a:#q
         te:You didn't type a number- try again!
         j:@a
```

This was used in section 11.3 somewhat prematurely, because it is the neatest way of back-tracking! The j:@ a can be combined with a conditional or relational test:

```
         jy:@a
         jn(v=9):@a
```

Notice that the conditioner always precedes the relation.

next match: j:@m

This jumps forwards to the next match instruction.

next problem: j:@p

This jumps forwards to the next pr: instruction (The pr: historically was used to separate each problem in a lesson, hence the name.)

How Many Labels?

SuperPILOT lets you have up to 50 labels in any one lesson. If you wish to use more labels, include the 'wipe labels' pr: instruction at an appropriate point:

```
pr:w
```

The effect of this instruction is to discard all current labels SO THAT THEY ARE NO LONGER ACCESSIBLE and you can then start using a new list of labels, which may include duplicates of the old ones.

12.2 Answer counting

Whenever an accept (a:) instruction is executed, a system variable %a is incremented by one. At the start of your program, %a is zero. Its value can be accessed directly if you wish:

```
t:What is 2+2?
a:#w
j(w=4):OK
t:No, you've had #(%a) attempts- try again.
j:@a
```

Note, again, how we can refer to a system variable by the use of #( ) but, as this is rather tedious, PILOT lets you access %a directly by use of the 'digit conditioner' which is simply an integer from 1 to 9. It is commonly used for providing hints; for example:

```
pr:l
*capital
t:What is the capital of France?
a:
m:paris
ty:Magnifique!
jy:next
t1:It begins with a P. Try again.
j1:capitals
t:The answer is Paris.
*next
.....
```

In this program, if the answer is incorrect for the first time of answering,
we give the user a hint. If more than one attempt is made, the answer is
given.

Here is another example of a program that uses answer counting. It draws
a picture on the screen and asks what it represents. It gives two hints (see
the t1: and t2: lines) and, on the third attempt, provides the correct
answer. Also, if the answer just contains the word 'triangle' (the fully
correct answer being matched in the ms: line requires the word 'right' to
precede 'triangle') AND if the user has had less than 3 tries then a different
sort of hint is given.

```
t:Here is a figure:
g:m50,250;d400,250;d50,400;d50,250
g:v0,39,16,23
th:What is it?
a:
ms:right&triang
ty:That's right
jy:stop
m:triang
ty(%a()3):Yes, it's a triangle, but what sort?
t1:Try again..
t2:Look at the 90 degree angle, and try
:again.
t3:Sorry, it's a RIGHT ANGLED TRIANGLE.
j3:stop
j:∂a
*stop e:
```

This program illustrates just how powerful PILOT can be in expressing quite complicated ideas in a very short program.

12.3 Subroutines

A subroutine is a section of code that is generally used more than once in a program. Alternatively, it may be a section of well-proven code that has been developed independently or in some other program. In fact IT IS GOOD PROGRAMMING PRACTICE to develop your larger programs as well-tested subroutines, and to string then together later into the single, large program That way, you can be sure that each part of your program is thoroughly de-bugged. It is MUCH EASIER to de-bug a small subroutine than a large program.

A subroutine begins with a label and ends with an e: (end) statement. To use the subroutine, you must use a u: op-code, followed by the name (i.e. the label) of the subroutine. After the subroutine has been processed, control returns to the statement immediately following the u:, as shown in Figure 12.2

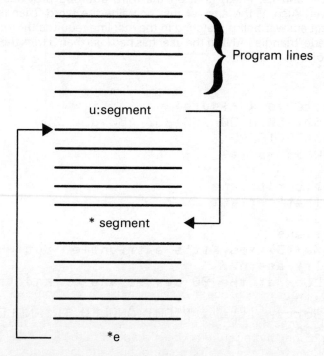

Figure 12.2 Control of program flow with a subroutine call.

For example, this program calls a subroutine to check if a user wishes to continue with the lesson:

```
t:Do you want to carry on?
a:
u:test
tn:OK, that's the end of the lesson.
en:
ty:Right, let's continue.
jy:next
*test r:This subroutine tests for the various ways of saying yes.
ms:yes!ok!right!sure!course
e:
```

A subroutine can not call itself but, it can call other subroutines, as shown in Figure 12.3.

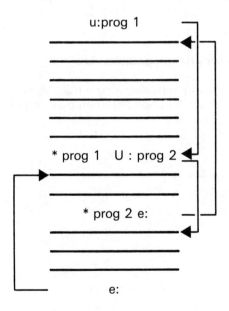

Figure 12.3 A Subroutine calling another Subroutine.

PILOT keeps track of complex calls like this by keeping a list of addresses to which each subroutine returns. When a u: command is encountered, PILOT stores the address of the next instruction as the return point. For each u:. one more return address is added to the list. And, as each e: is encountered at the end of a subroutine, the last address in the list is deleted. For this reason, do NOT leave a subroutine by a JUMP (j:)

instruction, or you will mess up the list, with unpredictable consequences. Also, it is good practice to keep all subroutines together either at the beginning or end of a program AND to make very sure that your program does not accidentally fall into a subroutine. If it does, you will get an error message to the effect that there is a 'return with no prior gosub' - even worse, your program will crash. For this reason, I often put subroutines at the beginning of a program, with a jump over them to the real start of the program, as shown below. This way, I avoid the fall-through problem:

```
j:start
*sub1
....
e:
*sub2
....
e:

etc.....

*start
r:This is where the program starts
```

The very first jump can alternatively be a j:@p if the main part of your program begins with a pr: option list, thereby using one less label.

Chapter 13

Calculations and Logical Operations

If we were describing any other programming language, the statements required for calculations would have been described long ago. But, PILOT and the other author languages are mainly used to facilitate dialogue with the student, and are used to a much lesser extent for calculations. Even so, we often need to perform calculations in a CBL lesson-for example, to increment student scores. Also, we may need to process alphanumeric strings- for example, by measuring their lengths, or by joining two together and so on. All dialects of PILOT provide adequate facilities for each type of calculation.

13.1 Numerical calculations using constants and variables.

The op-code for computation is C: and a simple use of it is:

    c:x=3

this assigns the value of 3 to x. As you will recall, x is a numeric variable, and such variables are denoted by a letter or a letter followed by a digit. A more useful computation might be:

    c:b2=(x-3)*(y-9)/6-8

Normal rules of precedence apply: exponentiation is done first, then multiplication and division, and finally addition and subtraction. Some versions of PILOT (e.g. Commodore 64) can only do integer arithmetic, whereas SuperPILOT works in real (decimal) mode. This means that the two liner:

    c:x=5/3
    t:#x

will print the answer 1.66666 (accurate to six digits) for SuperPILOT but the answer 1 (truncated) for an integer implementation. Very large or very small numbers that are calculated in a computer statement are printed out in scientific notation. For example, 6.24E-5 and 1.2345E11, where 'E' means '10 raised to the power'. In comparison with BASIC (yes, even BASIC) computations in PILOT are slow. To speed things up, SuperPILOT lets you write multi-statement lines (spaces must NOT occur after the ; separator):

c:t1=b*b-4*a*c;t2=-b+sqr(t1);t3=t2/(2*a)

In this line, you'll notice that the semi-colon is used as a separator. Notice also that 'sqr' is used to evaluate a square root. This is one of several functions, in COMMON PILOT:

Example	Explanation
c:a=abs(x)	absolute value of x
c:a=atn(x)	arctangent of x
c:a=cos(x)	cosine of x (all angles in radians)
c:a=sin(x)	sine of x
c:a=log(x)	base 10 (common) logarithm
c:a=ln(x)	base e (natural) logarithm
c:a=exp(x)	e (2.71828) raised to the power x
c:a=fix(x)	truncate x
c:a=int(x)	find the integer less than or equal to x
c:a=rnd(x)	If x<1 then a will be between 0 and 1. If x>=1, a will be an integer from 0 to x-1
c:a=sgn(x)	signum (sign) of x

If you are using SuperPILOT, you may wish to experiment with the calculation features by putting the system into immediate mode (CTRL-I from the 'Run a lesson' option on the author page). If you want to be really adventurous, SuperPILOT additionally has four input functions PDL(x) for games paddle x, BTN(x) for the button on paddle x, KEY(x) which returns the ASCII value of any key, and TIM(x) to measure the response time. See the manual for details of these.

One function that merits a little more explanation is the random number function, RND. Apart from its obvious uses of generating lots of random numbers (e.g. in arithmetic tests) it can be used to control random branching, as in:

j(rnd(1)<.3):cavern

186

gives a 30 percent probability of entering the sequence starting with label 'cavern'. Note that rnd gives a series of pseudo-random numbers, which are good enough for most purposes but are nevertheless predictable.

Using C: in Recording Scores and in Matching Sequences

One common use of the compute statement is in recording scores. To do this, you usually use the 'y' or 'n' conditioner:

```
t:The first man on the moon was:
t:
t:1. Buzz Aldrin
t:2. Neil Armstrong
t:3. Yuri Gagarin
t:
th:Choose 1,2, or 3:
as:#x
je:@a
m:2
cy:s=s+1
```

The last, vital line increments the score by one. Equally, we could replace the last two lines by:

```
c(x=1):s=s+1
```

A rather neat trick is to use a variable to detect the degree of correctness of an answer. For example, if you had the match statement:

```
m:milk!butter!cheese
```

then you would not know, in the event of a successful match, if the student typed one, two or all three keywords. Consider this alternative:

```
c:t=0
m:milk
cy:t=t+1
m:butter
cy:t=t+2
m:cheese
cy:t=t+4
```

What we have done here is to increment t by 1,2 or 4. If there were more matches, we would increment by 8, 16 and so on-- in increasing powers of 2. The end result is that the value of t tells us exactly what was matched:

t	Matched
0	nothing
1	milk
2	butter
3	milk and butter
4	cheese
5	milk and cheese
6	butter and cheese
7	milk and butter and cheese

So, we could add a line such as:

        t(t=5):You typed 'milk and cheese'

That makes for a very powerful matching feature. The order of occurrence of the keywords within the answer is, of course, irrelevant.

A more complete example is shown below:

```
t:Exact matching.
t:This is how to match just one word or
:a set sequence of words. This next
:match will only accept 'apple
:computer' as the correct answer- no
:extra letters or words are allowed:
t:
t:What sort of computer is this?
a:
t(%b="apple computer"):That's right.
t(%b<>"apple computer"):Wrong!
t:
as:
t:
t:Often, you want to know how correct a
:partially correct answer is.
```

188

```
t:For example, the following piece of
:code gives suitable responses for an
:answer that contains RED and/or
:GREEN and/or BLUE in any combination.
t:
t:Try typing in some combination:
a:
c:s=0
m:red
cy:s=s+1
m:green
cy:s=s+2
m:blue
cy:s=s+4
t(s=0):none right.
t(s=1):just red.
t(s=2):just green.
t(s=4):just blue.
t(s=3):red and green correct.
t(s=5):red and blue correct.
t(s=6):green and blue correct.
t(s=7):all correct.
as:
```

Combining Compute and Graphics Statements

Since, for most graphical problems, you need to calculate where to plot a line or a point, the two statements go together quite nicely. For example, here is a program that uses turtle graphics to draw spirals. It starts off by moving to the centre of the screen, then draws straight lines of length 't', such that each line is at an angle x to its predecessor:

```
t:angle?
a:#x
g:es
g:a45;m400
c:t=0
*step
g:dt;sx
c:t=t+1
j(t<100):step
```

Next, here is a program using ordinary graphics commands to draw a circle, using simple trigonometry. You may need to change the factor of 1.094 to make the circle look circular on your monitor:

```
th:Radius (up to 200)?
a:#r
g:o250,250;mr,0
c:i=0;d=0.2
*rpt
r:compute coordinates and allow for
:aspect ratio of 560:512
c:x1=r*cos(i);y1=1.094*r*sin(i)
g:dx1,y1;mx1,y1
c:i=i+d
j(i<=6.28):rpt
```

Similarly, this is a program to draw a picture of a sine wave. Notice how the amplitude is scaled by the factor f2 to give a nice big wave. You can apply the technique to any other mathematical function.

```
t:Sine wave plotter.
g:o0,250
g:m10,100;t+1
g:m0,100;d0,-100
g:m10,-100;t-1
g:m0,0;d500,0
c:a=0;p=3.1428/180;f1=1.2;f2=100
*loop c:x=f1*a;y=f2*sin(a*p);a=a+12
g:dx,y
j(a<=360):loop
```

13.2 Numerical calculations with arrays.

Arrays can be of one or two dimensions. A one dimensional array contains elements referenced by one index:

190

x(1), x(2)............x(n)

whereas a two-dimensional array (or table) requires two indices:

t(1,1), t(1,2)...........t(1,n)
t(2,1), t(2,2)...........t(2,n)
.....
.....
t(m,1), t(m,2)...........t(m,n)

Most versions of PILOT permit only limited storage space for arrays. In SuperPILOT, a total of 200 storage locations is allowed for all elemts of numeric arrays and simple variables. Before an array can be used, the amount of space that it will use must be specified in a d: (dimension) statement. This also sets all of the elements of the array to zero. For example, we could set up an array 's' to store the scores of 50 students by writing:

d:s(50)

However, this actually reserves 51 locations, since the zero'th element, in this case, s(0), is also automatically reserved. As for the simple variables, one-dimensional array names can be one letter or a letter followed by a digit.

Similarly, we could set up a table to store the scores on 5 tests for 20 students, using array 'y' - in the case of a two-dimensional array only a single letter is allowed:

d:y(5,20)

Again, extra 'zero' locations - in this case y(0,0), y(0,1).....y(0,20) and y(1,0), y(2,0).....y(5,0) are automatically reserved in a border to the left and over the top of where you imagine the table should be. In most cases, so long as storage space is not a problem, forget about these zero locations, because:

PILOT treats x, x(0) and x(0,0) as being synonymous.

and

The normal mathematical notation is to begin all arrays with the index, or indices, set at 1.

If you are short of space, you can make good use of the zero elements. For example, suppose you had a program which had accumulated the scores for 20 students in the array x(20), which had already been dimensioned. You could find the average score by writing:

```
c:t=0
*next c:t=t+1
c:x(0)=x(0)+x(t)
j(t<20):next
c:m=x(0)/5
t:The average is #m
```

And, a similar trick could be done with the table of 5 results for each of 20 students. The average per student could be stored in y(0,i) and the average per subject in y(j,0).

As with most programming languages, you must not re-dimension an array. In PILOT, this does not usually cause an immediate error, but it duplicates space already reserved, which we can ill afford.

Array elements can be included in type (t:) statements, so long as they are enclosed in parentheses, but may not be used in accept (a:) statements. So, this is acceptable

```
t:The score for student #i was #(x(i))
```

but this is not

```
a:#(x(i))
```

A useful feature of some implementations of PILOT (that does not appear to be mentioned in the SuperPILOT manual) is that arrays can be dynamically dimensioned with a variable, rather than a constant. This is handy when you don't know how big an array should be, and you don't want to waste space. For example:

```
t:How many students?
a:#n
d:s(n)
```

So, if we answer the question as '10' the last statement will reserve 11 locations (ten plus the zero'th).

Finally, SuperPILOT and some others permit several arrays to be dimensioned on one line, saving some space and speeding up the program slightly:

d:x(10);t(3,4);y1(80)

13.3 Computing with strings

A string is simply a sequence of printable characters. A string constant is enclosed within quote marks, e.g. "What's all this then?". A string variable is denoted by a letter, or a letter and a digit, followed by a dollar sign. So, a$ and x4$ are valid names for string variables. In PILOT, before a string variable can be used, it must be dimensioned to its maximum expected length. For example:

```
d:a$(50)
c:a$="short string"
```

Most versions of PILOT do not support string arrays as such, although they can be simulated by 'string slicing', as shown below. As for numeric variables, string storage space is at a premium- SuperPILOT permits up to 2000 characters of string storage.

Various operations can be carried out on strings:

CONCATENATION

Two or more strings can be joined together with a double exclamation mark:

```
d:a$(10);b$(10);c$(20)
c:a$="Good "
c:b$="Morning".
c:c$=a$!!b$
t:$c$
```

This would print the message   Good Morning., without the quotes, of course.

STRING SLICING

A part of the string can be accessed by means of one or more indices. Taking string c$, above, we could write

```
c:a$=c$(2,3)
```

which means "begin at position 2 and use the next 3 characters". So, a$ is

193

now the 3-character string "ood". If the second index is omitted, a length of 1 is assumed:

    c:a$=c$(6)

would assign the single, sixth character "M" in c$ to a$.

Some versions of PILOT contain the equivalents of the BASIC functions LEFT$, RIGHT$ and MID$, but SuperPILOT and many others do not. This is no serious problem, as shown by these examples based on the possible operations on a string, q$, containing exactly I characters:

LEFT$(q$,n)   equivalent to   q$(1,n)   i.e. the first n characters.

RIGHT$(q$,n)   equivalent to   q$(I-n+1,I) i.e. the last n characters.

MID$(q$,m,n)   equivalent to
MID$(q$,m,n)   equivalent to   q$(n,n+m-1) i.e. m characters.
                                                 beginning at character n.

SIMULATING STRING ARRAYS

By a similar subterfuge, a string variable can be made to simulate a string array, which is not available in SuperPILOT and many other versions. Imagine that we have a string of length 100. We can equally well think of it as being 10 sub-units, or sub-strings each of length 10. All we need to do is to set a pointer (i*10+1) which takes the values 1, 11, 21..... for i equal to 1, 2, 3..... . This enables us to simulate a string array with, in this case, 10 elements each of length 10. For example, this sequence inputs all ten names and prints them out again:

```
d:s$(100); a$(10)
c:i=0
*input c:i=i+1; p=i*10+1
t:Please type name #i
a:$a$
c:s$(p,10)=a$
j(i<10):input
c:i=0
*output c:i=i+1; p=i*10+1
c:a$=s$(p,10)
t:$a$
j(i<10):output
```

Notice that when a substring appears on the left of an expression (e.g. c:s$(p,10)=a$) the whole substring is replaced by whatever is on the right, truncated or padded on the right with blanks; the rest of the main string and its length are unaffected. When used in this way, such substrings are referred to as PSEUDO VARIABLES. (For another method of string array simulation, see the end of section 17.5).

EDITING STRINGS

The c: command can be used for the quite different purpose of string editing. In this mode, we follow the c: with a slash-mark, then the string to be edited, and then the editing option(s). For example, if string a$ contains "Sigma Technical", then this is how the editing would occur, in sequence:

c:/a$ u   Change to upper case, SIGMA TECHNICAL
           PRESS
c/a$ l   Change to lower case, sigma technical press
c:/a$ c   Capitalise first letter, Sigma technical press

There are two more options- for replacing and for deleting characters:

c:/a$ /iy/   Replace every i with a y, Sygma technycal
           press
c:/a$ /a/   Delete all the a's, Sygm technicl press

One use of a string edit is, having copied the user input into a string variable, to change it to lower case just for the purpose of matching. Otherwise, most editing is more easily done under the automatic pr: specifiers.

MISCELLANEOUS STRING FUNCTIONS

Just as we had numerical functions, there is also a range of string functions:

c:x=ASC(x$)   Returns ASCII decimal code for first character of x$
c:x$=CHR(x)   Converts the number (between 0 and 255) into a single character ASCII string.
c:x=FLO(x$)   Obtains the numeric value of the first number (if any) found in string x$.
c:x=INS(x,y$,z$)   Search for string z$ contained within y$, starting at position x in y$. The result is either zero (string not found) or an integer equal to

195

the character position at which z$ was located.
e.g. x=1, y$="household", z$="use" would
return a value of 3.

c:x=LEN(x$)   Returns the length of the string.
c:a$=STR(x)   Convert the number x into string form.

The use of upper and lower case in the above examples is arbitrary. The
FLO and STR function are invoked automatically if an assignment is
attempted where the types on either side of the equation are not matched:

    c:x="abc"   sets x to zero
    c:x="qwer45.8ght"   sets x to 45.8

13.4 Logical relations and operations

Logical operations include the comparison of numbers or strings that may
have been created by a compute statement- hence the reason for
including them in this chapter. In fact, we have already mentioned the use
of logical relations which use logical operations, in the context of Jump
statements, such as

    j(x<5 & x>7):range

The & operator stands for 'and' -meaning that both conditions must be
true. The & can be replaced by the word 'and' in SuperPILOT; similarly, we
use! for 'or' and < for 'not', with the symbols and words being interchangeable
in SuperPILOT.

In fact, any PILOT statement can contain a relation, and the relation can
contain just a simple logical test, or any expression which can appear on
the right hand side of a compute statement. So, these are all valid relational
tests:

    t(x>9):The value of x is greater than 9

    j(p<1 sqr(y-3)):next

    jn(a+b+c=sin(c)-abs(cos(d)-6)): end

The 'equals' in the last example is, of course, the logical test for equality,
not an assignment operator. It is, however, of interest that logical
operators can be used in assignments, for example:

    c: x=t & v

196

For the expression t&v to be true, both t and v must be greater than 0; within an expression, zero is 'false' and any non-zero element is 'true'. The result of such a test is either 1 (both values non-zero) or 0 (t and/or v are zero). So, if t is 4 and v is -89, x is 1. You can have other such expressions, such as:

```
c:p=∧x              (if x is zero, p is zero)
c:p= x ∧ y          (if x or y are non-zero, p is 1)
```

There are probably lots of uses for compute statements of this type, but I haven't found any!

Rather more useful is the fact that, at least in SuperPILOT, relational expressions can contain an arbitrary number of logical tests. This is not mentioned in the manual, but it is quite permissible to write a statement such as:

```
t(x=4 and yp and q$="hello" and y$="yes"):All conditions true!
```

The precedence order of the ! and & operators is equal when used in a logical expression, whereas the & operator has a greater precedence than ! when used in a match. So, if you have 3 variables, such that x=1, y=2 and z=, then the statement will print 'OK' because the expression is evaluated as 'true':

```
t(x=1 ! y=9 & z=3): OK
```

whereas this one prints nothing, as the test fails:

```
t(x=1 ! y=9 & z=8): OK
```

In other words, the first pair of tests read "if x is 1 or if y is 9" and these are evaluated as a single unit. Logically, the result is TRUE. Contrast this with the use of ! and & in match statements, where they have the same precedence.

13.5 An example program

By this stage we need to see an example program that pulls together a lot of what we learned so far. The program listed below uses graphics, text, compute and match commands. As befits this chapter, the emphasis is on numerical calculations and matching.

The program to be described illustrates quite a lot of PILOT in a short space, whilst also being useful for children learning to read scales, understanding volume measurements and giving some practice in mental arithmetic.

What the program does is to draw a beaker in the centre of the screen. On the side of the beaker there is a graduated scale, and an arrow is set to point at a random position on the scale.

The user has to read the scale and tell the computer how much 'liquid' to add in order to fill the beaker up to the arrow. It is not necessary to add it all at once, you can keep on adding small amounts until the level is either correct, to within one litre, or until too much liquid has been added. If the beaker is filled correctly, our young user has to calculate how much liquid has been added in total.

You should find the program easy to follow. The main programming 'trick' is in the subroutine *fill which uses turtle graphics commands to draw ascending left and right lines, to simulate liquid being added to the beaker. If you don't have SuperPILOT, you could substitute graphics commands using normal Cartesian axes.

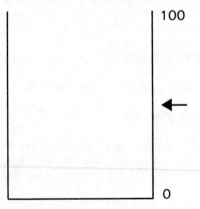

How much to add? 10

```
*start g:es0;v0,39,0,8
t:This beaker can hold 100 litres. I'm
:going to mark the side of it, and you
:tell me how much water to add.
t:
t:If you don't add enough, just add
:some more, but make a note of the
```

```
:total water added.
r:draw container
g:m210,50;t0;m180,250;t100
g:m220,250;d229,250;d229,49;d331,49;d331,250;
d340,250
c:a1=rnd(200)+1;x1=231;y1=51;x2=324;y2=5
:1;a=a1/2
r:insert arrow- note use of parentheses
:.
g:m335,(50+a1);d365,(50+a1);m345,(60+a1
:);d335,(50+a1);d345,(40+a1)
c:w=0;t=0
*add th:How much to add?
a:#w
c:y2=y2+2*w
u:fill
c:y1=y2
c:t=t+w
t((a-t)(1 or t)a):Stop!
jc:added
j:add
*added th:How much have you added?
a:£m
t(abs(m-t)(=1):That's right to 1 litre.
jc:stop
t1:No, try again.
t2:That's not right either- try again.
t3:One more try....
t4:No.
j4:stop
j:added
*stop t:You added #t  litres.
t:The arrow was pointing at #a  litres
as:
j:start

*fill r:x1,y1 to x2,y2
c:x3=x2-x1;y3=(y2-y1)/2
g:mx1,y1;*y3(a90;dx3;s-90;m1;s-
:90;dx3;s90;d1)
e:
```

Chapter 14

Pilot Files and Computer Managed Learning

Computer Managed Learning (CML) is used to store information about test scores, passwords, lists of students, how many times a student has taken a lesson, how many times a particular question is answered 'right' or 'wrong'- in fact, any sorts of data that you might use as a teacher to control the progress of your students through a course. In this sense, you can use a CML package JUST to record such data, though more commonly the CML and CAL techniques are normally used together. (A notable exception is in many military applications which use databases to display trends in student performance, and personal data so that you can select, say, all apprentices who have passed the vehicle maintenance course, are between 18 and 22 years of age, and come from a particular ethnic group.)

Often, a CBL user has the choice of either constructing his/her own CML package, or using the standard one that was purchased with the CBL authoring system. This is usual with mainframe systems such as IBM's IIS and Control Data's PLATO system. The CML components of these are very comprehensive, but some users find that they collect too much data, which is rarely examined.

Although a microcomputer user does not usually have the luxury of a ready-made CML system, SuperPILOT does have a unique instruction to simplify record keeping. So, we'll describe that first, then look at how to make do without it.

14.1 The SuperPILOT K: (keep) instruction

This is well-described in the language manual but, briefly, what happens is this:

1. The author creates a lesson text file called SYSTEM.LOG. Alternatively, a file of this name can be created automatically by initialising a blank disk and naming the disk SYSLOG. When this alternative is used, it is presumed that the student will use the Apple with a lesson disk in drive 1 and the SYSLOG disk in drive 2.

2. At suitable points in the lesson, the author includes k: (keep) instructions. These are almost identical in operation to the t: op-code, except that they direct their output data to SYSTEM.LOG.

For example, at the beginning of a lesson, you may have:

        t:Please type your name.
        a:n
        k:Student name: n

Then, a test score might be output. Let's presume the score is in the variable 't':
        t:Score on test 1: #t

3. Up to this stage, the data has been stored in a buffer, and to transfer it physically to the disk, we use the 'save' modifier:

        ks:

You can use the ks: in place of each k:, but as it is a rather slow operation, it is best placed at strategic points. Any additional modifiers, conditioners or expressions that are normally used with a t: can also be used with k: .

By this stage, you may be thinking that you might just as well construct your own CML package, for all the good that k: appears to be. But, when you are using k: with a SYSTEM.LOG file, the following additional information is automatically stored: the lesson name, links to other lessons, and an indicator of lesson completion.

Also, there is a separate statistical analysis package, SuperPILOT.LOG, which analyses SYSTEM.LOG files for inter-student comparisons, statistical validity of test items and the like. We have been unable to obtain details of this package from the supplier, maybe you will be more fortunate!

14.2 Do-it-Yourself CML

Apple PILOT (the predecessor to SuperPILOT) and all other versions of PILOT do not have a CML feature. Therefore, you have to do a little more work. Fortunately, there are two simple commands for sending data to a file, and for reading it back. These are:

> fo: record-number, string variable
> fi: record-number, string variable

where fo: means file output (i.e. from the program TO the file) and fi: means file input (i.e. from the file to the program). It is presumed that the file is on disk, and we'll shortly look at this machine-specific area. The file is random access (i.e. any record can be accessed equally rapidly) and the length of each record is usually a maximum of 256 characters (255 on the Apple). Pascal enthusiasts may need to know that two such records are stored in each Pascal data block.

As an example, we might have the following lines within a program:

> t:Please type your name:
> a:n
> fo:1,n$

That would store the student name in record 1. Then, suppose you had a test score in variable 't'. This can not be output directly into a file, but must first be converted into a string:

> c:t$=str(t)
> fo:5,t$

In this example, we've assumed that some other data has gone into record 4. to get the data out again, we simply use the fi: commands:

> fi:1,n$
> fi:5,t$
> c:t=flo(t$)
> t:Student n got a score of #t.

Opening and Closing Files

The only problem with this is that it will not work, since you invariably have to tell the hardware to 'open' the files you need before you use them. In other languages, you also have to close files after using them, but PILOT looks after that for you. In most implementations, you may only only have one file in use (i.e. 'open') at a time.

If you are using an Apple, you must use a FOX: command to open a new

202

file (i.e. one which has not already been used). This statement must be used before either data input or output is attempted. Its format is:

    fox:largest-record-number, file name

The effect of this statement is to reserve the correct amount of disk space for the file. For example:

    fox:200, results

or   c:a$=results;v=200
    fox:v,a$

Not so surprisingly, when you recall how arrays are set up, the above statements each reserve 201 records, not 200, since there is always a zero'th record. I find this extra record useful for storing system information, such as the current length of the file.

The FOX op-code can also be used to delete a file, by making the length equal to zero:

    fox: 0,students

This would delete file 'students'.

An existing file must be opened for both input and output with a FIX command. For example:

    fix:10,students

This opens the file 'students' and specifies a maximum record number of 10 . Any attempt to refer to a larger number than the specified maximum record number will cause an error.

Generally, you should try to keep the maximum number of records consistent for both FOX and FIX operations on a given file. There is no easy way of doing this if the number keeps changing, though one method is to store the current number of records in record zero, open the file for reading with a length of 1 record, and then read record zero to see what the length should really be. Then, you can re-open it with the correct length. Or, you can just be lazy and open it with the maximum length that you expect- which can waste storage space and take longer than necessary.

It can be useful to know that both versions of Apple PILOT store files with a .DATA extension under the UCSD filing system. Since neither version has any editor command to list .DATA files, the only easy way you can find out which files you have is with a Pascal language system. Another, more awkward, way is to copy the disk and make a note of each file name as it is reported on the screen.

14.3 What sort of data should be stored in a file?

This depends very much on your own lessons, but suitably general data that usefully be stored in files includes:

> lists of students
> test results
> the date on which a lesson was used
> lessons completed by each student
> student comments
> failure frequency for each question

You will normally need more than one file for such operations, so it makes sense to minimise the amount of data collection.

14.4 An example- student registration

The easiest way to understand file operations is to see an example. The following program also gives us an opportunity to revise some of the things we have seen so far.

The purpose of this program is to enable a teacher to maintain a list of students. Names can be added to, or deleted from the file. Also, the file can be listed and, when necessary, the whole file can be deleted. There is no pretence that this program is other than a demonstration- you would certainly need to add to it extensively in any real application. Each record is of the form:

> <name> <grades>

where <name> is up to 36 characters and <grades> is a sequence of 4 characters which might indicate if the student has passed, failed, or not yet attempted one of four lessons. Initially, <grades> is set to <nnnn> to indicate that the student has attempted nothing so far. If you were using the file created by this program, you would need to update <grades> as each student completed a lesson. You could use it other ways, too: require the student to 'sign on' and check that the <name> is on the list of allowed users, for example.

The program is split up into small sections and subroutines. This is the first part:

```
r:Simple file maintenance program
d:b$(40);f$(20);r$(40);a$(10);n$(36)
r:this string starts with 36 blanks
c:b$="
:   nnnn"
```

This reserves space for the various strings and sets up a string b$ with 36 spaces (for the student name) followed by 'nnnn'.

The next part sets up the file that you require:

```
t:What is the name of your file?
a:$f$
fix:1,f$
je(1):newfile
fi:0,r$
c:r9=flo(r$)
j:start
*newfile th:Maximum number of records?
a:#r9
te:Please type a number (e.g.10)
je:@a
t:
t:Initialising new file...
t:
fox:r9,f$
c:r$=str(r9)
fo:0,r$
*start fix:r9,f$
t:File '$f$ '   now available with
:#r9   records.
r:( You could amend this section so
:that it enabled you to extend the
:file)
```

Having obtained the file name, it attempts to open it as an existing file of length 1. If this can be done, it reads record zero (fi:0,r$) and converts the string r$ into a numeric variable, r9. This represents the actual length of the file, so we do a second FIX, using r9 this time. If the first FIX failed, there being no file of the name we typed in, then the 'error flag' will be

205

raised. In one statement, je(1):newfile, we detect the error condition, lower the flag, and jump to the label 'newfile'. At this label, we are asked how long to make the file, which is then initialised with a FOX.

In the next section, we jump to the subroutine required. We simply jump to one of 5 labels, using the INS function. There are neater ways of doing it than this (see the xi: version of the MENU program in the next chapter, for example.)

```
*menu t:Press any key to continue....
as:
g:es
t:Press one letter to:
t:A(dd or D(elete a record
t:R(emove or L(ist a file
t:or Q(uit
as:$a$
c:d=ins(1,"adrlq",a$)
j(d=0):@a
u(d=1):add
u(d=2):delete
u(d=3):remove
u(d=4):list
e(d=5):
j:menu
```

The next section reads each record until a blank one is found. The new record is constructed by copying string b$ (36 blanks, then nnnn) into r$ and putting the student name into the left hand side of r$.

```
*add g:es
t:Insert new record.
t:
t:Finding first blank record..
c:r=1
*addfi fi:r,r$
j(r$=""):addhere
c:r=r+1
t(r)r9):FILE FULL!!
jc:addend
j:addfi
*addhere t:Name to be added?
a:$n$
```

206

```
r:construct new record
r:Note- do not leave blanks in a multi-
:compute statement before variable
:names (otherwise, unrecognised
:variable)
c:l=len(n$);r$=b$;r$(1,l)=n$
fo:r,r$
*addend e:
```

The deletion section inspects each record for a specified name and, when it finds it, replaces it with a blank record.

```
*delete g:es
t:Delete old record
t:
t:Name to be deleted?
a:$n$
c:r=1
t:Searching for name '$n$'...
*delfi fi:r,r$
j(ins(1,r$,n$)=1):delhere
c:r=r+1
t(r)r9):Name not found!
jc:delend
j:delfi
*delhere th:Type DELETE if you are sure
:that you want to delete the record for
:'$n$':
a:$a$
j(a$<>"delete"):delend
c:r$=""
t:Record deleted
fo:r,r$
*delend e:
```

The file removal section is very simple: it just re-opens the file with a length of zero, after asking you to confirm that you really do want to remove it:

```
*remove g:es
t:File removal
t:
t:Type REMOVE if you want to erase file
```

```
:$f$
a:$a$
fox(a$="remove"):0,f$
tc:File $f$  removed.
e:
```

The file listing will be easy to understand if you've got this far. The only special points are the use of the SuperPILOT command, ts:p, to send output to the printer and ts:q to stop it.

```
*list
g:es
t:File listing option.
t:
th:Output also to printer (y/n)?
as:$a$
ts(a$="y"):p
g:es
t:Listing of file '$f$ '
ts:g5,5
t:STUDENT NAME
c:r=1
*lisfi fi:r,r$
t:$r$
c:r=r+1
j(r<=r9):lisfi
r:stop output to printer
ts:q
e:
```

And that's it!

The program is hopelessly inefficient in terms of 'clever' file handling tricks, but it has been kept simple deliberately to focus attention on the PILOT file commands. If you want to give a file maintenance program a bit more zip, you should read a book on file processing methods. In particular, you might look at hashing and table translation methods. Modesty does not prevent me from recommending my own book on the subject ('Successful Software for Small Computers', pub. by Sigma Technical Press), though I feel that a very simple program like this one, or SuperPILOT LOG is sufficient for most purposes.

Chapter 15

Advanced Features

Using only the features discussed so far, you can write stimulating and useful CBL lessons. There are some other features, however, that become more important as you build more complex or larger lessons. We'll discuss some of them here, although you may need to refer to your manual on specific points.

15.1 The GOTO and ESCAPE options

When you are de-bugging a large program, it is tedious to execute all of the code up to the erroneous section. One way around this is to use the 'g' for GOTO option in the pr: list. In its simplest form, you write

> pr:g

Although you may have other options set, as in:

> pr:gls

which sets the GOTO, converts to lower case, and removes spaces automatically from the student answer. With g option chosen, whenever the program stops at an accept (a:) instruction, you can type 'goto' followed by a label name, and the program will jump to that point. For example,

> goto check

will cause a jump to label 'check' if it exists. So, when de-bugging a program, put a pr:g followed by an accept statement at the beginning of the program, and you can jump to any part of the program. An alternative use of the goto option is to branch a student to part of the program, having shown him/her a list of possible destinations.

The escape option has a similar function, and this is enabled by typing:

        pr:e

or you can include the 'e' in a longer list of options. If the program now
stops at an accept statement, and if the user input begins with the '@'
symbol, control will be transferred to a subroutine labelled *sysx. If there
is no such label, program execution continues to the next statement. **You**
must supply the *sysx subroutine, and what you do inside it is up to you.
For example, you could tell the student that, at any point in the lesson,
he/she could type:

        @comment

to send a message into a comment file. Or, @end could be used to stop the
lesson. The subroutine needed for these two functions might be like this:

        @sysx d:a$(80)
        r:Subroutine for comments or quit
        mj:comment
        t:What is the number of the lesson on which
        :you wish to comment?
        a:#n
        t:What is your comment on lesson #n ?
        a:a
        fix:100,comments
        fo:n,a$
        j:back
        m:end
        tn:After the @ type END or COMMENT
        jn:@a
        t:That's the end of the lesson!
        e:
        *back e:@a

The first thing that this subroutine does is to examine the input for the
word 'comment'. In other words, was the last response '@comment'? If
so, we ask the number of the lesson on which the comment is to be made,
the nature of the comment, and then write this comment into a file for us to
examine at leisure. Then, we jump to the label 'back' which terminates the
subroutine and takes us back to the previous accept (i.e. the one that got
us here) to make more comments or to end the lesson, or just to carry on. If
the response were @end we execute a simple e: to end the lesson.

Other uses for a @sysx subroutine include:

        Displaying the values of program variables.

Providing a calculator facility (see XI:, next section).
Adding learner control.

That last suggestion would make a nice little project for somebody. The idea is that you divide your lesson up into 'frames' that you would like your users to move between. Then, you give them the facility to type:

@NEXT - to go to the next frame

@BACK - to go to the preceding frame

@HELP - to get help (from a help frame)

All you'd need to do is to keep track of the current frame names in string variables. The result is a very scaled down version of some of the functions of TICCIT or PLATO.

15.2 Execute Indirect (XI:)

This is an instruction which is difficult to explain easily, because what it does is to execute (i.e. carry out) the contents of a string variable, so long as that variable contains a valid PILOT statement. So, this sequence:

```
d:v$(8)
c:v$="So What!"
xi:v$
```

is entirely equivalent to

```
t:So What!
```

Which does not, on the face of it, seem very useful. But, xi: is useful when we build up a string from smaller parts and execute the whole string, indirectly.

Menu Programs with XI:

Here's an example that makes good use of the XI: instruction. Suppose we had a menu selection for five different parts of a lesson- here's how we could use xi: in a simple way:

```
th:Which part do you want to study?
as:$a$
```

```
m:1!2!3
jn:@a
c:m$="u:part"!!str(x)
xi:m$
```

After getting a value from 1 to 5, the compute statement combines the string "u:part" with the string value of x, to give m$. This new string must now contain u:part1, u:part2, u:part3, u:part4 or u:part5. The final xi: executes one of these valid statements and causes a jump to the subroutine with the appropriate label. Effectively, the xi: has saved us a sequence of tests and jumps (did he type 1, if so jump to part 1, etc.).

Although the menu will work well, you might like to make it look more professional. As written, if the user makes an illegal choice the menu will scroll upwards before inviting another reply. You can avoid this by backspacing over the present reply, erasing with a blank space, and back spacing again, which gets you back to where you started. In SuperPILOT you can do this by preceding the jn:@a statement with

```
tsn:x8,32,8
```

which is a 'special effects' type instruction, with an 'n' conditioner. The 'x' transmits the ASCII characters 8 and 32 (backspace and space) in the correct order. You can simulate this in other PILOTs by something like:

```
c:b$=chr(8)
c:c$=chr(32)
c:d$=b$!!c$!!b$
tn:d$
```

A version of the MENU program using these techniques is listed below:

```
d:x$(7)
*start
g:es
t:Please choose from:
ts:g4,4
t:1. See a demonstration.
ts:g4,7
t:2. Try one yourself.
ts:g4,10
t:3. Finish for now.
*arrow ts:g5,15
th:Please choose 1,2 or 3 -->
```

212

```
as:$x$
m:1!2!3
tsn:x8,32,8
jn:arrow
c:x$="u:part"!!x$
xi:x$
j:start


*part1
t:This would be the demo.
e:


*part2
t:This would be the try-out section.
e:


*part3
t:This is where we quit.
e:
```

There are plenty of other applications of the powerful XI: command. For example, you might like to write programs that:

Let the user try out statements in interactive mode (already available in SuperPILOT).

Simulate the match command (see the program at the end of section 11.2)

Provide a calculator facility in a *SYSX subroutine. This is easy, just let the user type @CALC and use a sequence like this inside *SYSX, presuming that e$ has been dimensioned:

```
*CALC  t:Expression?
a:$e$
c:e$="c:x="!!e$
t:Answer is #x
```

Another application of xi: would be to execute strings that had been stored as records in a file. This is an intriguing and potentially useful idea that we retun to in Chapter 17

15.3 The Link Commands (SuperPILOT)

These are specific to the Apple versions of PILOT. The normal link is
simply L: and there are modified forms, LX: and LP: .

Link to a PILOT lesson (L: and LX:)

These have two forms:

l:name (label)   or   lx:name (label)

The first form causes the present program to transfer control to the
beginning of a new program or, if an optional label is specified, to the label
within a program, whilst preserving the values of all variables. The second
form does the same thing but erases all variables, thus releasing storage
space. The major uses of these commands is in running very large
programs, or in the management of large suites of lessons or in providing a
turnkey package. By this, we mean a lesson that executes automatically as
soon as the Apple is 'booted'. The Apple PILOTs respond to this operation,
if in LESSON mode, by executing a program with the name HELLO. This
invites the user to choose from the various lessons on that particular
lesson disk. If you don't trust the user to do this, you can replace the
standard HELLO lesson with the one-liner:

l:mylesson

This will cause the Apple, on being switched on, to run 'mylesson' without
any user intervention.

Link to a Pascal Program (LP:)

To me, it was pleasant to find that I could link from PILOT to Pascal and
vice versa. I found that this was a useful trick when I came to write a PILOT
code generator, as you'll see later. Also, you may have existing Pascal
programs that you wish to use, or you may find it preferable to write CML
packages, for example, in Pascal which has better data structures and is
faster than PILOT.

Pascal Notes

Since the Apple PILOTs are written in, and are fully compatible with Apple
Pascal, it comes as no surprise to find that SuperPILOT (but not Apple
PILOT) enables you to link from a PILOT program to a Pascal program. To

do so, the Pascal program must be in compiled form and must have the .CODE extension. As such, it will not be possible for you to display its name under any of the PILOT editor menus, although you can do so under the Apple Pascal filer. As the information in the SuperPILOT manual is sketchy, and as I had several traumas myself, I propose to explain the procedure for linking to Pascal programs in a few simple steps:

1. Get yourself an Apple Pascal system and, if finances allow, equip your Apple with an 80 column card to preserve your eyesight and sanity.

2. Presuming you have 2 disk drives, boot your Apple with the disk labelled Apple 1 in drive 1, and Apple2 in drive 2.

3. Follow the instructions in the manual to create a file called SYSTEM.WRK.TEXT containing your Pascal program. To do this, you use the editor which is, thankfully, similar to that of PILOT. The Apple1 disk in drive 1 must not be write protected as the .TEXT file will be written to this disk- therefore, you must use a backup, not the original Apple1. If you intend to return to PILOT after executing the Pascal program, you must include the statement USES CHAINSTUFF at the very beginning (i.e. after the program header) and the statement SETCHAIN('SYSTEM.STARTUP.') immediately after the outer BEGIN of your Pascal program, to enable it to find its way back to PILOT.

4. Compile AND TEST RUN the program- it will be stored automatically in compiled form as SYSTEM.WRK.CODE on Apple1.

5. Replace the Apple2 disk in drive 2 with a formatted SuperPILOT lesson disk.

6. Using the F (filer), select the T (transfer) command and tell Pascal to transfer from #4.SYSTEM.WRK.CODE to #5.name.CODE where 'name' is the name you want to give to the Pascal program. Perhaps you could call it 'test' to be original! You can replace #5 with the diskette name (see the PILOT Language Manual for disk names, or the Pascal manual for how to change the name).

7. Turn off the Apple, and re-boot it under SuperPILOT leaving the lesson disk containing the Pascal program in drive 2.

8. Save this one-line lesson onto the same disk that contains your Pascal program:

    lp:test

where 'test' is the name of the Pascal program.

9. RUN this one line program- the Pascal program should execute and return you to the SuperPILOT welcome page.

That sequence demonstrates the usual method of linking to Pascal. You just include a statement of the form lp:name to link to any Pascal program with a .CODE extension. Note that you must NOT put .CODE at the end of an lp: instruction, the extension is added automatically. When the Pascal program finishes SuperPILOT will re-start unless you omitted the statement in step 3 (above).

If you wish to execute a Pascal program, then return to a specified PILOT lesson, you use a statement of the form:

    lp:name1;name2

where name1 is the name of the Pascal program, and name2 is the PILOT program that will be entered after the Pascal program has finished.

It is also possible to let the student select the return PILOT lesson after the Pascal program- I've not tried this, but you may like to do (see the SuperPILOT language manual!).

15.4 Sound Output and the sound editor (SuperPILOT)

Again, the content of this section is specific to the Apple II, although there may be other implementations. The sound command is of the form:

    s:pitch,duration (;pitch,duration.....;pitch,duration)

The pitch can be from 0 to 50, and the duration from 0 to 255. So, s:30,10 gives a short, mid-range 'beep' and s:10,30 gives a longer one; s30,10;10,30 gives a beep-beep.

Full details are in the manual, and details are also give of the Sound Editor. With this, you can compose a tune, give it a name such as 'Mozart' and play it back in a lesson with the statement:

    sx:Mozart

The sx: being an abbreviation for Sound eXecute.

15.5 Video Output (SuperPILOT)

Although it is possible to incorporate computer graphics into PILOT lessons (e.g. with the G: command or, better, with a graphics editor), it is less tedious for the author and more stimulating for the student if the computer can use images that are stored on video tape or disk. These can be in full colour and to TV standard.

Whatever the version of PILOT, you will need an interface circuit board between your computer and the video unit. The interface performs many functions, which include:

Providing start and stop signals for the video.

Searching for a given section of videotape or sequence of video disk.

Processing the input signals from the video unit so that they are compatible with the TV or monitor being used.

Most inexpensive interfaces enable the monitor to receive video OR computer generated signals, but not to overlay one on top of the other. With more cash at hand, overlaying is allowed. Interfaces are often provided with some additional software to facilitate accurate videotape location (video disk is no problem). For example, the CAVI 400 board from BCD Associates Inc enables the user to write frame numbers onto the second audio track of the video tape. Many interface boards are available for most popular micros or, the ambitious can make their own (see, for example, "Interactive Control of a Videocassette Recorder with a Personal Computer", R C Hallgren, in BYTE, July 1980, pp116-134).

That takes care of the physical connections. But, how can we communicate with the interface from within a PILOT lesson? The answer is: it all depends! For example, if your PILOT permits you to drop into and out of BASIC or machine code, you could POKE the desired video frame numbers into a data port or some other area of memory (see, for example, the above article by Hallgren). In a similar vein, try to find a control character (i.e. non-printing ASCII) that selects a particular port or slot in your micro, then you can select the port with a type statament (e.g. t:#x) and all subsequent output will be directed to it.

Alternatively, you could add a special command to PILOT by modifying the interpreter. If the interpreter is written in a high level language such as Pascal, this should not be too difficult. This is what Apple did to PILOT when it was upgraded to SuperPILOT. There is now a V: instruction, with the format:

V:command (;command....;command)

Because Apple do not know which video hardware you intend to use, it is still necessary to make the necessary modifications to the Author disk. For example, your commands could be the start and stop frame numbers on a video disk, so your customised V: instruction should be allowed to have just two commands following it. The only standard thing is that V: sends its output to slot #2 of the Apple, which is where you're expected to plug in your interface card. Full details are in the SuperPILOT Technical Support Manual. Unfortunately, we have had no success in locating this extra goody from the Apple dealer network!

15.6 The Character Editor (SuperPILOT)

The Apple PILOT's enable you to re-design all or part of the standard character set. Whilst this seems an unlikely advantage, it can be very useful indeed. For example. I once needed to display a lot of symbols for valves on a diagram of a chemical plant. One way would have been to draw them with individual graphics instructions, but it was far faster to create a small character set called 'symbols' in which the letters a,b,c, and d were redefined to look like this:

These were created with the character set editor which uses a grid in which you can design characters, as shown in Figure 15.1. To invoke this character set, we simply type:

tx:symbols

And then, all type statements will display the new characters. So, the statement

t:ab

will not print 'ab' but, instead, a chemical valve!

To return to the normal (ASCII) set we simply invoke the blank (default) set:

```
tx:
```

There are lots of examples of how to use alternate character sets in the manuals. The sample SuperPILOT lesson diskette includes a Greek character set, various character sets in different type-fonts, oversized letters, and parts of a little man in various poses. The following program uses the Maxwell character set (provided on the SuperPILOT sample disk) to walk a little man across the screen:

```
d:r1$(15);r2$(15);r3$(15)
c:r1$=" a / bc/ de";r2$=" fg/ hi/
:jk";r3$=" lm/ nop/ qr"
*cc tx:
t:speed?
a:#v1
c:v1=100-v1
tx:maxwell
ts:g10,10;*30(ar1$;dv1;ar2$;dv1;ar3$;dv
:1;wr)
j:cc
```

15.7 In conclusion......

Well, that's the end of our review of PILOT. To find out more, get lots of practice and read the manual when things go wrong, or you need to try really tricky things. I hope that the preceding chapters have revealed how to use the language and that you will either become a regular user yourself of PILOT or, perhaps, some other author language.

In case this book has, so far, seemed at times like a sales aid for Apple (as a competitor has suggested), let me say a few words to some other micro manufacturers: Why try to foist a simple language ON IT'S OWN to the unsuspecting public? PILOT alone is not really sufficient for CBL unless you are already a programming freak, which most teachers and trainers are not. These people need authoring aids such as video commands, editors and the like, in order to create good lessons quickly.

Most PILOTs on offer are just the raw language with either very simplistic editors, or no editors at all. Some versions enable you to do simple things such as design a new character or two as a 'bit-pattern' or to produce video-game objects (e.g. sprites) but there are very few others (none that I have seen) that give a similar range of graphics, sound and character editors as SuperPILOT. That is what puts SuperPILOT on a par with many more expensive authoring systems, and is indeed what qualifies it for the name 'system' as opposed to 'language'. So, I'm still not suggesting that Apple is the best computer nor that SuperPILOT is the best system. Indeed, I would be the first to agree that some of the mainline systems such as PLATO and its competitors may often be a better choice for big applications, or where the 'hand-holding' support of a large company is thought necessary. And, there are many areas where fast, real time response is needed, where no version of PILOT (or any other micro authoring language) is adequate.

But, by the time this book is published, there will be new systems on the market for your computer. Just be sure to check out the specification before you buy.

Chapter 16

An Example Application: training a librarian

No one can predict the applications that might be chosen by a CBL author, but you may be interested to read about one reasonably-sized application that was completed 'for real' on a standard Apple II, in SuperPILOT,during the course of preparation of this book. The PILOT programming is very simple, although the program itself is reasonably large.

16.1 The training problem

Our local library is involved in the training of librarians, and they were keen to see if computer based learning might be of use. This was considered to be particularly relevant because the library network in our county is installing computer-based book issuing equipment, so the staff were already using computers in their everyday work. We jointly discussed the possible form of a small project that might be used as a demonstration of the possibilities of CBL as a training medium, and finally chose the problem of training a person in the completion of a simple form.

The form in question is referred to internally as a 'C30 Form' and it used by library staff to track down a book that has been requested by a reader. The form is only used if the book is not in the particular library, and if it is not listed on the computerised network.

Subject to these limitations, a librarian normally finds the details of the book on a microfiche record (stored at the library) which includes bibliographic data (exact author name, publisher, edition, etc.) and a series of codes which indicate the libraries which normally have the book in question in stock. All of these details are then copied on to the form, making sure that the libraries which should have the book are listed in a particular order. This order is simply the sequence of visits made by the van driver, who follows a regular route between all of the libraries, and this route is supposedly known by the librarian.

221

All of this sounds like an easy problem, but is similar to a thousand and one other simple training problems encountered every where that procedures are to be followed- be it in an office, the Civil Service, the armed forces, the police force, and many more. Let's see how we tried to solve it.

16.2 The plan.

First of all, a sample form was examined, to see if it could be easily represented on the computer screen. The form is shown below.

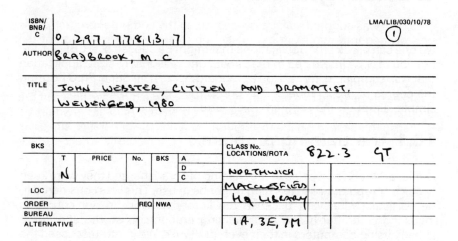

Most of the form is easy to understand. The ISBN section is used for the International Standard Book Number (or certain other standard numbers) and must be filled in correctly. The class number is based on the Dewey Decimal System, although certain internal library codes may alternatively be used for particular categories of book. The locations/rota section is used to prescribe the order in which other libraries are to be requested for the book. If a library does not have the book, the form is passed on to the next one on the rota. Any library which does have the requested book returns the form with the book to the library requesting it. The sections labelled BKS, LOC and so on did not need to be understood at this stage.

The main elements of the form were transcribed to a design sheet (Chapter 5) and were then designed interactively on the computer screen using the SuperPILOT graphic editor. The editor enables you to check the cursor position (row, column, x and y coordinates) simply by pressing the W (for What Info?) key. The only sacrifice made in the computer representation of the form was to allow 5, rather than 10 entries in the 'locations' section of the form. The design was stored as the 'quickdraw' file, 'form!'.

For this type of instruction, which is an example of 'REMEMBER-PROCEDURE', Component Display Theory suggests that we should use the following sequence:

> Tell the generality (of the procedure).
> Give Example(s).
> Give practice with representative examples.
> Have the student describe the generality.

This plan was adopted as far as necessary in the computer program: this was divided into two main modules- one to see a demonstration of the form being filled in, the other to have practice in filling in typical forms, using the keyboard and screen. The first stage (to tell the general procedure of filling in the form) was thought to be inappropriate since it could easily be done by a human. Nevertheless, we did leave space in the program for this section also to be computerised. Also, little would be gained in this case in having the student describe the generality, since it is so simple. In any case, this could always be covered in a face-to-face interview.

16.3 The program

This is listed on the next few pages.

In the 'demo' section, you will see calls to various subroutines v1, v2, v3 and so on. These are at the end of the program and are used to select particular viewports on the screen that correspond to each part of the form. The usual procedure followed is for the explanation to be displayed at the bottom of the screen, whilst part of the form was being completed. The w: (wait) command was used to slow things down, giving the student time to read each section.

The 'prac' (practice) section begins by eliciting today's date which is placed on the correct part of each simulated form. The data for each practice problem is stored in one of ten subroutines, labelled *prob1, *prob2...*prob10 and these are selected at random until the student has completed all of them. To ensure that the same problem is not selected twice, the string q$ is set to a sequence of ten ones. When problem 'i' is chosen, character i in string q$ is set to zero, marking that problem as 'dead' for future choices. A second string, s$ is set to '00000'. This is also used as a marker, but this time it is used to check which parts of the particular form have been completed. There are five parts for the student to complete and, whenever one part is successfully completed, the corresponding character in s$ is set to one. This seems the correct approach because in real life the student would be able to complete the form in any order. You will see the coding that corresponds to all of this between the labels *choose and *menu.

```
pr:1
d:q$(10);a$(80);i$(13);d$(10);t$(80);x$
:(2);p$(6);n$(70);n1$(70);b$(100);b1$(1
:00);c$(20);11$(16);12$(16);13$(16);14$
:(16);15$(16);s$(5)
ts:g5,5
t:WILMSLOW LIBRARY presents....
ts:g10,11
t:How to
ts:g15,12
t:complete
ts:g15,13
t:a C30 form.
t:
th:Press any key to start the lesson:
as:
*start g:v
ts:i
g:es3
t:Before you begin, make sure that you
:have a copy of the instructions!
ts:g4,4;n
t:Do you want to....
ts:g6,6
t:1. Have an explanation of
ts:g9,7
t:the reservation system?
ts:g6,9
t:2. See a demonstration of
ts:g9,10
t:how to fill in a C30 form?
ts:g6,12
t:3. Practice filling in
ts:g9,13
t:the forms?
```

```
ts:g6,15
t:4. Finish?
*arrow ts:g1,17
th:Please press 1,2,3 or 4 ->
as:
m:1
jy:intro
m:2
jy:demo
m:3
jy:prac
s:30,10
m:4
ey:
ts:x8,32,8
j:arrow


*intro
t:This section is not yet available.
:Please consult the librarian for an
:explanation of the system.
as:
j:start


*demo
g:es
t:        Completing the Form.
t:
t:
t:
w:2
t:This section takes you through, step
:by step, how to complete the
:reservation form.
t:
th:When you want the computer to
:continue, just press RETURN.
```

```
as:
gx:form!
u:v1
th:This is (roughly) what the form looks
:like.
u:v1
th:It is filled in by you and is
:sent to other libraries in the order
:that YOU specify. You must fill the
:form in correctly to get the best
:service!
u:v1
th:The first thing to do is to write
:the
:book number in the ISBN space, like
:this (watch the space)...
w:3
u:v2
th:0 14 048061 7
u:v1
th:Notice that the number must EXACTLY
:fill the space provided. All spaces
:must be included....
u:v1
th:You write the place (Wilmslow) and
:today's date in the top right-hand
:box...
w:2
u:v3
th:WILMSLOW
w:1
th:    17/6/83
u:v1
th:Now, write the author's name (or
:names) and the book title in the
:correct boxes...
w:2
u:v4
th:SINGH, M
w:2
u:v5
```

```
th:Himalayan Art for Librarians- a new
:perspective.
u:v1
th:It is very important to add the
:edition,(if specified) the publisher and
publication
:date...
w:1
u:v5
ts:g0,2
th:2nd Edn, Collier, 1971.
u:v1
th:On the COM fiche, you can see the
:Class Number. Write this in, complete
:with any category symbol.
w:1
u:v6
t:709.973
w:1
ts:g0,1
th:KA
u:v1
th:Finally, you find (from the COM) in
:which libraries the book is located.
:These are entered in the box marked
:LOCATIONS/ROTA.
u:v1
th:In order of priority, list them
:according to the route that the inter-
:branch van follows FROM WILMSLOW.
u:v1
th:The reason for this is that the
:libraries nearest to you will then be
:visited first, and the book will be
:reserved more quickly.
u:v1
th:Let's presume that there are just
:three libraries that have
:this book. Handforth is nearest, so
:that goes at the top...
u:v7
```

```
w:2
t:HANDFORTH
w:1
t:DITTON
w:1
t:NESTON
u:v1
t:And that's all there is to it!
t:Press RETURN to get back to the
:main menu.....
as:
j:start


*prac
g:v
g:es
ts:g0,5
t:Do you want instructions ?
t:Type 'yes' or 'no' then press the
:RETURN key on the right of the
:keyboard:
a:
m:%no%
jy:prac1
t:This section lets you practice
:filling in some sample forms. Your
:score is not being recorded- just
:practice until you get the hang of it.
t:
t:To fill in the form on the computer,
:type the name of the section you wish
:to complete (e.g. 'title' for the
:title section), then type in what you
:think should appear in that section.
as:
g:es
t:When you have finished typing your
:answer, press the RETURN key on the
:far right hand side of the keyboard.
as:
```

```
t:And, if you make a mistake, just
:erase it by using the LEFT ARROW key,
:just under and to the left of the
:RETURN key.
t:
t:Now, let's begin...
as:
*prac1
u:v1
t:What is today's date (type it in the
:form of 21/6/83, for example)?
a:$d$
th:Thank you.
c:q$="1111111111"
*choose
gx:form!
u:v3
w:2
th:WILMSLOW    $d$
c:x=rnd(10)+1
j(q$(x,1)="0"):choose
c:q$(x,1)="0"
r:set answer summer
c:s$="00000"
u:v1
t:Please refer to your copy of the
:microfiche for problem number £x .
t:Then press RETURN
c:t$="u:prob"!!str(x)
xi:t$

*menu
u:v1
t(s$="11111"&q$="0000000000"):You have
:completed all of the examples.
:Press RETURN to see the main menu.
asc:
jc:start
t(s$="11111"):This form is now complete
tc:Like to try another (Y or N)?
asc:
```

```
mc:y!Y
jyc:choose
mc:n!N
jyc:start
jnc:@a
t:Which section to complete?
a:
m:isbn!bnb!%c%!number
jy:isbn
ms:auth
jy:author
ms:title
jy:title
ms:class
jy:class
ms:locat
jy:loc
t:No such section, try again.
j:@a
*isbn
t:Please type the book number.
a:$a$
c:t$="m:"!!i$
xi:t$
cy:s$(1)="1"
ty:That's right
uy:v2
tyh:$a$
jy:iend
t3:In fact the answer is  $i$.
j3:iend
t:Sorry, that's not right.
t(len(a$)(13):Have you left out the
:spaces?
t:Try again....
j:@a
*iend j:menu
*author
t:Please complete the author section:
a:$a$
c:t$="m:"!!n$
xi:t$
```

```
cy:s$(2)="1"
ty:That's right.
uy:v4
tyh:$a$
jy:aend
t3:You should have typed $n1$ .
j3:aend
t:No.. have you checked your spelling?
t:Try again....
j:@a
*aend j:menu
*title
t:Please complete the title section:-
a:$a$
c:t$="m:"!!b$
xi:t$
cy:s$(3)="1"
ty:Quite correct!
uy:v5
tyh:$a$
jy:tend
t3:The correct answer is $b1$ .
j3:tend
t:Not quite. Make sure that you include
:bibliographic data (publisher etc).
t:Try again...
j:@a
*tend j:menu
*class
t:Type in the class information:-
a:
c:t$="m:"!!c$
xi:t$
cy:s$(4)="1"
ty:That's right.
cy:/c$ /&
uy:v6
tyh:$c$
jy:cend
c3:/c$ /&
t3:The correct answer is $c$ .
```

```
j3:cend
t:No. The number must be exactly as
:written AND you must include any other
:codes.
t:Try again.
j:@a
*cend j:menu
*loc
u:v1
t:Please enter the locations in order:
c:i=0
*loc1 c:i=i+1
r:allows for up to 5 locations.
c(i=1):t$="ms:"!!11$
c(i=2):t$="ms:"!!12$
c(i=3):t$="ms:"!!13$
c(i=4):t$="ms:"!!14$
c(i=5):t$="ms:"!!15$
t:Which is location &i ?
*loc2 ax:$a$
xi:t$
ty:Correct.
uy:v7
tsy:g0,(i-1)
tyh:$a$
jy:locend
t:No, try again.
j:@a
*locend u:v1
j(i(1):loc1
c:s$(5)="1"
j:menu

*prob1
c:i$="0 297 77813 7"
c:n$="bradbrook"
c:n1$="Bradbrook, M.C."
c:b$="webster&citizen&dramatist&weidenf
:&1980"
c:b1$="John Webster, Citizen and
:Dramatist, Weidenfield, 1980"
```

232

```
c:c$="822.3&gt"
c:l=3
c:l1$="north"
c:l2$="macc"
c:l3$="hq"
e:

*prob2
c:i$="b67012993"
c:n$="axelrod"
c:n1$="Axelrod, H.R."
c:b$="guppies&purns&1965"
c:b1$="Guppies, TFM Purns, 1965"
c:c$="639.375&hq"
c:l=4
c:l1$="poyn"
c:l2$="runc"
c:l3$="widn"
c:l4$="warr"
e:
```

The rest of the program is mainly concerned with matching student inputs
to pre-stored answers fairly exactly. One point of coding interest lies
between the labels *loc1 and *locend which concatenates two strings into
a valid match statement, and then executes it indirectly. This demonstrates
how the xi: command can often save repetitious coding.

The subroutines *prob1....*prob2 simply contain a number of compute
statements to store the data for each form in a set of strings. The integer 'l'
refers to the number of locations in the rota, and these locations are
abbreviated so that a successful match will result even for careless
spelling (the actual match is done with the approximate spelling match,
ms:, to give even greater flexibility.

16.4 The documentation

Some interim documentation was produced, part of which is reproduced
below. But, just as if you needed convincing that someone, somewhere
will defeat your most careful instructions, take a look at the section headed
'Using the Package'. There, I'd written 'remove the diskette from its
protective sleeve'. Sure enough, someone peeled open the liner and
pulled out the magnetised plastic! This highlights the fact that if training
material is to be presented in a technological form which could be easily

damaged, then the instructions must be absolutely precise for the trainee, and tested to exhaustion for possible misinterpretation.

Here is an extract from the actual documentation:

Using the Computer

The computer is an Apple II (or IIe) with a 48K minimum RAM, at least one disk drive, and a black and white monitor.

Other than this, you only need to have a copy of the student lesson diskette.   The lesson is written in the SuperPILOT language, but you do not need to know this, and no other diskettes are required.

The keyboard on the computer is just like an ordinary typewriter, except that:

i)   There is a key marked RETURN on the right of the keyboard. Press this whenever you have finished typing or whenever there is a cursor symbol ▨ on the screen, which means "I am waiting to continue".   You make it continue by pressing RETURN.

ii)   There is a left-arrow key ← , also on the right.   You use this to rub-out any mistakes.   Each press of this key erases the last character that you typed.

iii)   There is a key labelled RESET.   DO NOT press this unless you wish to end the lesson!

Using the Package

i)   Turn on the computer and TV monitor.

ii)   A disk drive should start whirring, the light on the drive should illuminate, and the screen should display "Apple II".

iii)   Open the disk drive door.

iv) Remove the lesson diskette from its protective sleeve. DO NOT TOUCH THE DISKETTE SURFACE.

v) Insert the diskette into the drive, making sure that the label is facing upwards and the cut-out slot (through which the diskette surface is visible) is facing towards the drive.

vi) Close the disk drive door. The drive will make several noises, then the screen will display "WILMSLOW LIBRARY presents....."

You are now ready to start.

Most of the package is self-explanatory and you should work through it in the sequence suggested on the "menu screen".

Section 3 is the "practice" section, enabling you to complete C30 forms on the screen. To do this, you need to use the copies of the microfiche details in Part 3 of these notes.

Please note that, for ease of programming, whatever you type will be automatically converted into lower-case letters and displayed as such when you do the practice exercises. Thus, you might type WILMSLOW, but it will be displayed on the form as "wilmslow". We can easily reverse this feature if needed.

Microfiche Details

Each set of details is taken from the actual COM entry. Please note that these entries do not mention names of libraries but a library code (e.g. 6H for Holmes Chapel) so you either need to know them or refer to the sheet in Part 4 of these notes.

Problem Number 1

0 297 77813 7

Bradbrook, M.C.

John Webster, Citizen and Dramatist
Weidenfield 1980

822.3   GT

1A, 3E, 7M

Problem Number 2

B67012993

Axelrod, H.R.

Guppies
TFM Purns, 1965

639.375   HG

4D, 4M, 4S, 7R2

COMMON PILOT LANGUAGE SUMMARY

LABELS
--must begin with an *
--one to six alphanumeric characters
--first character must be alphabetic

OP CODES
PR: option list

Option List
U - upper Case
S - remove spaces
E - escape

L - lower case
G - Goto allowed
W - clear labels

R: remark
T: type text
A: accept answer
M: match answer
J: jump
U: use subroutine
E: end subroutine or program
C: compute a computational language statement or EDIT a string
XI: execute indirect
FI: file input
FO: file output
 : Type text continuation
D: dimension
G: graphics

MATCH INSTRUCTION SPECIAL CHARACTERS

* match any single character
% match a space or answer start or end
& AND -- match one word and another
! OR -- match one answer or another

JUMP DESTINATIONS

label	jump to label
@A	jump to last A;

@A	jump to last A:
@M	jump to next M:
@P	jump to next PR:

MODIFIERS
H   Suppress line feed with Type (TH:)

```
J       Automatic jump with Match (MJ:)
S       Spelling correction on Match (MS:)
X       Suppress input text editing (AX:)
```

EDIT OPTIONS
```
C                   Capitalize first letter
U               Translate string to upper case
/XY   Replace all character X by character y
```

```
/XY   Replace all character X by character Y
/X/     Remove all occurances of character X
```


CONDITIONERS

```
Y                       Execute if yes match
N                       Execute if no match
n   Digit conditioner, execute if match with Answer counter
E                       Execute if error condition set
C       Execute if last relational expression true
```

RELATIONAL EXPRESSIONS

op-code (relational): text -- Execute instruction only if relational expression is true (non-zero)

EXECUTION TIME COMMANDS

GOTO - Jump to new location
@ any text - escape

COMPUTATIONAL FEATURES VALID ON C: OP CODE OR RELATIONAL EXPRESSIONS

Floating point scalar variables, arrays, varying length strings

+ - * / ** !!

= < > < > <= >=

& - !

ABS   FIX   INT   SGN   RND   SIN   COS   ATN   SQR   EXP   LOG   LN

STR   FLO   ASC   CHR   LEN   INS

SYSTEM VARIABLES

%A   %B

SUBSCRIPTING

single dimension array
        X(N)   N may be a variable or constant 0-999

238

double dimension array

      X(N,N)

string

      A$(P)   P = Position (starting from 1)

A$(P,L) L = Length

GRAPHICS COMMANDS

OX,Y	OFFSET
Px,y	plot point
Qx,y	erase point
Dx,y	draw line
Rx,y	erase line
Mx,y	move beam
ES	erase screen
Cn	select color

SuperPILOT Language
Quick Reference Guide[*]

The Parts of an Instruction

These are all the possible elements of a SuperPILOT instruction, in correct order:

Element	Comment
*label	Usually on separate line.
instruction name	Required; 1 to 3 letters.
modifier	Usually just one; one letter.
conditioners	Up to 4; one character each.
(expression)	One allowed; in parentheses.
:	Required colon.
object	Depends on instruction.

Label

Optional; identifies a place in the lesson. The first six characters of the label are significant; preceded by an asterisk and followed by at least one space or end of line. When label appears in the object field of a branching instruction, asterisk is omitted.

Modifier

Optional; usually only one is used. Modifiers affect specific instructions. Here are the instruction-modifier pairs:

TH:	(Type-Hang)	No carriage-return after a Typed line.
AX:	(Accept-eXact)	Accept exact response, with no editing.
AS:	(Accept-Single)	Accept a single-character response.
MS:	(Match-Spell)	Allow up to one wrong character on a Match.
MJ:	(Match-Jump)	Jump to next Match if this Match is unsuccessful.
LX:	(Link-Erase)	Start a new lesson without preserving the old lesson's variables.
LP:	(Link-Pascal)	Link to the Pascal program named in object.
KS:	(Keep-Save)	Write data accumulated from Keep instructions onto system.log file.

Conditioners

Optional; up to four, plus an expression, may be useful on one instruction. Conditioners may be used with any instruction. An instruction is skipped unless all of its conditions are met:

Y	(Yes)	Execute if last Match was successful.
N	(No)	Execute if last Match was unsuccessful.
1-99	(Answer-Count)	Execute if conditioner number equals current Answer-Count.
E	(Error)	Execute if the Error Flag has been raised.
(..)	(Expression)	Execute if expression's value is non-zero.
C	(Last-expression)	Execute if last evaluated instruction-modifying expression was true (non-zero).

The SuperPILOT Instruction Set

Text Instructions

Remark	r: THIS IS A COMMENT.
	r: Version 3, 18 April '81

Comments to author; not executed.

Type	t:What is an apple?
	t:#n is right, s .

Displays and formats object text on student's screen. If text includes variable names, their stored values are displayed, instead.

Response Instructions

Problem	pr:egt20
	pr:us

Starts new section and sets options (if PR: sets any option, all options not restated are turned off).

E	(Escape)	pr:e

Response starting @ tells SuperPILOT to Use subroutine sysx .

G	(Goto)	pr:g

Response goto label tells SuperPILOT to Jump to label.

L	(Lowercase)	pr:l

Converts responses to small letters.

U	(Uppercase)	pr:u

Converts responses to capital letters.

S	(Spaces)	pr:s

Removes all spaces from responses.

Tx	(Time)	pr:t15

Sets maximum response time to x seconds (pr:t0 resets unlimited response time).

[*] Reproduced by kind permission of Apple Computer

W   (Wipe-labels)   pr:w
"Forgets" all labels previous to this point in lesson.
         (no options)   pr:
Starts new section without changing any set options.

Accept   a:
                    a:#n s
Accepts student's response. May assign response to variables.

Match   m:COMPUTER
                    m:yes!ok!right
Looks for object text in student's last response. Result of search used by Yes and No conditioners. Object text may include any number of controller characters:

*   (Wildcard)   m:comput*r
       Matches any response character.
%   (Start-word)   m:%apple
       Matches space or beginning of response.
!   (Or)   m:apple!pear
       Separates object texts. Match successful if response contains either of given texts.
&   (And)   m:apple&computer
       Separates object texts. Match successful if response contains both texts in the given order.

Control Instructions

Jump   j:next
                    j:@m
Branches to the specified label, or to the next pr: (j:@p), the next m: (j:@m), or the last a: (j:@a).

Use   u:score
                    u:@p
Branches like J: , usually to a labelled subroutine that ends with e: but "remembers" where to return.

End   e:
                    e:@a
Returns to instruction following the u: that called this subroutine, or (if there is an object) terminates subroutine and then branches like J:. If not reached by a u: , ends lesson.

Link   l:lesson2
                    l:lesson2,review
Starts new lesson, keeping all the variables from the old lesson. May start at a specified label.

eXecute Indirect   xi:q2$
                    xi:s$
Executes contents of the specified string variable as a SuperPILOT instruction.

Wait   w:5
                    w:n3
Pauses the specified number of seconds or until any key is pressed, whichever comes first. Object may be a simple numeric variable name.

Computation Instructions

Dimension   d:q2$(40)
                    d:r(4,5)
Sets maximum string size for string variable or maximum subscript for each dimension (one or two) of a numeric variable array.

Compute   c:q2$="APPLE"
                    c:m=417.95
                    c:h3=cos(flo(a$)-2)
Evaluates an arithmetic or string expression, and stores it in the variable to left of equal sign.

Compute   c:/q2$ /@/ c
    (used for string editing)
Edits contents of specified string variable, with these options:

U   (Uppercase)   c:/s$ u
       Converts all letters to capitals.
L   (Lowercase)   c:/s$ l
       Converts all letters to lowercase.
C   (Capitalize)   c:/s$ c
       Capitalizes first character if it is a letter.
/x/   (Delete)   c:/s$ /x/
       Removes every character x .
/xy   (Replace)   c:/s$ /xy
       Replaces every character x with the character y .

Special Effects Instructions

Graphics   g:c6;p23,40;d98,13
                    g:es2;m0,0;dx1,y1;dx2,y2
Executes the graphics commands that appear in the object field:

Vl,r,t,b   (Viewport)   g:v29,39,0,23
       Sets left, right, top, and bottom character positions for text viewport. Columns = 0 (left) to 39 (right), and rows = 0 (top) to 23 (bottom). Default is to full screen, 0,39,0,23.
ES   (Erase Screen)   g:es
       Erases the text viewport to the set text background color.
ESx   (Erase Screen in   g:es2
            Graphics Color)
       Erases screen to color x (0 to 10) without changing drawing color:
Cx   (Color)   g:c6
       Sets drawing color to x (0 to 10).
Ox,y   (Offset)   g:o99,230
       Defines absolute x,y as reference point for relative locations, and moves pen there. Graphics x = 0 (left) to 559 (right), y = 0 (bottom) to 511 (top).
Ax   (Angle)   g:a45
       Sets the direction, in degrees, for relative graphics commands.
Sx   (Spin)   g:s90
       Increments the set angle direction by the specified number of degrees.
Mx,y   (Move)   g:m20,77
       Moves pen to point at relative x,y .
Mx   (Move)   g:m100
       Moves pen specified distance in set angle direction.
Px,y   (Plot)   g:p300,450
       Plots point at relative x,y .

241

Px   (Plot)   g:p300

    Plots point at specified distance in set angle direction.

Qx,y   (Quit)   g:q300,450

    Plots black point at relative x,y .

Qx   (Quit)   g:q240

    Plots black point at specified distance in set angle direction.

Dx,y   (Draw)   g:d9,200

    Draws line to relative x,y .

Dx   (Draw)   g:d360

    Draws line of specified length in set angle direction.

Rx,y   (Redraw)   g:r300,450

    Draws black line to relative x,y.

Rx   (Redraw)   g:r210

    Draws black line of specified length in set angle direction.

Ttext   (Type)   g:tOhio River

    Places text on screen starting at current graphics cursor position.

Xx1,x2,x3   (Xmit)   g:x8,8,8,7,18

    Transmits screen-control characters whose ASCII codes are x1,x2,x3 .

*x(...)   (Repeat-Factor)   g:*3(d50;s90)

    Executes the commands in parentheses the specified number of times.

eXecute Graphics   gx:map

        gx:mirage

Redraws image from named file, step by step on student's screen. Does not erase screen before drawing.

eXecute Graphics   gx:photo2!

(Quick-Draw)   gx:monster!

Quickly replaces the screen with complete image from named file. File name includes ! character.

Type Specify   ts:*20(ax$;d25;wr)

Determines how and where text will appear on the screen; background and foreground colors; type styles and line spacings.

Vl,r,t,b   (Viewport)   ts:v0,39,0,4

    Sets left, right, top, and bottom boundaries for text viewport. Default is full screen. Columns = 0 to 39 (left to right), and rows = 0 to 23 (top to bottom).

Gx,y   (Goto)   ts:g10,15

    Move text cursor to x,y coordinates.

Sx   (Size)   ts:s1

    Sets single (x=1) or double (x=2) size.

Tx   (Thickness)   ts:t2

    Sets character thickness, where 1 is normal, 2 is boldface.

Mx   (Mode)   ts:m2

    Sets type style, where x=1 is normal, x=2 is overstrike, x=3 is exclusive-or.

Xx   (Transmit)   ts:x8

    Sends any character to the screen, by that character's ASCII number.

Lx   (Line Spacing)   ts:l2

    Sets spacing between lines, multiples from 1-15.

P   (Print)   ts:p

    Sends future characters to printer.

Q   (Quiet)   ts:q

    Turns off character flow to printer.

Ax$ (Animate)   ts:ax$

    Executes a fast, unformatted write of string variable x$.

Wlrud   (Walk)   ts:wrrd

    Moves text cursor one character position left (wl), right (wr), up (wu), or down (wd).

Dx   (Delay)   ts:d15

    Pauses for specified 60ths of a second.

Bx   (Background)   ts:b5

    Sets the background text color, 0-20.

Fx   (Foreground)   ts:f4

    Sets the foreground text color, 0-20.

I   (Inverse)   ts:i

    Future characters are printed in the background color on a background that is the foreground color.

N   (Normal)   ts:n

    Cancels Inverse ts:i instruction.

ES   (Erase Screen)   ts:es

    Erases text viewport in the set text background color.

ESx   (Erase Screen in   ts:es6

    Graphics Color)

    Erases screen to graphics color x .

*x(...)   (Repeat-Factor)   ts:*4(ab$;wr)

    Executes the commands in parentheses the specified number of times.

eXecute character-seT   tx:cyrillic

        tx:chess-set

Starts using characters in named diskette file.

eXecute character-seT   tx:

(no object)

Goes back to standard ASCII character set.

Sound   s:2,20;4,55;3,20

        s:30,200;0,20;40,200

Plays sounds of pitch,duration . Pitch = 1 (low note) to 50 (high note)

    Pitch = 0 is silent (rest)

    Duration = 0 (short) to 255 (long)

eXecute Sound   sx:tuneup

        sx:oursong

Plays sound effect stored in named diskette file.

Accept Point   ap:

Accepts x,y coordinates of graphics screen position indicated by student using game controllers or other pointing device.

Video Control   v:[commands]

Provides access to peripheral devices such as videotapes and videodisks.

File Handling Instructions

| Keep | k:#a tries, #w wrong |
| | k:Name: n |

Transfers object to lesson file system.log .

| Open new file | fox:25,p$ |
| | fox:j5,new |

Creates and opens new file with the given name or with the name stored in the specified string variable, to contain records 0 through the specified largest-record number.

| Open new file | fox:0,x$ |
| (with 0 records) | fox:0,new |

Finds existing file with given name or name stored in the specified string variable, and deletes that file from the diskette.

| Open existing file | fix:m2,q$ |
| | fix:25,new |

Opens existing file with given name or name stored in the specified string variable, for reading or writing records 0 through the specified largest-record number.

| File Output | fo:n,x$ |
| | fo:13,good times |

Stores given string or contents of specified string variable in the specified record of file now open.

| File Input | fi:n,x$ |
| | fi:13,p$ |

Reads specified record of file now open, and stores result in specified string variable.

SuperPILOT Colors

Graphics Colors

0 = Black1	4 = Black2	8 = Reverse
1 = Green	5 = Orange	9 = One Dot On
2 = Violet	6 = Blue	10 = One Dot Off
3 = White1	7 = White2	

Text Colors

0 = Black	8 = White/Black	13 = Green/White
1 = Green	9 = Green/Black	14 = Violet/White
2 = Violet	10 = Violet/Black	15 = Orange/White
3 = White	11 = Orange/Black	16 = Blue/White
4 = Black	12 = Blue/Black	17 = Green/Orange
5 = Orange		18 = Green/Blue
6 = Blue		19 = Violet/Orange
7 = White		20 = Violet/Blue

Variables and Functions

Variables

User Variables	Typical Names	Example
Simple numeric	f , q3	c:f = 15
Numeric array	p8(13), m(3,4)	c:p8(7) = 33
String	r$, u5$	c:r$ = "Apple"
Substring	r$(3) , u5$(4,7)	c:u5$(2,5) = r$

System Variables

%A	Answer-Count	(number of times last a: executed)
%B	Answer Buffer	(response to last a:)
%X	X-Coordinate	(response to last
%Y	Y-Coordinate	AP: instruction)
%C	Column-Coordinate	(Vertical and horizontal
%R	Row-Coordinate	text cursor position)
%S	Spin Angle	(current angle value)
%O	Game Port	(peripheral access)
%V	V: Parameter	(signed A/V access)
%W	V: Parameter	(unsigned A/V access)

Functions

Transcendental Functions

SIN(X)	Returns sine of angle x radians.
COS(X)	Returns cosine of angle x radians.
ATN(X)	Returns radian measure of angle whose tangent is x .

Arithmetic Functions

SGN(X)	Returns -1 if x<0 , 0 if x=0 , or 1 if x>0 .
ABS(X)	Returns absolute value of x .
FIX(X)	Returns integer found by discarding any decimal portion of x , without rounding (-32767.9 < x < 32767.9).
INT(X)	Returns largest integer less than or equal to x (-32767.9 < x < 32767.9).
RND(X)	If x<1 , returns random number from 0 to .999969. If x is from 1 to 32767, returns random integer from 0 through x-1 .
SQR(X)	Returns square root of x (x>0).
LOG(X)	Returns base 10 log of x (x>0).
LN(X)	Returns natural log of x (x>0).
EXP(X)	Returns e (2.71828) to power x .

String Functions

ASC(X$)	Returns decimal ASCII code for first character in x$.
CHR(X)	Returns character whose decimal ASCII code is x .
FLO(X$)	Returns first number in string x$.
STR(X)	Returns number x expressed as a string of characters.
INS(N,T$,P$)	Searches from n-th character of t$ for first occurrence of p$. Returns 0 if no occurrence found, or returns position in t$ of matching sequence's first character.
LEN(X$)	Returns number of characters in x$.

Input Functions

PDL(X)	Returns an integer from 0 to 255 indicating position of knob ("paddle") on game controller number x .
BTN(X)	Returns 1 if button on game controller x is being held down, or 0 if that button is not being pressed.
KEY(X)	Returns 1 if any key has been pressed since last a: or w: , or 0 if no key has been pressed.
TIM(X)	Returns response time in seconds for last a: or ap: or 0 if pr:tn timeout ended response.

Part Four:

Beyond Pilot

Nobody is pretending that PILOT - or even SuperPILOT - is the best answer for everybody.

This final section leads you gently into the idea of a system that is **Language-Free:** something that people with no knowledge of programming can use. The trick is that it **generates** lines of flawless PILOT code, unknown to the user.

This idea is presented as representative of some other systems, and some major examples are reviewed in the final chapter.

The last part of the final chapter grasps the nettle of "which is the most cost-effective system?" A simplified cost-benefit model is presented, with some startling results!

Chapter 17

Authoring Without Coding: a prototype program generator

This chapter forms a bridge between the programming approach of the last few chapters and the more exotic authoring systems, described in the next chapter, that claim to make lesson production easier by eliminating- or drastically reducing- the actual programming.

Throughout the history of CBL, various researchers and vendors have developed authoring systems that minimise the computer knowledge required by the user. This can mean that lesson input can be delegated to less skilled users, or that computer usage is more efficient, or both. As a side effect, it tends to imply that the author is working within a fairly rigid framework and can not exploit the full power of the system.

You, the expert on SuperPILOT or whatever, will have little need of such systems. Your fingers flash over the keys to produce error-free code with awe-inspiring productivity. But, you might just be interested in an approach that is similar to that used by some pretty expensive systems. The program described does not claim to be particulary efficient, but it might just enable you to develop a world-beater that will enable everybody else to write programs as well as you do.

This particular program is actually a 'program generator'. It engages the user in a 'dialogue' and generates program statements (in PILOT) that are guaranteed to be 100% syntactically correct.

17.1 What does a program generator do?

Well, they all work differently but, for our purposes, a generator outputs valid program statements into a file for later (deferred) execution. The dialogue between the user and the computer is carried out in terms of the intended application, and the user is not required to understand the details of the language statements being generated. In all cases, a generator is intended to be efficient in terms of user effort (e.g. many statements are generated in response to a simple question being answered) and some effort is made to trap errors of logic.

A particularly well-known generator is The Last One. This generates BASIC programs as the user is engaged in a dialogue about the files and so on to be processed in commercial applications. But generators are not intended to be general purpose. You would not use The Last One to write a space invader game!

In the same way, an Author-Language Program-Generator will only generate author language statements and will do so with reference to some sort of educational model. For example, IBM's IIAS system generates Coursewriter code, whilst some parts of the PLATO system generate TUTOR code. In each case, the system assumes that you are producing a lesson, in that it helps you in planning the number of attempts at a question or in selecting the touch-sensitive parts of the screen, in the case of PLATO, for example.

Even given the restrictions we've discussed, you can see that a generator could be useful to you, using only a microcomputer. You might use one to generate all sorts of simple programs, or you could simply use it to bash out the skeleton of a program and then embellish it with your own extra pieces of code. The important thing is that the generator is minimising effort.

It should be said that not all examples of this 'go-faster' software work this way; some use an empty 'shell' into which data is placed, whilst others string together chunks of commonly-used code into larger programs. The one we are going to describe is probably unique- it is written in PILOT (actually, SuperPILOT) and it generates PILOT statements. Although it is designed specifically for the Apple II or IIe, you should be able to adapt it easily for your computer.

If you want to find out more about generators, read the book 'Programs that write Programs', by Chris Naylor, published by Sigma Technical Press in 1983.

17.2 What does this one do?

It lets you select one of several actions from a 'menu'. It controls and checks your actions (e.g. Is the text laid out to your satisfaction?) and it then generates one or more valid PILOT statements. The statements are assembled together as a FRAME and, when the user is happy with the frame, the contents of it are output to a file. In SuperPILOT, the only type of file available is a DATA file which can not be run as a lesson directly. So, there's a special Pascal program provided with this program which converts the DATA file into a TEXT file, which will run quite happily as a normal SuperPILOT lesson.

This could be termed a 'one-shot' generator. Once the data file has been generated, you can't go back and edit it although you can edit each frame as you are composing it and, of course, you can use the ordinary (and excellent) SuperPILOT text editor to alter the program that you generate.

As written, the program will generate up to 50 frames of PILOT (this number is easily altered). It is quite a comprehensive example of PILOT programming- if nothing else- and you must regard it as an EXPERIMENTAL PROTOTYPE for you to play with, take the best bits out of, chop and change and so on. Perhaps you'll send me your improved version to evaluate!

17.3 Some deficiencies

I'm at pains to emphasise the weaknesses of this simple generator, even before you've seen it. Well, here are some of the improvements that could be made, and some general observations:

Because it is written in PILOT, it runs rather slowly. Perhaps it should be written in Pascal (with which SuperPILOT is compatible) although, obviously, you would need a full Pascal system.

Next, it does not generate graphics statements; instead, it uses picture files that have been created under the SuperPILOT graphic editor. You might want to add a graphics segment to it.

It is slightly hungry in terms of disk space, in that it outputs interim data into a temporary DATA file prior to conversion into a TEXT file. If you were really short of space, you could use the generator in drive 1 and an empty 'resource' diskette in drive 2 to give yourself more room. A resource disk is one with the minimum of system information, enabling you to store many more files than on a lesson disk: see page 260 of the SuperPILOT language manual.

One more thing- text is input into a 'window' that you choose on the screen. In the current version, the program will not let you design a window larger than 80 characters and you can only have one window per frame. This is no real problem as you can have several different frames or you can add the extra text, later, under the text editor.

And, you'll probably find lots more problems- so you'll write your own generator- and that's the way we make progress!

17.4 A session with the generator

The first thing to do is to plan your lesson as a number of inter-linked frames. For example:

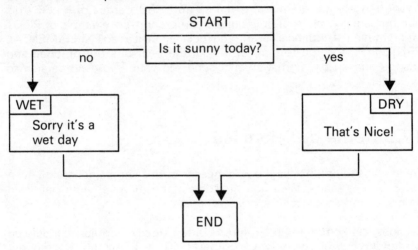

To do this properly, you will need to use the LESSON DESIGN SHEETS described earlier in this book. This will enable you to plan the appearance of each frame. Let's assume that the designer of the above simple lesson has already done this.

The example contains four frames, labelled START, WET, DRY and END. The frame START expects a student input, which it matches against 'rain' or 'sun' etc. causing a branch to frames WET or DRY. After displaying a suitable message, each of these frames goes to a frame called END. This program automatically puts the START label at the beginning of the lesson and the END label at the end, so you should be careful not to duplicate them.

Having planned your lesson, this is the sequence to follow:

1. Copy the SuperPILOT program GENERATOR and the compiled Pascal program COPY.CODE (see listings, later) onto a diskette with the name LESSONS (see SuperPILOT manual for details). If any other name is chosen, the Pascal conversion program will not run correctly.

2. If you wish use pre-edited graphics files, transfer them to the same disk as that containing GENERATOR or put the graphics disk into drive 2, remembering that you will have to refer to file names on that disk as '#5:filename' (because the Apple calls disk drive 2 "#5").

3. RUN the program, either with the LESSONS disk in drive 1 (possibly with a graphics disk in drive 2) or in drive 2 with the author disk in drive 1.

4. At the display:

    I)nput   K)ill   C)onvert   L)ist   S)top

choose I (for input). You will then be asked for a file name and the system will set up an empty file of length 50 records.

5. After a few seconds, the screen clears and you will see, on the top line:

    N)ew   G)ph   T)xt   A)cp   M)ch   J)mp   Q)t

These prompts refer to the actions that you can take within a frame. You normally choose G (select a graphic), T (place text inside a window). A (accept user input), M (match the input) or J (jump to a label. N)ew ends a frame and Q)t ends a lesson. The normal sequence within a frame is G,T,A,M,J but it is not obligatory and you can go back to any previous selection and alter its attributes.

6. Perhaps choose G. The program asks you 'Which Picture' to which you reply with the name of some pre-stored picture which will then be displayed if it is on the disk.

7. Then, you might choose T. Notice that the dialogue is conducted on the top line, so this is not available to you. You are asked for the dimensions of the window in which the text will be displayed (left, right, top and bottom edges in turn. By default- if you just press RETURN- values of 0,39, 1 or 23 will be entered for you for any particular edge). The window is displayed in inverse video and you are asked if it is OK. If it is, you input the required text (up to 80 characters) directly into the window.

8. If M is chosen next, you type in the keyword match expected. Any combination of keywords is allowed as specified in PILOT. After typing in

this 'match string' you are asked to type in a 'test string' as a sort of sample student answer. The program tells you if it matches and you are asked if you want to store the original 'match string'.

9. Normally, you would next choose J and tell the program where to jump to in the case of a successful or an unsuccessful match. You might just jump to a frame that says 'well done' or 'wrong' or you could carry on matching alternative answers in subsequent frames.

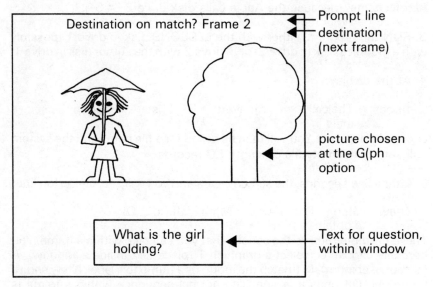

Figure 17.2 A partially completed frame

An example of what you might see by this stage is shown in Fig 17.2.

10. If you're happy with the frame, choose N)ew and the contents will be written to disk, taking about 10 seconds.

11. You are then invited to choose a frame name for the next frame, and this will be displayed on the same line as the prompts as a reminder of the frame you are creating.

You then carry on, remembering that terminal frames must point to the frame called END.

Finally, you choose Q (to quit lesson input) which takes you back to the main program menu. Your normal action here will be to choose the CONVERT option which links to a Pascal program and converts the data file into a runnable lesson. This lesson will be created as a PILOT file and will be listed on the lesson directory, just like any other lesson.

Notice that there is also a 'list' option to list the data file and a 'kill' option to remove datafiles no longer needed. This should be used immediately after conversion as disk space is extremely limited. Generally, try to keep just one active lesson on such a disk. If the disk becomes full, strange and undocumented errors may occur and the Pascal program (hidden inside the disk) may just seem to die. That's why you might like to modify the generator so that it sits in drive 1, with a resource disk in drive 2.

17.5 How it works

In this section, the program listing is interleaved with an informal description. The program is modular, and will be described by reference to the PILOT labels in the listing.

The program begins by allocating space for the various strings. The section labelled *start selects the input, kill, convert or list options.

*input

This section obtains a file name from the user, deletes any existing file of the same name, and re-opens it to be length f1 records (f1=50). Note that 2 PILOT data records fit into one block. By choosing 50 records, we consume 26 blocks, the extra one being used by the system.

The program then sets the file pointer to 1, this being the first record that will receive a generated frame of PILOT statements. Record 0 is left vacant since you might like to use it as a header record thought I might do this, but never did!)

Each frame consists of up to 9 strings, a1$,a2$...a9$. To start with, the contents of the first four strings are set to:

        j:start
        *end
        e:
        *start

These provide us with an 'end frame' and a label to 'start' to refer to. These four strings are the contents of a frame (remember that a frame can contain up to 9 such strings) and these are output to the data file by the subroutine labelled 'flush'.

251

```
d:f$(80):p$(100):a$(80):b$(10):x$(2):y
:$(2):l$(2):r$(2):u$(2):d$(2):a1$(15):a2
:$(14):a3$(16):a4$(83):a5$(10):a6$(2):
:a7$(80):a8$(9):a9$(9):n$(1):s$(255):z$
:(7)

r:set file length
c:fl=50

*start q:es

u:pos
th:(I)nput (K)ill (C)onvert (L)ist
:(S)top
as:$b$
e(b$="s"):
u(b$="i"):input
u(b$="k"):kill
u(b$="c"):con
u(b$="l"):list
j:start

*input
ts:es
t:Data File Input Option
t:
t:Lesson Name (deletes file of same
:name) or QUIT?
a:$f$
j(f$="quit" or f$="QUIT"):start
fox:0,f$
fox:fl,f$

r:set up an 'end' frame
c:f=1
c:a1$="j:start";a2$="*end";a3$="e:";a4$
:="*start";a5$="";a6$="";a7$="";a8$="";
:a9$="";z$=a4$
u:flush
q:es
*inmenu u:pos
```

```
th:$z$ :N)w G)h T)x A)c M)c J)m Q)t
as:$b$
u(b$="n"):new
u(b$="g"):graph
u(b$="t"):text
u(b$="a"):accept
u(b$="m"):match
u(b$="j"):jump
t(b$="q"):End of lesson input....
wc:3
r:flush out last frame
uc:flush
j(b$="q"):start
j:inmenu


*pos
ts:v0,39,0,0;es;v
e:



*flush
u:pos
th:Please wait
c:s$=""
c(a1$()""):s$=s$!!a1$
c(a2$()""):s$=s$!!"\"!!a2$
c(a3$()""):s$=s$!!"\"!!a3$
c(a4$()""):s$=s$!!"\"!!a4$
c(a5$()""):s$=s$!!"\"!!a5$
c(a6$()""):s$=s$!!"\"!!a6$
c(a7$()""):s$=s$!!"\"!!a7$
c(a8$()""):s$=s$!!"\"!!a8$
c(a9$()""):s$=s$!!"\"!!a9$
fo:f,s$
c:f=f+1
t(f)fi):Output file is full!
jc:fstop
c:a1$="";a2$="";a3$="";a4$="";a5$="";a6
:$="";a7$="";a8$="";a9$=""
*fstop e:
*new r:write out last frame to file
```

*inmenu

This displays the current frame name name and the various prompts available within a frame.

*new

This gets a valid name for the frame, creates a label by preceding the name by *, and adds the code required either to clear the screen or simply to place the text cursor at the top left. All of this is stored in a1$. Notice that the question 'erase last frame?' refers to the preceding logical frame, which is not necessarily the last one to be generated, so we always give the user a clear screen before going any further.

*graph

This obtains a name for a pre-stored picture, displays it using 'xi:a2$' and stores the code in a2$ if the user is happy with the picture.

*text

The user answers the questions about the dimensions of the window in which the text is displyaed. The window information is stored in a l$ which is a concentration of:

"g:v"!!l$!!","!!r$!!","!!u$!!","!!d$

The text is stored in a4$ which is simply "th:" followed by the text.

*accept

This checks the intended cursor X and Y values and concatenates their string equivalents into "ts:g"!!x$","!!y$ which you'll recognise as a graphics 'go to' statement, which is stored in a5$. The accept statement (a:) is stored in a6$.

*match

We get a 'match string' a$ and generate

a7$="m:"!!a$

The testing is done by an xi: on string a7$ to give the user a chance to change his mind.

*jump

```
u:flush
*new1 u:pos
th:Frame Name?
a:$z$
u(len(z$)>6):pos
tc:Too Long, try again...
wc:2
jc:new1
u:pos
th:Erase last frame (y/n)?
as:$b$
c(b$="y"):a1$="*"!!z$!!" g:es0"
jc:nend
c:a1$="*"!!z$!!" ts:g0,0"
*nend g:es
e:

*graph u:pos
*gstart th:Picture name?
a:$a$
c:a2$="gx:"!!a$
xi:a2$
u:pos
th:This Picture?
as:$b$
j(b$="y"):gend
g:es
j:inmenu
*gend e:

*text u:pos
c:l=0;r=39;u=2;d=23
*left u:pos
th:Window left (0...39)?
a:£l
c(%b=""):l=0
j(l1<0 or l1>39):left
*right u:pos
th:Window right (£l ...39)?
a:£r
c(%b=""):r=39
```

```
j(r(1 or r)39):right
*top u:pos
th:Window top (1...23)?
a:£u
c(%b=""):u=1
j(u(1 or u)23):top
c:d1=int(80/(r-1+1)+u-1)
*bottom u:pos
th:Window bottom (£u ...£d1 )?
a:£d
c(%b=""):d=d1
j(d(u or d)d1):bottom
c:l$=str(l);r$=str(r);u$=str(u);d$=str(
:d):a3$="ts:v"!!l$!!","!!r$!!","!!u$!!","!
:!d$
xi:a3$
ts:i;es:n
u:pos
th:OK (y/n)?
as:$b$
xi(b$()"y"):a3$
tsc:es
ec:
u:pos
th:Text for this Window?
xi:a3$
ax:$a$
c:a4$="th:"!!a$
ts:v
e:

*accept
r:cursor location
*curx u:pos
th:Cursor X position (0-39)?
a:£x
j(x(0 or x)39):curx
c:x$=str(x)
*cury u:pos
th:Cursor Y position (1-23)?
a:£y
```

This generates the required jump statements and ensures that the user is not trying to write a frame that jumps to nowhere. The strings are stored in a8$ and a9$.

There are various other sections of code that are very easy to follow. In the original version of the generator, there was quite an interesting piece of code in the subroutine *flush. It is worth mentioning this, even, though the particular programming technique is not used in the current version. What we wanted to do was to avoid that section in the subroutine which examines a1$, a2$...a9$, and concatentates them to s$. In an earlier version of the program, we created a string, t$, like this:

$$c:t\$="c:t\$=a"!!str(n)!!"\$"$$

If n were 2, then after this line had been executed, t$ would contain the string "c:t$=a2$". We then had a line:

$$xi:t\$$$

The effect of this was to execute t$ indirectly so that t$ actually contains the contents of a2$, which gives us a way of simulating one-dimensional string arrays, otherwise unavailable in PILOT. This works fine if the string 'array' is on the right hand side but I've not yet worked out a similar scheme for the array being on the left!

By the way, you might be wondering why this elegant method was discontinued: it was slower than our less elegant method used in the current listing.

```
j(y(1 or v)23):cury
c:y$=str(v)
c:a5$="ts:g"!!x$!!","!!y$
c:a6$="a:"
e:

*match u:pos
th:Match String?
a:$a$
c:a7$="m:"!!a$
u:pos
th:Test string?
a:
xi:a7$
u:pos
```

```
ty:That matched
tn:That failed
w:2
u:pos
th:Store the match (y/n)?
as:$b$
j(b$="y"):mend
j:match
*mend e:

*jump u:pos
th:Destination on match?
a:$a$
t(len(a$)>6):Too long
jc:jump
c(a$()""):a8$=" jy:"!!a$
*jump2 u:pos
th:Destination if no match?
a:$a$
u(len(a$)>6):pos
tc:Too long
wc:2
jc:jump2
u(a$=""):pos
jc:Must choose one or the other!
wc:2
jc:jump
c:a9$=" jn:"!!a$
e:


*kill
ts:es
t:DATA FILE  Kill Option
t:
th:Kill which file?
a:$f$
t:
t:Type 'delete' if you are sure you
:want to kill $f$  as a DATA
:file.
```

258

```
a:$b$
fox(b$="delete"):0,f$
tc:File deleted.
e:
*con
ts:es
t:Data File to Lesson convert option
t:
t:Now linking to Pascal....
lp:copy
e:


*list
ts:es
t:Data File List Option
t:
th:List which file?
a:$f$
fix:f1,f$
te:No such file
je(1):lend
c:l=1
*lrep
fi:l,p$
j(p$=""):lend
t:$p$
c:l=1+1
j:lrep
*lend as:
e:
```

17.6 A Pascal data file conversion program

Now that the data file has been generated, how can you use it as a program? You might think that one way would be to read each record in the data file, copy it into a string, and to execute indirect (xi:) the string.

This would wear your disk drives out rather quickly and, whenever a jump to a label was encountered, the program would fail because it would not

259

know the absolute record address to which it should jump. We've got to do better than that, so here's a better scheme:

There is a major snag: as we've already said, you can't run a data file, so it must be converted (in the case of SuperPILOT) into a text file (i.e. a Pascal file with a .TEXT extension). To do this it is, unfortunately, necessary to use Pascal, which is the native language of SuperPILOT. The most obvious thing is to rename the file. Let's say you've just generated a file called 'test'.

The data file will be stored as 'test.data' and will be revealed as such by the Apple Pascal filer. Try renaming it as 'test.text' and, unfortunately, the SuperPILOT lesson text editor does not list 'test' on its directory page.

Rather than wondering why this was so, I pressed a Pascal expert into service (My thanks to Roger Graham of Manchester Polytechnic for writing the first version of this program) who wrote the program FILECOPY to copy a data file (which is an 'untyped' Pascal file) across to a text file. Magically, the file IS then listed on the SuperPILOT text-editor directory of lessons just like any other lesson.

So, let's describe how the program works. One thing to remember is that each Pascal block stores 2 PILOT records, so the program spends much of its time chopping the blocks into records.

There are various other points to note:

1. The USES CHAINSTUFF and SETCHAIN('SYSTEM.STARTUP') are obligatory.

2. The file input and output names (INNAME and OUTNAME) are forced to begin with LESSONS. That is why your disk MUST be called LESSONS, since this enables the program to run in either drive.

3.The program deliberately skips character positions 0 and 256 within a block because they are not always non-printing, but they are not part of the generated data. The SuperPILOT language manual does specify that records are of length 255 characters (positions 1 to 255 and 257 to 511) but it is rather short of any more details. For anybody who wants the gory details, it would appear that SuperPILOT gratuitously throws in the odd random character in positions 0 and 256 if, and only if, the first character in the record (i.e. block positions 1 or 257) is a 't'. It's a bit bizarre- perhaps somebody knows the answer- but the procedure adopted of ignoring the problem works well enough.

Note that the Pascal program FILECOPY must be compiled and stored on the disk with the Pascal name COPY.CODE.

```
REPEAT
WRITELN('BLOCK NUMBER = ',BLOCKNUMBER);
INDEX := 1;
LIMIT :=255;
FOR RECOUNT := 1 TO 2 DO
BEGIN
REPEAT
ORDVAL := ORD(BUFFER+INDEX←);
IF ORDVAL = DLE THEN INDEX := INDEX
+ 2
ELSE
BEGIN
IF ORDVAL IN +32..127← THEN
BEGIN
(* PROCESS  PRINTING CHARACTER *)
WRITE(BUFFER+INDEX←);
WRITE(OUTPUTFILE,BUFFER+INDEX←)
END;
INDEX := INDEX + 1
END;
UNTIL INDEX ) LIMIT;

WRITELN;
WRITELN(OUTPUTFILE);
LIMIT := 511; INDEX := 257

END;
ORDVAL := ORD(BUFFER+0←);
FINISH := (ORDVAL (32);
ORDVAL := ORD(BUFFER+1←);
FINISH := (BLOCKNUMBER ) 0) AND (FINISH) AND
(ORDVAL (32);
BLOCKNUMBER:=BLOCKNUMBER + 1;
BLOCKCOUNT:=BLOCKREAD(INPUTFILE,BUFFER,1,
BLOCKNUMBER);
PAGE(OUTPUT)

UNTIL EOF(INPUTFILE) OR FINISH;
```

261

```
WRITELN;
CLOSE(INPUTFILE);
CLOSE(OUTPUTFILE,LOCK);
WRITELN('FILE ',INNAME,' COPIED TO ',OUTNAME)
END.
```

17.7 Conclusion- and, what next?

That's the end of it. It might seem laborious- in fact, it is- but it's nowhere near as large as some of the systems you'll see in the next chapter. It also has the advantage of costing nothing, once you've paid for SuperPILOT.

There are many other generators you could write, or you could add further options to this one. The generator we've discussed so far might be used for writing tutorial sequences, but you could easily write a generator for multiple choice tests. This might be of the 'shell' type in which you have up to, say, 6 possible answers that could be stored on consecutive records of a file. Another record would contain the correct answer and a few more PILOT statements (also stored on the file) would display the questions, perhaps in random order, and attend to storing the number of tries, the total score and so on. It's quite a nice application because writing the code for multiple-choice tests is such a boring job for a human, so why not let the compute do it! Just as with the generator, you will have to use the Pascal conversion program to convert the data file into a runnable program.

* A disk containing a runnable demonstration version of the software described in this package is available at nominal cost direct from the publisher. Please write for details.

Chapter 18

Other Authoring Systems-
or, the search for the real
princess!

Whilst the home-brew system of the previous chapter is of some interest, and SuperPILOT itself is adequate for many purposes, it is interesting to know about some of the other systems on the market. As to which is the BEST one, no one can really say because there are so many that are so similar. The quest for the perfect authoring system has been similar to the search for the Holy Grail. A more mundane analogy is the fairy tale 'The Princess and the Pea' in which our hero the prince is very choosy about his bride to be: some are too fat, some too thin, too tall or too small. And it's been a similar story with CBT. So, you will have to make up your own mind as to which, if any, of the goods on offer are suitable for your particular application. To help you, the last part of this chapter contains a simple mathematical model of cost-effectiveness that is intended to give an objective measurement of various competing systems.

We can not hope to include every authoring system in one chapter- a whole book would be needed and, even then, it would become rapidly outdated. Instead, three systems are described in some detail, and very brief details are given of others. The ones chosen for more detailed descriptions are PLATO, COMBAT and WISE. They each have unique characteristics, and they use contrasting hardware.

18.1 The PLATO System

We have talked about this, the archetypal CBL system, at many points in this book. It was developed originally by Illinois University and, over the past 20 years by Control Data Corporation at a cost of some $600 million. Originally, it was purely a mainframe system, with terminals attached to a Control Data Cyber either through cables or by telephone. As recently as 1979, public pronouncements from CDC implied that networked CBL was necessary, in order to exploit the full mainframe power, but recent developments in more powerful micros, combined with difficulties in selling PLATO (at least in the UK) as a standard bureau service, have forced rapid changes in the product. There are many users of mainframe PLATO in the USA, including universities and commercial undertakings, particularly airlines. In the UK, there are relatively few PLATO users compared to the USA, with Manchester University as the main academic user. We will describe the microcomputer versions of PLATO later; for details of the special terminals used, see chapters 1 and 2.

As we have already seen (in Chapter 1) the TUTOR language lies at the heart of PLATO. Here is a short program written in TUTOR which is a replica of the PILOT program in Chapter 12.

```
unit        geometry
at          1812
write       What is this figure?
draw        510;1510;1540;510
arrow       2015
specs       okcap
answer      <it,is,a> (right,rt) triangle
write       Exactly right!
wrong       it,is,a triangle
at          1605
write       Please be more specific:
            it has a special angle.
```

This is a complete UNIT of tutor. The 'draw' section simply draws a triangle on the high-resolution, touch sensitive PLATO screen, while the 'arrow' command places a small arrow on the screen where the student's response will appear as it is typed. The 'okcap' means that upper or lower case can be used. The matching is carried out in the 'answer' line and, if the response is correct, PLATO will respond agreeably with OK. The words in angle brackets <.....> are ignored by PLATO, and any extra words are simply underlined as being 'unexpected' but disregarded for matching purposes. Words inside round brackets (....) are necessary parts of the match, and are regarded as sysnonyms. It is quite easy for the PLATO user to build up dictionaries of ignorable and/or synonymous words rather than resort to coding each time.

If an answer does match the expected one, the user presses NEXT on the PLATO keyboard which takes him or her on to the next unit, or to the end of the lesson if there are no more units. If the answer does not match, PLATO replies NO and the user can try again. Most PLATO authors would include extra units accessible by pressing the HELP key. There are additonal special keys such as BACK, DATA and STOP which the author can also use for various purposes. For example, BACK can be used to review preceding units and DATA might recall a set of laboratory measurements for use in a science lesson.

The author can also specify parts of the screen as being touch sensitive. For example:

```
pause      keys=touch
keytype num,touch(1215),touch(100,200)
```

This tells PLATO to expect a touch-screen input and sets 'num' to 0 if the student touches a region of the screen close to location 1215, to 1 if the touch is near to 100,200 and to -1 for any other touch.

Naturally, we can only begin to scratch the surface of TUTOR here but you can see that is not dissimilar from the other languages which have emulated it, except that it does have many more commands; often a single TUTOR command will be equivalent to 5 or 10 lines of PILOT and will execute far more quickly.

The PLATO editors

As with most CBL systems, the text editor is at the centre of things. Whilst using the text editor, the user can press the HELP key for specific instructions. For details about how to write particular instructions, the author can access a feature unique to PLATO, called AIDS, simply by pressing Q and the NEXT key. This is itself a PLATO lesson through which an author can either browse or select just the item needed, either through an index or by typing in the word or phrase about which information is needed.

Having typed in the TUTOR code, the author 'condenses' it (into runnable code) by pressing the SHIFT-STOP keys; at this stage an errors in coding are revealed and the author may need to re-enter the editor and debug the program.

In the case of complex graphics, this would be a tedious process for pictures of any complexity, so PLATO provides a graphics editor with two modes: insert-display and show-display. In the insert mode, the author designs pictures on the screen interactively, using lines, text, rectangles, circles and so on. The process is similar to that for many other such editors, but the neat trick is that the author can select the show-display mode to view the picture in the same way that it will be seen by the student. Unlike other editors, this one generates the TUTOR code representation of the picture, just as it would be written manually (see the previous chapter on program generators).

CDC are developing other authoring tools aimed at making programming easier. The most important of these is the 'Local Authoring and Delivery System' described under Microcomputer versions of PLATO, below.

Though not strictly an editor, the PLATO CMI system (also called PLM-Plato Learning Management) is worthy of special mention. It is, in fact, a system of editors, generators and other software intended for the creation and maintenance of fairly large training systems with the minimum of effort. It is designed to administer tests, assign study activities and to keep records withot knowledge of a programming language. To do this, PLM provides the author with a skeleton structure into which learning materials and tests are stored. The largest unit is a CURRICULUM which is made up of COURSES, which in turn are broken down into MODULES (see Fig 18.3). A module is comprised of several INSTRUCTIONAL UNITS (IUs) each containing a number of questions designed to test the student's mastery of a given objective. Attached to each module is a pool of learning resources which might include books, video and, of course, PLATO CAL lessons. The structure of a module is shown in figure 18.1

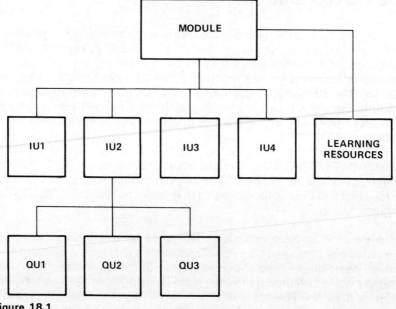

Figure 18.1

The author is responsible for inputting the contents of each IU, although he is prompted as to which type of question is needed (e.g. Touch-screen, short answer, multiple choice) so no programming is required. Also, he specifies which learning resource(s) is or are applicable to each IU so that, in the event of an IU not being mastered, PLM may allocate only those resources for study in an optimal, rather than a blanket fashion. This is illustrated in Figure 18.2.

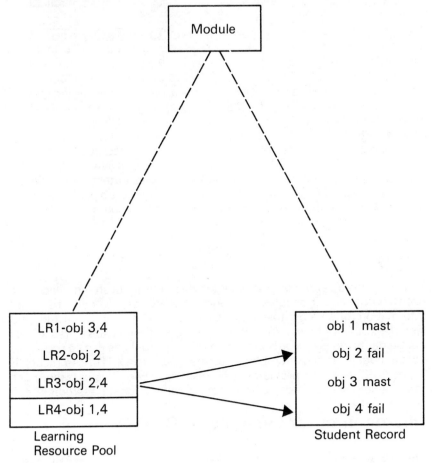

Figure 18.2

It is usual for a curriculum to use a database of modules which are allocated to courses and to individual students as necessary. To do this there is a complex piece of software in PLM called the Variable Management Strategy (VMS) and this is illustrated in Fig 18.3.

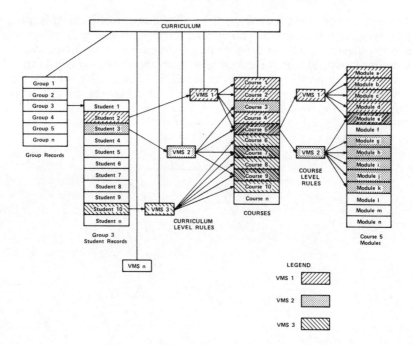

Figure 18.3

This includes a set of conditions as to which students are enrolled on to each course, and it enables the course administator to collect student information (often more than necessary!) and to find out when student X last used PLATO, how many times a particular IU was attempted and so on. Students whose records indicate particular problems can be prevented by the course administrator from further use of PLATO (the record is 'turned off') until the problems have been resolved. This is taken much more seriously than being barred from a conventional classroom!

Microcomputer versions of PLATO

The newer versions of PLATO terminals are, in fact, full blown Z80 based microcomputers. PLATO lessons can be produced, with full access to the ecntral mainframe and the lessons can then either be down-loaded to the terminal, the phone link disconnected, and used locally on disk. This latter approach has been taken by the Boeing company, whose pilot training system was described in chapter 2: when British Airways use the Boeing lessons, they do so entirely in the stand-alone mode.

Similarly, versions of PLATO lessons have been developed (sometimes as BASIC translations) so that they will run on popular microcomputers such as the Atari, IBM PC, Texas and Apple. These lessons were originally developed in American universities, and you are likely to see advertisements for them in American magazines such as Byte.

But, developing lessons in stand alone mode is a different matter. In 1981, CDC offered a subset of PLATO that would run on their own Viking terminal. It did not permit TUTOR authoring, but instead comprised a number of 'models' with which an author could interact. For example, there were models for tutorial lessons, drill and practice, and decision-tree simulations. Taking one such model, drill and practice, the author would enter up to a permitted maximum of multiple-choice answers to questions that could be edited on the screen; the result of such interactions was that a TUTOR program was generated which would run just as any other program. The model approach greatly reduces authoring time for certain categories of lesson and it can increase the standard of lesson presentation by freeing the author from the drudgery of coding.

In a similar vein, courseware development models are planned for authoring on the IBM Personal Computer, Sirius and Zenith machines and delivery systems are planned for Apple, Commodore and BBC computers to get away from the high price image of PLATO (a stand alone Viking terminal currently costs £3,900 and with PLATO software the total comes to £17,000). Prices are not yet available for these non-CDC implementations. Models are soon to be available for the Viking range that can control external devices such as videodisk or tape/slide.

18.2 COMBAT

This is an acronym for COMputer BAsed Training and is a British product, developed by Mills and Allen Communications Ltd. It was developed initially on the PDP-11/23 minicomputer equipped with a VT100 terminal and a combination of hard and floppy disks. It was envisaged that the PDP-11 would be the 'preparation system' and that a smaller 'delivery system' would be used to run the courseware on cheaper micros (delivery systems), notably the Apple II. The common link here is that both of these micros support UCSD Pascal, in which COMBAT was written.

More recently, COMBAT has been offered on the IBM PC which can be used to run both the preparation and delivery systems, and the cost of the software has fallen to about £1000. Further implementations are being developed and the Delivery System is already available for the Superbrain, Torch and BBC Model B with Torch Z80 Disk Pack.

One part of COMBAT is the Template Preparation System, in which the author builds a lesson from frames. There are various sorts of frame, one for each instructional strategy, such as decision tree, tutorial, or testing.

A frame specifies a sequence of operations, such as

-presentation of information
-interaction with trainee
-feedback based on trainee response
-selection of the next frame

The author sets up a lesson using a number of editing programs, allowing the selection of the lesson, editing of a frame, creation of a text or graphic image and so on. The editing programs may, at the author's choice, be menu or command driven.

A second part of COMBAT, referred to as Author-Pascal, is best regarded as a collection of Pascal tools: i.e. a large number of Pascal procedures (c.f. subroutines in BASIC or PILOT) that have been prepared for the author. For example, there are procedures to justify text, to present graphics and to match student responses. The author simply calls up the procedure required, and provides it with the parameters required (e.g. the keywords to be matched). At the end of all this the author has produced a Pascal program for his lesson, but much more quickly than if the procedures were wriiten from scratch.

A third component of COMBAT is its Management System. Among its functions are:

- course management allowing lessons to be linked into courses
- student registration, to control and monitor student access
- performance analysis, to print and interrogate student records
- transfer of courseware between different computers

18.3 WISE and SMART (see also Section 2.3)

These are offerings from Wicat Inc. The name 'Wicat' is an acronym for World Institute for Computer Assisted Training, a Utah-based school, and WISE is an acronym of Wicat Interactive System for Education. Like PLATO Wicat also offer a CML package, which is called SMART.

The emphasis here is on menu-driven features. There is no programming language so far as the author is concerned, although WISE itself is written in Pascal, and all interactions are with screen-oriented editors and a repertoire of simple 2-letter commands. If these are forgotten, WISE will help an author!

The hardware on which WISE and SMART are delivered is the Wicat range of 16-bit microcomputers with high resolution graphics screens. Provision is made for a larger Wicat to act as the centre of a network to a number of smaller machines and, with the software installed on the network, several authors and/or students can work simultaneously.

WISE: the WISE system offers the author 11 types of frame which are assembled into a lesson. These include 'display and wait' frames which just display text and graphics, menu frames for multiple-choice questions, short-answer matching, calculations and so on. As each frame is completed, the author can see what it looks like to the student, justifying their claim to 'what you see is what you get'.

Having chosen a particular type of frame the interacts with a menu and uses simple commands to specify its contents. For example, if a multiple-choice question frame is being completed, the author completes such details, on the screen, as:

    the name of the frame;
    the number of attempts permitted;
    scores for each answer;
    the destination frames;

No computer language is needed, just a fill-in-the-blanks approach.

Similarly, if a graphics frame is being created, the author will use a different menu to choose where to position the text or graphics to be presented. A variety of simple commands are also used, such as cc (create circle), cl (create line), ca (create arc), rt (rotate), mf (modify font), od (object delete) and, of course, he for help! In response to each of these commands, WISE quizzes the author for the various parameters (such as the size of a circle, the position of text etc.)

A strong feature of WISE is its ability to control videodisks, and a number of professional disks, particularly in the medical training field have been produced by Wicat.

SMART: is the CML companion to WISE, and shares its menu-driven approach to user acceptability. It is able to manage a whole network of

Wicat machines connected on a network. Comprehensive data is collected automatically by SMART for the generation of reports which can include:

Sudent status: which objectives are mastered, which are incomplete, how the student is progressing compared with the rest of the class and a prediction of when the student will complete the course.

Group status:a list of student status reports for all students in a particular group.

Objective status: the performance of all students on any objective is summarised, in order to assess the validity of that objective (e.g. does nobody master it?).

Item analysis: as for objectives, the performance of each question can be validated.

Prescriptions: to show which students are on which objective.

In order to set up SMART, the author uses menu screens and answers on-screen prompts. For example, the system asks the author to specify an objective for part of the course and what the prerequisites for that objective are. SMART is smart enough(!) to detect specified but undefined objectives and other logical errors of course planning, and call them to the attention of the author.

There are many other features of SMART that we can not describe fully here. In many ways it is similar in complexity to PLATO's PLM, but is perhaps easier for the inexperienced user (on-line help and tutorial assistance are available) and has the unique advantage of 'intelligent' features in being able to spot logical errors. SMART also includes a 'mail' feature for inter-terminal correspondence (e.g. from an instructor to a student).

18.4 Other systems

There are literally hundreds of others, but the main ones that the reader may come across are:

STAF: a text-oriented authoring language that runs on many CP/M micros. It is of particular interest for the various levels of answering matching that the author can specify and, because it is written in FORTRAN, for its easy portability across a range of computers. It was originally developed during the National Development Programme in Computer Assisted Learning as a subset of the Leeds Author Language. It has recently been enhanced as STAF-2 and is available from Leeds University and a some other outlets in the UK. For example, the Microcomputer/Videotex terminal 'Teleputer 3' from Rediffusion Computers supports STAF-2.

The language is a little unusual in its format (some feel that it resembles assembler) although this simply reflects its non-verbose nature. For example, a simple 'frame' of STAF could be:

```
#A00,0*
Where is Sigma Technical Press?
@0 WILMSLOW CHESHIRE /A70
@0 CHESHIRE /A80
A20;
```

The first line is the node-label, the @0 signifies the type of matching (these range from 0 to 7, 0 being the most lax) and the is a branch instruction to some other frame in the event of a successful match. Thus, if the student answer includes WILMSLOW and CHESHIRE, a branch will occur to frame A70, if the answer contains just CHESHIRE, the branch is to frame A80, otherwise a branch will occur to frame A20.

STAF could possibly run also on the Systime CATS system. This is somewhat more comprehensive than STAF alone, using the Leeds Author Language (Systime call it the Low level Authoring Language) from which STAF was derived. Built on top of this are three 'compilers' or generators of LAL statements. These are the multiple-choice (MCQ), General Authoring Language (GAL) and Frame Oriented Author Language (FOAL). MCQ provides pre-set formats for test questions, GAL is a means of linking together various frames, and FOAL provides a library of standard format frames for presenting information and questions in textual form. FOAL screens can be overlaid to produce composite effects. The CATS system also has facilities for recording student data and for running simulations.

MENTOR-2: this is a relatively new system, available from PMSL Computer Services, Hays Lane, Mixenden, West Yorkshire. It is an enhanced version of VCIS which is developed in Utah, in the USA. The two systems have a close technical interchange.

As with the Wicat WISE system (which also, coincidentally, was developed in Utah), MENTOR-2 runs on hardware that supports the UCSD p-system, but it is the intention to develop it for other microcomputer operating systems, including MS-DOS. The system ideally runs on fairly top-end micros with a minimum of 128K of RAM and twin floppies with approximately 1 Mbyte of storage.

MENTOR implementations have been achieved, at the time of writing, on TERAK and Sirius microcomputers and on the GOULD/SEL mini with multiple terminals. VCIS has been implemented on the TERAK and is currently being developed on the Hewlett-Packard, Zenith and IBM PC microcomputers. The Zenith version uses an MS-DOS compatible operating system. A minicomputer version for the Gould -SEL 32/27 is also available.

Lessons are normally created as a series of frames, which are compared to overhead transparencies in that such frames can be overlaid to obtain any desired effect. MENTOR is almost entirely menu driven; there are separate editors for the creation of text and graphics with no programming skills required in either case. An animation sequence editor is available on the TERAK and is being implemented on the Sirius. Video tape sequences can be used by both machines and video disk can be used with the TERAK. Video disk and slide control is planned for the Sirius.

Any combination of these visual representations may then be recombined by a series of commands using the training material BUILDER program. This is a menu driven facility which allows the timed display of frames and the acceptance of student responses, up to 80 characters long, either as comments or to posed questions. Multiple path branching is available with answer matching against author-defined anticipated answer options on up to 254 paths, and one unanticipated answer path. Each path, with or without further displays, can be terminated with repeat or other path terminator options to prevent a student progressing further until satisfying the present answer criteria. Functions such as extra numerical accumulators can be programmed in Pascal as Specials, and then used easily by an author within the BUILDER program.

The system includes management features, such as trainee registration, assignment of lessons to courses, number of correct/incorrect answers per lesson with score facility, time spent on a lesson and courses, trainee comments and unanticipated answers. Most of these can be selected by an author, others can be programmed in Pascal to meet users' requirements. Scoring and other numerical measures are accessible to the author as one measure of student achievement, and more enhanced facilities are currently being developed.

The system is available, at the time of writing, at a cost of £3,500 for a 10 year authoring/delivery licence and £750 for a 10 year delivery only licence.

TICCIT: this runs on a Data General minicomputer. Its particular strengths are its inbuilt 'learner control' models as an aid to authors and its use of standard colour TV. Students use a special keyboard through which they can select a 'map' to view the course as a whole and through which they control the progress of the lesson with keys such as BACK, REPEAT, EASY, HARD and HELP. Authors may use a proven strategy for preparing lessons, with the APT (Authoring Procedure for TICCIT) editor. It is of interest that the underlying learning model is Component Display Theory, developed by David Merrill, and described earlier in this book. TICCIT also offers an authoring language, TAL, for use by authors who wish to 'go their own way'.

Although TICCIT is beyond the budget of many users, micro-TICCIT is now available. This uses the ADAPT authoring system, similar to APT, but able to run on relatively small mini/microcomputers such as the Data General microECLIPSE connected to much less expensive micros through the ARCNET local area network. The nice thing about MicroTICCIT is that lessons, once developed, will run on an IBM Personal Computer as a delivery system. At this time (late 1983) prices have not been finalised for the UK but it is expected that the price of a 4-terminal network system will be about $52,000, expandable to 40 terminals at $4,000 per terminal

TICCIT is available in the UK from Hazeltine Corporation, Worton Hall, Worton Road, Isleworth, Middlesex.

MICROTEXT: is a screen-oriented authoring system for the BBC and CBM machines, with Apple and CP/M versions available soon. Microtext was developed at the National Physical Laboratory, with the intention of making simple things simple to do, so that an author can in a few minutes set up a simple branching presentation. At the same time, Microtext contains a wide range of sophisticated features so that as an author gains experience, he can implement more complicated applications tailored to specific needs. We have already described some aspects of Microtext, including a short example, in chapter 9.

The authoring process is centred around editing frames of text on the screen, using the integrated editor and language interpreter. This means that one can immediately switch between seeing the text in student mode, and editing both the text and control structure in author mode. Individual commands are entered (machine dependent) for any screen graphics needed. Text and graphics are stored as series of linked frames, and presentation and branching can be modified by the state of internal variables. Response matching includes single character or keyword analysis, with optional numeric validation and range checks.

Microtext can be used for a wide range of applications, in addition to training or education, such as interviewing. form filling or giving practical assistance. Professional versions support user-defined commands to control peripherals such as light pens, touch screens, slide projectors or video-disk players.

The cost of the BBC Computer version is currently £60.

USE: this language has been evolved since 1979 by consultants at Urbana Software Enterprise, who have benefited from their use of the TUTOR langauage over a period of some 20 years. The result is a stand-alone system termed the RC-2 (the original model was the RC-1) using the Z80 processor and a number of powerful co-processors. It is manufactured by Regency Systems Inc and marketed in the UK by Rediffussion Simulation Ltd. A CML package and the RCG courseware generator are available. The RCG package is essentially similar to the language-free template systems that we have discussed previously, with the important enhancement of an option to link into the full USE author language when the template approach is too limited. The RC-2 has powerful graphical manipulation features, including a bit-pad graphics package, that will be of great interest to engineers and others wishing to display complex shapes in various orientations. A video interface package is accessible through USE to control most types of European and American standard video devices.

The system has a high degree of compatibility with PLATO-developed courseware and seems to demonstrate very adequately how to squeeze many of the important features of PLATO into an 8-bit micro!

PASS: this is supplied by Bell and Howell for the Apple II. Like some other systems, it has two editors: a prompting one for novices and another one for more advanced authors. In addition to the PASS authoring language and editor, there is also an administration package to collect student records. The non-prompting version of PASS requires the author to design a lesson as a series of interlinked instructional units. Each unit is composed of optional information, question, answer, response and review parts. A strong feature of PASS are the graphics and character editors. In many ways, PASS and SuperPILOT compete for the same market (and on the same computer) but PASS may be rather easier for the novice.

DIALOG: this was originally developed as an IBM mainframe system by Janotta-Falkus Computer-Ausbildung GMBH, but is now also offered by McGraw-Hill as a product for the IBM PC equipped with 128K RAM, two 320K dual-sided disk drives, and optional colour card. The current price is £1495.

Dialog is basically a screen-oriented frame-handling system, with menu-driven features. For example, a user can select from one of several types of screen, including: presentation; menu; multiple-choice; matching lists; or fill-in-the-blank. Of particular interest to commercial users is the ability to generate commercial simulations quickly and easily, by virtue of the "application screen simulation facility". This enables the user to design screens which are an exact mimic of the real application (either as it would appear on the PC or a mainframe such as a 3270) with up to 20 user inputs on one screen. The normal range of PC colours can be used, together with graphics symbols, though there are no high resolution graphics commands as yet. Interactive video features are available to supplement the graphics. Although the system is written in Pascal, it is not possible to generate the bulk of a lesson with Dialog and then enhance it with extra lines of Pascal code, as can be done with COMBAT. This feature will probably not be too important to the non-programming audience to whom Dialog is presumably targeted.

18.5 Counting the cost: which system is best?

Now we come to the crunch: a prospective user wishes to decide which CBL system to buy. It can be an emotive choice, or it can be dictated by the hardware already available if there is surplus capacity.

In this short section, we present a model of cost-effectiveness that was originally developed by Richard Stanley of Control Data Ltd. To that extent, you may suspect bias, but it seems an unbiased and objective model that uses simple mathematical equations, honest financial assumptions and publicly-available 'hard' data such as prices. It also contains subjective data and, if you do not like the data used here, use your own and see what answers you get! Your answer may be just as good as mine, but the important thing is the underlying model. I have incorporated the model into a short BASIC program, but you may prefer to use a spreadsheet package.

The Financial Model

In one man-month of length MM hours, we can produce MM/CH hours of courseware, where CH is the number of coding hours to produce one hour's worth of lesson. The value of CH is obviously contentious, in that it depends heavily on the type of lesson being produced. We will take a deliberately vague stance, and say that it is an 'average' lesson with a good mix of text and graphics, but one that does not require such advanced features as videodisk control, complicated file handling or very advanced calculations. Typical of an average lesson would be any of those we described in Chapter 2, with the exception of MicroQUERY, LOGO or Flight Simulation.

One hour of lesson will be more effective than an hour of traditional chalk and talk, by a factor L. This is called the learning rate, and will always be greater than or equal to 1. (Its exact value will depend on such factors as the response speed of the system, how necessary it is to use printed matter etc. Accepted values are 1.0 to 1.5) So, to produce the equivalent of one hour of chalk and talk, we need:

$$M = CH/(MM*L) \quad \text{months}$$

Of course, we can employ more than one author at a terminal: one author can be bashing the keys while others are planning a lesson. If each hour of lesson requires DT hours of planning, then

$$A = (DT + CH)/CH$$

authors can, in principle, be co-authoring. This fact is interesting, but often irrelevant if there is only one author. DT is a fairly constant quantity, so smaller values of CH lead to greater efficiency.

Next, we'll devise a factor which, when multiplied by the capital cost of a piece of equipment or software, gives the approximate monthly cost of ownership. To calculate this, we need to know the maintenance cost (typically 10% of the purchase price) and the interest rate that we are paying on our presumably-borrowed money (or what we would have got it we had not spent the money). Assuming depreciation over D years, averaged interest at 1% per year, we obtain the factor P, which is simply the sum of the three terms:

$$P = (M/100 + I/(2*100) + 1/D)/12$$

which, when multiplied by the original price, gives the cost of ownership per month.

There are two main elements of cost:

278

1) The host computer (which may be the only one or the central one in a network) and its associated software. MUltiply the cost of this by P and call the answer P1.

2) The terminals (if any) connected to the computer. The monthly cost of each is obtained by multiplying its cost by P. Call the answer P2.

Now we can compute the cost of developing one hour of lesson. This is:

$$DC=(CH/(MM*L))*(A*AP*MM + CT + P2) + P1*Y$$

where the new terms are:

AP=author's payment, per hour
CT=authoring access charge/ terminal/ month (levied by some bureau services, e.g. mainframe PLATO)
Y =duration of the development project, in months

The factor A can be eliminated by substitution to give:

N=number of attached terminals

$$DC=(CH/(MM*L))*((DT+CH)*AP*MM + CT + P2) + P1*Y$$

For simplicity, we will use just one terminal (N=) during the development phase. In reality, this is often the case, though you can use any value.

Once the course has been developed, the presentation cost per retained hour is simply:

$$PC=(N*P2 + P1)/(R*N*MM*L)$$

The quantity R (the retention factor) is included because there is good evidence that CBL is retained better than classroom instruction. R will increase with the 'richness' of the system in terms of graphics, video, 'help' keys and so on. In everyday language, we are equating R to how well something "sticks in our mind" after being taught in some particular way.

For example, you will probably agree that personal experience under the personal guidance of a highly skilled teacher is more effective than a classroom presentation from an average teacher addressing a class of 100. To this extent, we can construct a graph similar to that in Fig 18.4, which shows the cost/ quality trade-off, with classroom instruction under average conditions taken at an R value of 1.0. The cost figures used are roughly averaged to include both total development costs and ongoing delivery costs. As can be seen, there is no obvious relationship, though CBL is clearly (along with video) a good compromise. The factor L (the learning rate) appears again, in the above equation, because of one hour at the terminal being worth more than one classroom hour.

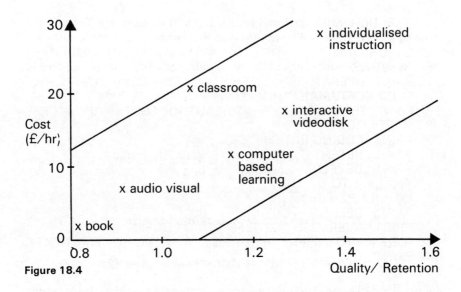

Figure 18.4

It is also possible to compute the break-even population, i.e. when it is more worthwhile to use CBL than classroom instruction. This is not included in the program because its exact value is a little complicated to determine. A rough measure is:

Break-even= (CH * AP)/(AV - PC) where AV is the average cost of traditional instruction.

The Program

This is written in fairly standard BASIC (Applesoft, actually) and is listed below:

```
1 Y = 3:NT = 5:MM = 120
2 M = 10:I = 15:D = 3
3 MF = (M / 100 + I / 200 + 1 / D) / 12
4 DIM P(5): REM - STUDENT POPULATION
5 P(1) = 1:P(2) = 100:P(3) = 500:P(4) = 1000:P(5) = 2000
6 J = 1: REM -INDEX FOR LOOP
8 READ N: REM  NUMBER OF SYSTEMS
9 READ A$
```

```
10 READ OC,HH,HS,TC,AP,CT,CH,R,L
26 PRINT "PRESS ANY KEY TO CONTINUE:"
27 INPUT B$
28 HOME
30 P1 = OC + MF * (HH + HS)
40 P2 = MF * TC
50 D = (CH / (MM * L)) * ((DT + CH) * AP * MM / CH + CT + P2) + P1 * Y
60 PRINT A$
70 PRINT "OPERATORS' COSTS= ";OC;" HOST COMPUTER= ";HH;"
   HOST SOFTWARE=";HS
80 PRINT "TERMINAL COST= ";TC;" AUTHOR COST= ";AP;" ACCESS
   COST= ";CT
90 PRINT "CODING RATIO= ";CH
100 PRINT "RETENTION= ";R;" LEARNING RATE= ";L
110 PRINT "DEVELOPMENT COST= ";D
120 FOR I = 1 TO NT
130 PC = (I * P2 + P1) / (R * I * MM * L)
140 PRINT "DELIVERY COST (";I;")=";PC
144 PRINT "AVERAGED COSTS FOR THIS CONFIG.
146 FOR K = 1 TO 5: PRINT "POP. ";P(K);" AV= ";PC + D / P(K): NEXT K
148 PRINT
150 NEXT I
200 J = J + 1
210 IF J < = N GOTO 9
220 END
290 DATA 10
300 DATA  PLATO,0,0,0,3900,20,730,50,1.5,1.5
310 DATA  CDC VIKING-110 LOCAL AUTHORING AND DELIVERY,0,0,
14000,3900,20,0,16,1.3,1.3
320 DATA  COMBAT (IBM-PC),0,0,1000,3000,15,0,100,1.2,1.3
330 DATA  SUPERPILOT,0,0,120,1750,12,0,120,1.2,1.2
340 DATA  PASS,0,0,7500,1750,13,0,80,1.2,1.2
350 DATA  BASIC (PET),0,0,0,1200,12,0,200,1.1,1.0
370 DATA  WISE,0,7500,15000,4500,15,0,80,1.5,1.4
380 DATA  REGENCY,0,14300,0,5750,20,0,80,1.5,1.5
390 DATA  MENTOR II,0,0,3500,3000,15,0,80,1.5,1.4
400 DATA  MICROTEXT (BBC),0,0,60,1200,12,0,80,1.3,1.3
```

The variables set to constant values at the beginning of the program are:

MM=120 hours of use per month
M =10% maintenance charge
I =15% interest charge
D =3 year depreciation period
Y = 3 month development period

DT=10 hour planning period
NT=maximum number of terminals considered (5)

The variable items for each system are stored in DATA statements in the following order:

Cost per month of operations staff (OC)
Cost of host computer (HH)
Cost of authoring software (HS)
Cost of terminal (if applicable) (TC)
Payment to author, $ per hour (AP)
Access charge to host computer (CT)
Coding ratio, hours per hour of lesson (CH)
Retention factor (R)
Learning rate (L)

The variable names into which each item of data goes is in brackets, in the above list.

If you look at the program listing, you should be able to recognise the equations used. The loop at the end of the program is used to determine the presentation cost using 1,2,3,4 or 5 terminals.

The Results

A typical run follows the listing, using data for just a few systems; you can easily plug in the data for any other. What we have done is to choose a range of systems, from the ultra-cheap to what is considered pricey in anyone's terms. L and R are subjective values, the other data is publicly available.

The figures that we have used are the ones suggested to us by the various manufacturers, and it is up to you to believe them or not (e.g you may wish to increase the coding ratio in certain cases).

Nevertheless, the results may surprise you in putting PLATO in quite a favourable light, along with a system like SuperPILOT and especially Microtext (the winner according to this model!) both of which are generally thought of as low-cost. The problem is, of course, that we are not really comparing like with like, so far as their authoring capabilities are concerned. The rather shattering fact that the local authoring version of PLATO is apparently more expensive than its mainframe parent is due solely to the fact that we have assumed that the entire authoring system is retained for the life of the project, whereas in reality perhaps it would be

282

leased for a month or so, in which case the delivery cost would fall to £0.61 and the development cost would be lower. But, we haven't done this for any other system (partly because of the ongoing need for an authoring station for de-bugging faulty courses, partly for uniformity, and partly due to sheer exhaustion on the part of the author at the end of a long book) so perhaps it's not too unfair. A further proviso is that we have made no allowance for telephone and other costs that may be incurred by the online PLATO user (£730 is just the basic access cost).

One general observation that can be made is that any system which is 'split', in the sense of requiring separate development and delivery hardware, comes out of the ranking very unfavourably. This is because the development system lies idle once the lesson has been developed. However, the recipient of developed software may well reap the benefit.

Notice the high cost of developing a BASIC program, purely due to the suggested 200:1 coding ratio (it could well be even higher) so you are warned against being seduced by cheapness alone.

You are strongly recommended to check the prices used in the program, which are in pounds sterling in the Autumn of 1983, before coming to any conclusions. Also, I am well aware that price is not the only factor, and there may be many more important factors. For example, you may feel it important to have a networked system so that you can distribute lessons to a large number of users. Or, you may feel it important to have a system such that lessons can be input by relatively unskilled personnel.

The cost model does not take into account these factors, which leaves you with quite a problem:

You just might have to decide for yourself!

	PLATO	PLATO Local Authoring Delivery	COMBAT (IBM PC)	SUPER PILOT	PASS	BASIC (PET)	WISE	REGENCY	MENTOR II	MICRO TEXT
Operators/mth	0	0	0	0	0	0	0	0	0	0
Host Computer	0	0	0	0	0	0	7500	14300	0	0
Host access/mth	730	0	0	0	0	0	0	0	0	0
Software	0	14000	1000	120	7500	0	15000	0	3500	60
Terminal	3900	3900	3000	1750	1750	1200	4500	5750	3000	1200
Author (£/hr)	20	20	15	12	13	12	15	20	15	12
Coding ratio	50	16	100	120	80	200	80	80	80	90
Retention	1.5	1.3	1.2	1.2	1.2	1.1	1.5	1.5	1.5	1.2
Learning Ratio	1.5	1.3	1.3	1.2	1.2	1.1	1.4	1.5	1.4	1.2
Development (£/lesson-hour)	915	2042	1362	1277	1861	2485	3807	2992	1362	772
Basic Delivery (£/lesson-hour, 1 terminal)	0.61	3.74	0.90	0.45	2.27	0.38	4.54	3.14	1.09	0.26
Basic Delivery (£/lesson-hour, 5 terminals)	0.61	1.39	0.72	0.43	0.80	0.38	1.51	1.35	0.62	0.25
Averaged delivery cost (£/lesson-hour, 3 terminals, 100 population)	9.76	22.21	14.38	13.21	19.65	25.23	40.09	31.57	14.32	7.98
Averaged delivery cost (£/lesson-hour, 3 terminals, 1000 population)	1.52	3.83	2.11	1.72	1.97	2.87	5.82	4.64	2.06	1.02

* assume LAD is retained

Table 18.1 Summary
Viking 110

284

INDEX

A message from the publisher

Sigma Technical Press is a rapidly expanding British publisher. We work closely in conjunction with John Wiley & Sons Ltd. who provide excellent marketing and distribution facilities.

Would you like to join the winning team that published these highly successful books? Specifically, **could you successfully write a book that would be of interest to the new, mass computer market?**

Our most successful books are linked to particular computers, and we intend to pursue this policy. We see an immense market for books relating to such machines as:

DRAGON
THE BBC COMPUTER
APPLE
TANDY
SINCLAIR
OSBORNE
ATARI
IBM PC
SIRIUS
NEWBRAIN
COMMODORE
and many others

If you think you can write a book around one of these or any other popular computer — or on more general themes — we would like to hear from you.

Please write to: Graham Beech
Sigma Technical Press,
5 Alton Road,
Wilmslow,
Cheshire, SK9 5DY,
United Kingdom.

Or, telephone 0625-531035